Praise for *Programming AWS Lambda*

If you're a Java programmer hoping to unlock the benefits of serverless architectures, you finally have the book you've been looking for!

—*Dr. Tim Wagner, Vendia CEO and Cofounder*

Mike and John have been my go-to people for all things Java and serverless over the past several years. This book very nicely captures many of their core learnings and "gotchas" in this space. A great addition to my bookshelf. Many thanks to them both!

—*Daniel Bryant, Java Champion*

If you're a Java developer who wants to reap the benefits of serverless computing while avoiding the pitfalls, this is the book you've been looking for.

—*Brian Gruber, Principal Architect at Meetup*

For developers who want to leverage their Java experience while taking advantage of new architectural possibilities offered by AWS Lambda, this book provides a thorough guide to building robust, scalable serverless applications.

—*Stuart Sierra, Software Architecture Consultant*

A clear and comprehensive introduction to programming lambdas in Java. This book goes way beyond "hello world" to cover how to write, deploy, run, and support Java-based lambdas that take full advantage of serverless architectures rather than just "lifting and shifting" your application code.

—*Sarah Wells, Technical Director for Operations & Reliability at Financial Times*

Programming AWS Lambda

Build and Deploy Serverless
Applications with Java

John Chapin and Mike Roberts

Beijing · Boston · Farnham · Sebastopol · Tokyo   

Programming AWS Lambda

by John Chapin and Mike Roberts

Copyright © 2020 Symphonia LLC. All rights reserved.

Published by O'Reilly Media, Inc., 1005 Gravenstein Highway North, Sebastopol, CA 95472.

O'Reilly books may be purchased for educational, business, or sales promotional use. Online editions are also available for most titles (*http://oreilly.com*). For more information, contact our corporate/institutional sales department: 800-998-9938 or *corporate@oreilly.com*.

Development Editor: Virginia Wilson	**Indexer:** Judith McConnville
Acquisitions Editor: Kathleen Carr	**Interior Designer:** David Futato
Production Editor: Katherine Tozer	**Cover Designer:** Karen Montgomery
Copyeditor: Kim Wimpsett	**Illustrator:** Rebecca Demarest
Proofreader: Charles Roumeliotis	

March 2020:   First Edition

Revision History for the First Edition

2020-03-18:   First Release

See *http://oreilly.com/catalog/errata.csp?isbn=9781492041054* for release details.

The O'Reilly logo is a registered trademark of O'Reilly Media, Inc. *Programming AWS Lambda*, the cover image, and related trade dress are trademarks of O'Reilly Media, Inc.

The views expressed in this work are those of the authors, and do not represent the publisher's views. While the publisher and the authors have used good faith efforts to ensure that the information and instructions contained in this work are accurate, the publisher and the authors disclaim all responsibility for errors or omissions, including without limitation responsibility for damages resulting from the use of or reliance on this work. Use of the information and instructions contained in this work is at your own risk. If any code samples or other technology this work contains or describes is subject to open source licenses or the intellectual property rights of others, it is your responsibility to ensure that your use thereof complies with such licenses and/or rights.

978-1-492-04105-4

[LSI]

Table of Contents

Foreword

AWS Lambda—and both serverless and backend as a service in general—have had a hugely disruptive effect on the software industry. They've greatly improved the productivity of millions of developers by eliminating many of the hassles, costs, and "undifferentiated heavy lifting" of dealing with servers, from security patching to autoscaler tuning. More importantly, though, serverless has changed the very definition of an application, from a blob of code that we drop onto server farms into a configuration of multi-tenanted cloud services that we orchestrate with code in the sky. Serverless is the next stage of cloud evolution—just as it once felt impossible to build a company without its own data center, it's quickly becoming possible for companies never to own a server. It's a fascinating transformation to watch and be part of!

When I was first coming up with the ideas that eventually became AWS Lambda, I had many discussions with the AWS leadership team about the risks and opportunities. The opportunities were massive—the chance to reimagine how compute and applications were constructed and to change the very nature of software development in the cloud. But the risks were equally great. The innovative "spark gap" of Lambda was high, and crossing that chasm required a lot of energy: to gain the advantages of serverless—pay per use, per-request scaling, built-in fault tolerance, and so much more—*we'd have to ask developers to give up conventional server- and container-based deployments*. They'd have to approach architecture in a completely different way, one built around doing as *little* as possible rather than owning as *much* as possible. Back in 2014 when we unveiled Lambda to the world, this was our biggest fear: *would developers make that leap and come on that journey with us?*

Fortunately the answer over the last five years has proven to be a resounding "yes," and at the heart of that success are books like the one you're reading now. A revolution like serverless requires spreading the message to millions of developers—many of whom will have existing code, in-place processes and tools, and a wealth of language and library knowledge that they need to preserve. Mike and John, the founders of Symphonia and authors of *Programming AWS Lambda*, bring many years of experience and expertise not just in working with AWS and Lambda but also in working with countless Java developers and mission-critical enterprise Java applications. This insight helps them bridge the new world of serverless and the existing knowledge and practices of enterprise Java developers and their teams. It's this marriage of understanding—the best of old and new together—that gives these authors their unique insight and makes this material so essential.

If you're completely new to serverless, this book will help you understand not just what it makes possible but also *why* and *how*. If you're getting started or have used services like AWS Lambda in other languages, it will be your trusted companion as you learn the best practices for architecting, developing, deploying, testing, and monitoring serverless Java applications of all types—from highly distributed mobile apps to highly scalable data processing pipelines. Regardless of your skill level, this book will help you design and deliver Java applications faster and more reliably.

Welcome to the serverless world, and enjoy your journey—your expert tour guides await!

— Dr. Tim Wagner
Vendia CEO and Cofounder,
Original creator of AWS Lambda

Preface

About This Book

Welcome to *Programming AWS Lambda*. We're glad you're here!

Serverless computing is a revolutionary way of building systems. At its heart, serverless is about performing the minimum technical work necessary to sustainably provide value to our users. A serverless approach does this by making the most of services provided by cloud vendors, like Amazon Web Services (AWS).

In this book, you'll learn how to architect, build, and operate serverless applications that use *AWS Lambda*—the original, and widely adopted, serverless compute platform. AWS Lambda is rarely used by itself, however, and so while reading this book, you'll also learn how to successfully integrate Lambda with other serverless AWS services, like S3, DynamoDB, and more.

Why We Wrote This Book

We have been using Lambda since 2015, ever since Lambda's support for Java was first announced. Within just a few weeks we saw the amazing ability that Lambda had to let teams build new features far faster than we'd ever seen before. By removing a lot of low-level aspects of developing and running systems, and instead focusing on a clean, event-driven approach, we realized that many of the complexities that got in the way of our teams no longer applied when using Lambda. Lambda also let us amplify our use of the rest of the AWS platform—it had a multiplicative impact on our effectiveness.

We initially had two concerns about Lambda—that it wouldn't support the programming knowledge and software inventory that we'd built over the years in Java and that it would be far too expensive to run at scale.

What we found instead surprised us.

Lambda's support for Java was not merely an "add on." In fact, Java is a first-class runtime within the Lambda platform. Building Lambda applications in Java freed us to get back to the essence of programming, letting us use our skills and existing code.

Further, Lambda turned out to be less, not more, expensive to run than equivalent, traditionally built systems. The efficiency of Lambda's "pay-per-use" model, to subsecond precision, allowed us to create systems that processed hundreds of millions of events per day and yet were cheaper than their predecessors.

This combination of speed of development, embrace of existing languages, and cost effectiveness led us to believe that serverless compute platforms, with Lambda at their forefront, were the start of something special in our industry. In 2016 we started our business, Symphonia, with the mission to help companies make the leap to this new way of building systems.

Who This Book Is For

This book is intended primarily for software developers and software architects, but it will be useful to anyone involved in the technical aspects of building software applications in the cloud.

We assume that you already know or can learn the basics of the Java programming language. You don't need to have knowledge of, or experience with, any Java application frameworks (like Spring) or libraries (like Guava). We do not assume that you have any prior knowledge of Amazon Web Services.

Why You Need This Book

In many ways serverless, and Lambda with it, is one of the most significant changes to building server-side software in decades. While our code may look similar line by line, and perhaps even class by class, to how it was written before, the architectural constraints and capabilities of Lambda drive designs that have a very different shape than what you've seen in the past.

Over the last few years we've come to understand how to successfully build systems with Lambda. This book will give you a jump-start into learning these same lessons.

From getting started techniques to advanced architecture, from programming and testing to deployment and monitoring, we cover the lifecycle of what you need to understand to build production-quality systems with Lambda at scale.

What makes this book unique is we do all of this in the context of the Java programming language. We've both been Java programmers for more than two decades each, so in this book we help you use your existing Java skills in a whole new way.

So strap in, and welcome to the age of serverless!

Using the End-of-Chapter Exercises

Each chapter of this book ends with some exercises. Some of these exercises encourage you to take the lessons of the chapter and see them working "for real" in the AWS Cloud. While certain elements of Lambda can be simulated locally, you'll only really get a feel for what Lambda development is like by using it in the context of the AWS platform. The good news is that AWS provides a healthy "free tier" (*https://aws.amazon.com/free*) that should allow you to experiment without incurring any costs.

Other exercises are intended to make you consider how you might work differently with Lambda compared with other technologies. Serverless architecture is often a very different way of thinking, and working through these exercises will start adapting your brain in this way.

Conventions Used in This Book

The following typographical conventions are used in this book:

Italic
> Indicates new terms, URLs, email addresses, filenames, and file extensions.

`Constant width`
> Used for program listings, as well as within paragraphs to refer to program elements such as variable or function names, databases, data types, environment variables, statements, and keywords.

`Constant width bold`
> Shows commands or other text that should be typed literally by the user.

`Constant width italic`
> Shows text that should be replaced with user-supplied values or by values determined by context.

> This element signifies a tip or suggestion.

> This element signifies a general note.

This element indicates a warning or caution.

Using Code Examples

Supplemental material (code examples, exercises, etc.) is available for download at *https://github.com/symphoniacloud/programming-aws-lambda-book*.

If you have a technical question or a problem using the code examples, please send email to *bookquestions@oreilly.com*.

This book is here to help you get your job done. In general, if example code is offered with this book, you may use it in your programs and documentation. You do not need to contact us for permission unless you're reproducing a significant portion of the code. For example, writing a program that uses several chunks of code from this book does not require permission. Selling or distributing examples from O'Reilly books does require permission. Answering a question by citing this book and quoting example code does not require permission. Incorporating a significant amount of example code from this book into your product's documentation does require permission.

We appreciate, but do not require, attribution. An attribution usually includes the title, author, publisher, and ISBN. For example: "*Programming AWS Lambda* by John Chapin and Mike Roberts (O'Reilly). Copyright 2020 Symphonia LLC, 978-1-492-04105-4."

If you feel your use of code examples falls outside fair use or the permission given above, feel free to contact us at *permissions@oreilly.com*.

O'Reilly Online Learning

 For more than 40 years, *O'Reilly Media* has provided technology and business training, knowledge, and insight to help companies succeed.

Our unique network of experts and innovators share their knowledge and expertise through books, articles, conferences, and our online learning platform. O'Reilly's online learning platform gives you on-demand access to live training courses, in-depth learning paths, interactive coding environments, and a vast collection of text and video from O'Reilly and 200+ other publishers. For more information, please visit *http://oreilly.com*.

How to Contact Us

Please address comments and questions concerning this book to the publisher:

O'Reilly Media, Inc.
1005 Gravenstein Highway North
Sebastopol, CA 95472
800-998-9938 (in the United States or Canada)
707-829-0515 (international or local)
707-829-0104 (fax)

We have a web page for this book, where we list errata, examples, and any additional information. You can access this page at *https://oreil.ly/programming-aws-lambda*.

Email *bookquestions@oreilly.com* to comment or ask technical questions about this book.

For more information about our books, courses, conferences, and news, see our website at *http://www.oreilly.com*.

Find us on Facebook: *http://facebook.com/oreilly*

Follow us on Twitter: *http://twitter.com/oreillymedia*

Watch us on YouTube: *http://www.youtube.com/oreillymedia*

Acknowledgments

Thanks to our technical reviewers for giving their time and improving this book for you: Brian Gruber, Daniel Bryant, Sarah Wells, and Stuart Sierra. Thanks to our former coworkers at Intent Media who joined in with using a wild new technology four years ago and showed us how it could transform teams. Thanks to all of Symphonia's clients, partners, and friends—we're grateful for your continued trust and confidence. Thanks to everyone at O'Reilly, especially our editorial team; it's amazing to write our own "animal" book two decades and more after we started reading them. And thanks to all of the folk in the serverless community who we've been sharing this ride with!

Further thanks to the members of the AWS serverless team, especially Ajay Nair, Chris Munns, Noel Dowling, and Salman Paracha, for producing a revolutionary product and for chatting with us over the last few years. Finally thanks to Tim Wagner for leading Lambda through its infancy and for writing the foreword to this book!

John's acknowledgments: First and foremost, thank you to my parents, Mark and Bridget, who gave me the privilege and freedom to choose my own path in life and the love and support to not fall off of it. Thanks of course to my coauthor and business partner, Mike, without whom this book and our company would have never existed—one day I'll teach him how to write American English (but not today). And endless thanks to my wife Jessica, who kept my spirits up and never asked what the word count was.

Mike's acknowledgments: There's too many people to thank here, but I'll give it a go. Thanks to my senior school computer studies teacher, Ray Lovell, and to my college tutor, Carroll Morgan. Thanks to my colleagues through the years, especially from my time at ThoughtWorks. Daniel Terhorst-North has been a mentor and brain-twister through most of my career; Daniel, please keep making me go "huh!?" Thanks to Brian Guthrie, Lisa van Gelder, and the rest of the NYC eXtreme Tuesday Club community. And to Mike Mason who has been a colleague (twice), a roommate (on several occasions), and the closest of friends for far more than half of my life. (Yes, Mike, The Phrase is in the book—it's your turn again now!)

My most significant appreciation, however, goes to three people "without whom…" First, thanks to Martin Fowler for inspiration, for friendship, and also for publishing my article on serverless architectures that led to what you're reading here. Next, thanks to my coauthor John for joining me in the roller coaster that is our company, Symphonia. Finally, of course, thanks to my wonderful spouse, Sara, who supports both the strange hours of me being self-employed and apparently me now being a published author.

CHAPTER 1

Introduction to Serverless, Amazon Web Services, and AWS Lambda

To start off your serverless journey, we're going to take you on a brief tour of the cloud and then define serverless. After that, we dive into Amazon Web Services (AWS)—this will be new to some of you and a refresher to others.

With those foundations set, we introduce Lambda—what it is, why you might use it, what you can build with Lambda, and how Java and Lambda work together.

A Quick History Lesson

Let's travel back in time to 2006. No one has an iPhone yet, Ruby on Rails is a hot new programming environment, and Twitter is being launched. More germane to us, however, is that at this point in time many people are hosting their server-side applications on physical servers that they own and have racked in a data center.

In August 2006 something happened that would fundamentally change this model. Amazon's new IT division, AWS, announced the launch of Elastic Compute Cloud (EC2) (*https://aws.amazon.com/ec2*).

EC2 was one of the first infrastructure-as-a-service (IaaS) products. IaaS allows companies to rent compute capacity—that is, a host to run their internet-facing server applications—rather than buying their own machines. It also allows them to provision hosts just in time, with the delay from requesting a machine to its availability being on the order of minutes. In 2006 this was all possible because of the advances in *virtualization* technology—all EC2 hosts at that time were *virtual machines*.

EC2's five key advantages are:

Reduced labor cost

Before IaaS, companies needed to hire specific technical operations staff who would work in data centers and manage their physical servers. This meant everything from power and networking to racking and installing to fixing physical problems with machines like bad RAM to setting up the operating system (OS). With IaaS all of this goes away and instead becomes the responsibility of the IaaS service provider (AWS in the case of EC2).

Reduced risk

When managing their own physical servers, companies are exposed to problems caused by unplanned incidents like failing hardware. This introduces downtime periods of highly volatile length since hardware problems are usually infrequent and can take a long time to fix. With IaaS, the customer, while still having some work to do in the event of a hardware failure, no longer needs know what to do to fix the hardware. Instead the customer can simply request a new machine instance, available within a few minutes, and reinstall the application, limiting exposure to such issues.

Reduced infrastructure cost

In many scenarios the cost of a connected EC2 instance is cheaper than running your own hardware when you take into account power, networking, etc. This is especially valid when you want to run hosts for a only few days or weeks, rather than many months or years at a stretch. Similarly, renting hosts by the hour rather than buying them outright allows different accounting: EC2 machines are an operating expense (Opex) rather than the capital expense (Capex) of physical machines, typically allowing much more favorable accounting flexibility.

Scaling

Infrastructure costs drop significantly when considering the scaling benefits IaaS brings. With IaaS, companies have far more flexibility in scaling the numbers and types of servers they run. There is no longer a need to buy 10 high-end servers up front because you think you might need them in a few months' time. Instead, you can start with one or two low-powered, inexpensive virtual machines (VMs) and then scale your number and types of VMs up and down over time without any negative cost impact.

Lead time

In the bad old days of self-hosted servers, it could take months to procure and provision a server for a new application. If you came up with an idea you wanted to try within a few weeks, then that was just too bad. With IaaS, lead time goes from months to minutes. This has ushered in the age of rapid product experimentation, as encouraged by the ideas in Lean Startup (*http://thelean startup.com*).

The Cloud Grows

IaaS was one of the first key elements of the cloud, along with storage (e.g., AWS Simple Storage Service (S3) (*https://aws.amazon.com/s3*)). AWS was an early mover in cloud services, and is still a leading provider, but there are many other cloud vendors such as Microsoft and Google.

The next evolution of the cloud was platform as a service (PaaS). One of the most popular PaaS providers is Heroku. PaaS layers on top of IaaS, abstracting the management of the host's operating system. With PaaS you deploy just applications, and the platform is responsible for OS installation, patch upgrades, system-level monitoring, service discovery, etc.

An alternative to using a PaaS is to use containers. Docker (*https://www.docker.com*) has become incredibly popular over the last few years as a way to more clearly delineate an application's system requirements from the nitty-gritty of the operating system itself. There are cloud-based services to host and manage/orchestrate containers on a team's behalf, and these are often referred to as containers-as-a-service (CaaS) products. Amazon, Google, and Microsoft all offer CaaS platforms. Managing fleets of Docker containers has been made easier by use of tools like Kubernetes (*https://kubernetes.io*), either in a self-managed form or as part of a CaaS (e.g., GKE from Google, EKS from Amazon, or AKS from Microsoft).

All three of these ideas—IaaS, PaaS, and CaaS—can be grouped as *compute as a service*; in other words, they are different types of generic environments that we can run our own specialized software in. PaaS and CasS differ from IaaS by raising the level of abstraction further, allowing us to hand off more of our "heavy lifting" to others.

Enter Serverless

Serverless is the next evolution of cloud computing and can be divided into two ideas: backend as a service and functions as a service.

Backend as a Service

Backend as a service (BaaS) allows us to replace server-side components that we code and/or manage ourselves with off-the-shelf services. It's closer in concept to software as a service (SaaS) than it is to things like virtual instances and containers. SaaS is typically about outsourcing business processes, though —think HR or sales tools or, on the technical side, products like GitHub—whereas with BaaS, we're breaking up our applications into smaller pieces and implementing some of those pieces entirely with externally hosted products.

BaaS services are domain-generic remote components (i.e., not in-process libraries) that we can incorporate into our products, with an application programming interface (API) being a typical integration paradigm.

BaaS has become especially popular with teams developing mobile apps or single-page web apps. Many such teams are able to rely significantly on third-party services to perform tasks that they would otherwise have needed to do themselves. Let's look at a couple of examples.

First up we have services like Google's Firebase (*https://firebase.google.com*). Firebase is a database product that is fully managed by a vendor (Google in this case) that can be accessed directly from a mobile or web application without the need for our own intermediary application server. This represents one aspect of BaaS: services that manage data components on our behalf.

BaaS services also allow us to rely on application logic that someone else has implemented. A good example here is authentication—many applications implement their own code to perform sign-up, login, password management, etc., but more often than not this code is similar across many apps. Such repetition across teams and businesses is ripe for extraction into an external service, and that's precisely the aim of products like Auth0 (*https://auth0.com*) and Amazon's Cognito (*https://aws.amazon.com/cognito*). Both of these products allow mobile apps and web apps to have fully featured authentication and user management, but without a development team having to write or manage any of the code to implement those features.

The term *BaaS* came to prominence with the rise in mobile application development; in fact, the term is sometimes referred to as *mobile backend as a service* (MBaaS). However, the key idea of using fully externally managed products as part of our application development is not unique to mobile development, or even frontend development in general.

Functions as a Service

The other half of serverless is functions as a service (FaaS). FaaS, like IaaS, PaaS, and CaaS, is another form of compute as a service—a generic environment within which we can run our own software. Some people like to use the term *serverless compute* instead of FaaS.

With FaaS we deploy our code as independent functions or operations, and we configure those functions to be called, or triggered, when a specific event or request occurs within the FaaS platform. The platform itself calls our functions by instantiating a dedicated environment *for each event*—this environment consists of an ephemeral, fully managed lightweight virtual machine, or container; the FaaS runtime; and our code.

The result of this type of environment is that we have no concern for the runtime management of our code, unlike any other style of compute platform.

Furthermore, because of several factors of serverless in general that we describe in a moment, with FaaS we have no concern for hosts or processes, and scaling and resource management are handled on our behalf.

Differentiating Serverless

The idea of using externally hosted application components, as we do with BaaS, is not new—people have been using hosted SQL databases for a decade or more—so what makes some of these services qualify as backends as a service? And what aspects do BaaS and FaaS have in common that cause us to group them into the idea of serverless computing?

There are five key criteria that differentiate serverless services—both BaaS and FaaS—that allow us to approach architecting applications in a new way. These criteria are as follows:

Does not require managing a long-lived host or application instance
> This is the core of serverless. Most other ways of operating server-side software require us to deploy, run, and monitor an instance of an application (whether programmed by us or others), and that application's lifetime spans more than one request. Serverless implies the opposite of this: there is no long-lived server process, or server host, that we need to manage. That's not to say those servers don't exist—they absolutely do—but they are not our concern or responsibility.

Self auto-scales and auto-provisions, dependent on load
> Auto-scaling is the ability of a system to adjust capacity requirements dynamically based upon load. Most existing auto-scaling solutions require some amount of work by the utilizing team. Serverless services self auto-scale from the first time you use them with no effort at all.

> Serverless services also auto-provision when they perform auto-scaling. They remove all the effort of allocating capacity, both in terms of number and size of underlying resources. This is a huge operational burden lifted.

Has costs that are based on precise usage, up from and down to zero usage
> This is closely tied to the previous point—serverless costs are precisely correlated with usage. The cost of using a BaaS database, for instance, should be closely tied to usage, not predefined capacity. This cost should be largely derived from actual amount of storage used and/or requests made.

> Note that we're not saying costs should be solely based on usage—there may be some overhead cost for using the service in general—but the lion's share of the costs should be proportional to fine-grained usage.

Has performance capabilities defined in terms other than host size/count
> It's reasonable and useful for a serverless platform to expose some performance configuration. However, this configuration should be completely abstracted from whatever underlying instance or host types are being used.

Has implicit high availability
> When operating applications, we typically use the term high availability (HA) to mean that a service will continue to process requests even when an underlying component fails. With a serverless service we expect the vendor to provide HA transparently for us.
>
> As an example, if we're using a BaaS database, we assume that the provider is doing whatever is necessary to handle the failure of individual hosts or internal components.

What Is AWS?

We've talked about AWS a few times already in this chapter, and now it's time to look at this behemoth of cloud providers in a little more detail.

Since its launch in 2006, AWS has grown at a mind-boggling rate, in terms of the number and type of service offered, the capacity that the AWS cloud provides, and the number of companies using it. Let's look at all of those aspects.

Types of Service

AWS has more than a hundred different services. Some of these are fairly low level—networking, virtual machines, basic block storage. Above these services, in abstraction, come the component services—databases, platforms as a service, message buses. Then on top of all of these come true application components—user management, machine learning, data analysis.

Sideways of this stack are the management services necessary to work with AWS at scale—security, cost reporting, deployment, monitoring, etc.

This combination of services is shown in Figure 1-1.

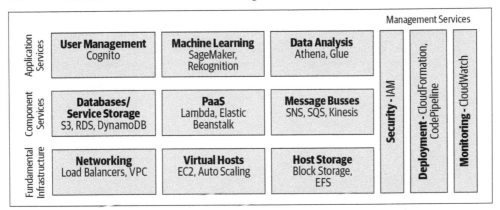

Figure 1-1. AWS service layers

AWS likes to pitch itself as the ultimate IT "Lego brick" provider—it provides a vast number of pluggable types of resources that can be joined together to create huge, massively scalable, enterprise-grade applications.

Capacity

AWS houses its computers in more than 60 data centers spread around the world as shown in Figure 1-2. In AWS terminology, each data center corresponds to an *Availability Zone (AZ)*, and clusters of data centers in close proximity to each other are grouped into *regions*. AWS has more than 20 different regions, across 5 continents.

That's a lot of computers.

While the total number of regions continues to grow, so does the capacity within each region. A vast number of US-based internet companies run their systems in the us-east-1 region in Northern Virginia (just outside Washington DC)—and the more companies that run their systems there, the more confident AWS is in increasing the number of servers available. This is a virtuous cycle between Amazon and its customers.

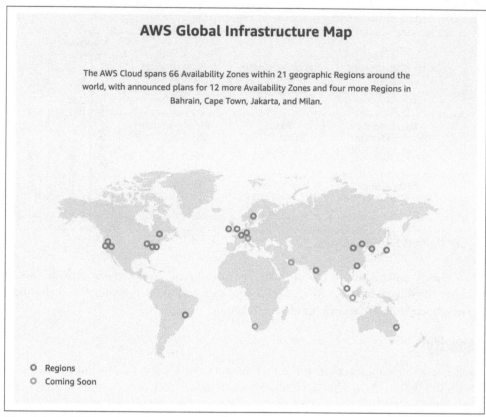

Figure 1-2. AWS regions (source: AWS (https://oreil.ly/61Ztd))

When you use some of Amazon's lower-level services, like EC2, you'll typically specify an Availability Zone to use. With the higher-level services, though, you'll usually specify only a region, and Amazon will handle any problems for you on an individual data center level.

A compelling aspect of Amazon's region model is that each region is largely independent, logistically and from a software management point of view. That means that if a physical problem like a power outage, or a software problem like a deployment bug, happens in one region, the others will almost certainly be unaffected. The region model does make for some extra work from our point of view as users, but overall it works well.

Who Uses AWS?

AWS has a vast number of customers, spread all around the planet. Massive enterprises, governments, startups, individuals, and everyone in between use AWS. Many of the internet services you use are probably hosted on AWS.

AWS is not just for websites. Many companies have moved a lot of their "backend" IT infrastructure to AWS, finding it a more compelling option than running their own physical infrastructure.

AWS, of course, doesn't have a monopoly. Google and Microsoft are their biggest competitors, at least in the English-speaking world, while Alibaba Cloud competes with them in the growing Chinese market. And there are plenty of other cloud providers offering services suited to specific types of customer.

How Do You Use AWS?

Your first interaction with AWS will likely be via the AWS Web Console (*https://console.aws.amazon.com*). To do this, you will need some kind of access credential, which will give you permissions within an *account*. An account is a construct that maps to billing (i.e., paying AWS for the services you use), but it is also a grouping of defined service configurations within AWS. Companies tend to run a number of production applications in one account. (Accounts can also have *subaccounts*, but we won't be talking about them too much in this book—just know that if you're using credentials supplied by a company, they might be for a specific subaccount.)

If you haven't been given credentials by your company, you'll need to create an account. You can do this by supplying AWS with your credit card details, but know that AWS supplies a generous *free tier*, and if you just stick to the basic exercises in this book, you shouldn't end up needing to pay AWS anything.

Your credentials may be in the form of a typical username and password or may be via a single sign-on (SSO) workflow (e.g., via Google Apps or Microsoft Active Directory). Either way, eventually you'll successfully log in to the web console. Using the web console for the first time can be a daunting experience, with all 100+ AWS services craving your attention—Amazon Polly shouting "PICK ME!!!" in equal measure to a strange thing called Macie. And then of course what about all of those services known only by an acronym—what *are* they?

Part of the reason for the overwhelming nature of the home page of the AWS Console is because it really isn't developed as one product—it's developed as a hundred different products, all given a link on the home page. Also, drilling into one product may look quite different from another because each product is given a good amount of autonomy within the AWS universe. Sometimes using AWS might feel like a spelunking exercise in navigating the AWS corporate organization—don't worry, we all feel that way.

Apart from the web console, the other way of interacting with AWS is via its extensive API. One great aspect that Amazon has had from very early in its history, even before the times of AWS, is that each service must be fully usable via a public API, and this means that for all intents and purposes anything that is possible to configure in AWS can be done via the API.

Layered on top of the API is the CLI—the command line interface—which we use in this book. The CLI is most simply described as a thin client application that communicates with the AWS API. We talk about configuring the CLI in the next chapter ("AWS Command Line Interface" on page 26).

What Is AWS Lambda?

Lambda is Amazon's FaaS platform. We briefly mentioned FaaS earlier, but now it's time to dig into it in some more detail.

Functions as a Service

As we introduced before, FaaS is a new way of building and deploying server-side software, oriented around deploying individual functions or operations. FaaS is where a lot of the buzz about serverless comes from; in fact, many people think that serverless *is* FaaS, but they're missing out on the complete picture. While this book focuses on FaaS, we encourage you to consider BaaS too as you build out bigger applications.

When we deploy traditional server-side software, we start with a host instance, typically a VM instance or a container (see Figure 1-3). We then deploy our application, which usually runs as an operating system process, within the host. Usually our application contains code for several different but related operations; for instance, a web service may allow both retrieval and updating resources.

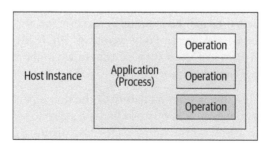

Figure 1-3. Traditional server-side software deployment

From an ownership point of view, we as users are responsible for all three aspects of this configuration—host instance, application process, and of course program operations.

FaaS changes this model of deployment and ownership (see Figure 1-4). We strip away both the host instance and the application process from our model. Instead, we focus on just the individual operations or functions that express our application's logic. We upload those functions individually to a FaaS platform, which itself is the responsibility of the cloud vendor and not us.

Figure 1-4. FaaS software deployment

The functions are not constantly active in an application process, though, sitting idle until they need to be run as they would in a traditional system. Instead, the FaaS platform is configured to listen for a specific event for each operation. When that event occurs, the platform instantiates the FaaS function and then calls it, passing the triggering event.

Once the function has finished executing, the FaaS platform is free to tear it down. Alternatively, as an optimization, it may keep the function around for a little while until there's another event to be processed.

FaaS as Implemented by Lambda

AWS Lambda was launched in 2014, and it continues to grow in scope, maturity, and usage. Some Lambda functions might be very low throughput—perhaps just executing once per day, or even less frequently than that. But others may be executed billions of times per day.

Lambda implements the FaaS pattern by instantiating ephemeral, managed, Linux environments to host each of our function instances. Lambda guarantees that only one event is processed per environment at a time. At the time of writing, Lambda also requires that the function completes processing of the event within 15 minutes; otherwise, the execution is aborted.

Lambda provides an exceptionally lightweight programming and deployment model —we just provide a function, and associated dependencies, in a ZIP or JAR file, and Lambda fully manages the runtime environment.

Lambda is tightly integrated with many other AWS services. This corresponds to many different types of event source that can trigger Lambda functions, and this leads to the ability to build many different types of applications using Lambda.

Lambda is a fully serverless service, as defined by our differentiating criteria from earlier, specifically:

Does not require managing a long-lived host or application instance
  With Lambda we are fully abstracted from the underlying host running our code. Furthermore, we do not manage a long-lived application—once our code has finished processing a particular event, AWS is free to terminate the runtime environment.

Self auto-scales and auto-provisions, dependent on load
  This is one of the key benefits of Lambda—resource management and scaling is completely transparent. Once we upload our function code, the Lambda platform will create just enough environments to handle the load at any particular time. If one environment is enough then Lambda will create the environment when it is needed. If on the other hand hundreds of separate instances are required, then Lambda will scale out quickly and without any effort on our part.

Has costs that are based on precise usage, up from and down to zero usage
  AWS charges for Lambda only for the time that our code is executing per environment, down to a 100 ms precision. If our function is active for 200 ms every 5 minutes, then we'll be charged only for 2.4 seconds of usage per hour. This precise usage cost structure is the same whether one instance of our function is required or a thousand.

Has performance capabilities defined in terms other than host size/count
  Since we are fully abstracted from the underlying host with Lambda, we can't specify a number or type of underlying EC2 instances to use. Instead, we specify how much RAM our function requires (up to a maximum of 3GB), and other aspects of performance are tied to this too. We explore this in more detail later in the book—see "Memory and CPU" on page 59.

Has implicit high availability
  If a particular underlying host fails, then Lambda will automatically start environments on a different host. Similarly, if a particular data center/*Availability Zone* fails, then Lambda will automatically start environments in a different AZ in the same *region*. Note that it's on us as AWS customers to handle a *region-wide* failure, and we talk about this toward the end of the book—see "Globally Distributed Applications" on page 238.

Why Lambda?

The basic benefits of the cloud, as we described earlier, apply to Lambda—it's often cheaper to run in comparison to other types of host platform; it requires less effort and time to operate a Lambda application; and the scaling flexibility of Lambda surpasses any other compute option within AWS.

However, the key benefit from our perspective is how quickly you can build applications with Lambda when combined with other AWS services. We often hear of companies building brand new applications, deployed to production, in just a day or two. Being able to remove ourselves from so much of the infrastructure-related code we often write in regular applications is a huge time-saver.

Lambda also has more capacity, more maturity, and more integration points than any other FaaS platform. It's not perfect, and some other products in our opinion offer better "developer UX" than Lambda. But absent any strong tie to an existing cloud vendor, we would recommend AWS Lambda for all of the reasons listed earlier.

What Does a Lambda Application Look Like?

Traditional long-running server applications often have at least one of two ways of starting work for a particular stimulus—they either open up a TCP/IP socket and wait for inbound connections or have an internal scheduling mechanism that will cause them to reach out to a remote resource to check for new work. Since Lambda is fundamentally an event-oriented platform and since Lambda enforces a timeout, neither of these patterns is applicable to a Lambda application. So how *do* we build a Lambda application?

The first point to consider is that at the lowest level Lambda functions can be invoked (called) in one of two ways:

- Lambda functions can be called *synchronously*—named `RequestResponse` by AWS. In this scenario, an upstream component calls the Lambda function and waits for whatever response the Lambda function generates.

- Alternatively, a Lambda function may be invoked *asynchronously*—named `Event` by AWS. This time the request from the upstream caller is responded to immediately by the Lambda *platform*, while the Lambda *function* proceeds with processing the request. No further response is returned to the caller in this scenario.

These two invocation models have various other behaviors, which we get into later, starting with "Invocation Types" on page 43. For now let's see how they are used in some example applications.

Web API

An obvious question to ask is whether Lambda can be used in the implementation of an HTTP API, and fortunately the answer is yes! While Lambda functions aren't HTTP servers themselves, we can use another AWS component, *API Gateway*, to provide the HTTP protocol and routing logic that we typically have within a web service (see Figure 1-5).

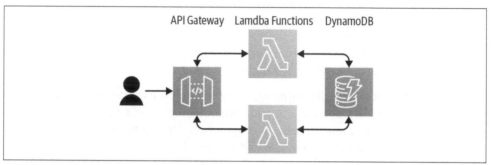

Figure 1-5. Web API using AWS Lambda

The above diagram shows a typical API as used by a single-page web app or by a mobile application. The user's client makes various calls, via HTTP, to the backend to retrieve data and/or initiate requests. In our case, the component that handles the HTTP aspects of the request is Amazon API Gateway—it is an HTTP server.

We configure API Gateway with a mapping from request to handler (e.g., if a client makes a request to GET /restaurants/123, then we can set up API Gateway to call a Lambda function named RestaurantsFunction, passing the details of the request). API Gateway will invoke the Lambda function *synchronously* and will wait for the function to evaluate the request and return a response.

Since the Lambda function instance isn't itself a remotely callable API, the API Gateway actually makes a call to the Lambda platform, specifying the Lambda function to invoke, the type of invocation (RequestResponse), and the request parameters. The Lambda platform then instantiates an instance of RestaurantsFunction and invokes that with the request parameters.

The Lambda platform does have a few limitations, like the maximum timeout we've already mentioned, but apart from that, it's pretty much a standard Linux environment. In RestaurantsFunction we can, for example, make a call to a database—Amazon's DynamoDB is a popular database to use with Lambda, partly due to the similar scaling capabilities of the two services.

Once the function has finished its work, it returns a response, since it was called in a synchronous fashion. This response is passed by the Lambda platform back to API

Gateway, which transforms the response into an HTTP response message, which is itself passed back to the client.

Typically a web API will satisfy multiple types of requests, mapped to different HTTP *paths* and *verbs* (like GET, PUT, POST, etc.). When developing a Lambda-backed web API, you will usually implement different types of requests as different Lambda functions, although you are not forced to use such a design—you can handle all requests as one function if you'd like and switch logic inside the function based on the original HTTP request path and verb.

File processing

A common use case for Lambda is file processing. Let's imagine a mobile application that can upload photos to a remote server, which we then want to make available to other parts of our product suite, but at different image sizes, as shown in Figure 1-6.

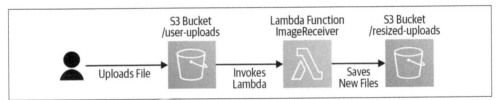

Figure 1-6. File processing using AWS Lambda

S3 is Amazon's Simple Storage Service—the very same that was launched in 2006. Mobile applications can upload files to S3 via the AWS API, in a secure fashion.

S3 can be configured to invoke the Lambda platform when the file is uploaded, specifying the function to be called, and passing a path to the file. As with the previous example, the Lambda platform then instantiates the Lambda function and calls it with the request details passed this time by S3. The difference now, though, is that this is an *asynchronous* invocation (S3 specified the Event invocation type)—no value is returned to S3 nor does S3 wait for a return value.

This time our Lambda function exists solely for the purpose of a *side effect*—it loads the file specified by the request parameter and then creates new, resized versions of the file in a different S3 bucket. With the side effects complete, the Lambda function's work is done. Since it created files in an S3 bucket, we may choose to add a Lambda trigger to that bucket also, invoking further Lambda functions that process these generated files, creating a processing pipeline.

Other examples of Lambda applications

The previous two examples show two scenarios, with two different Lambda event sources. There are many other event sources that enable us to build many other types of applications. Just some of these are as follows:

- We can build message-processing applications, using message buses like Simple Notification Service (SNS), Simple Queue Service (SQS), EventBridge, or Kinesis as the event source.

- We can build email-processing applications, using Simple Email Service (SES) as the event source.

- We can build scheduled-task applications, similar to cron programs, using CloudWatch Scheduled Events as the trigger.

Note that many of these services other than Lambda are *BaaS* services and therefore also serverless. Combining FaaS and BaaS to produce *serverless architectures* is an extraordinarily powerful technique due to their similar scaling, security, and cost characteristics. In fact, it's such combinations of service that are driving the popularity of serverless computing.

We talk in depth about building applications in this way in Chapter 5.

AWS Lambda in the Java World

AWS Lambda natively supports a large number of languages. JavaScript and Python are very popular "getting started" languages for Lambda (as well as for significant production applications) partly because of their dynamically typed, noncompiled nature allowing for very fast development cycles.

We both got our start, however, using Lambda with Java. Java occasionally has a bad reputation in the Lambda world—some of which is fair, and some not. If what you need in a Lambda function can be expressed in 10 lines or so, it's typically quicker to put something together in JavaScript or Python. However, for larger applications, there are many excellent reasons to implement Lambda functions in Java, a couple of which are as follows:

- If you or your team is more familiar with Java than the other Lambda-supported languages, then you'll have the ability to reuse these skills and libraries in a new runtime platform. Java is as much a "first-class language" in the Lambda ecosystem as JavaScript, Python, Go, etc., are—Lambda is not limiting you if you use Java. Further, if you already have a lot of code implemented in Java, then porting some of this to Lambda can be a significant time-to-market advantage, in comparison to reimplementing in a different language.

- In high throughput messaging systems, the typical runtime performance benefit of Java over JavaScript or Python can be significant. Not only is "faster" normally "better" in any system, with Lambda "faster" can also result in tangible cost benefits due to Lambda's pricing model.

For JVM workloads, Lambda natively supports, at the time of writing, the Java 8 and Java 11 runtimes. The Lambda platform will instantiate a version of the Java Runtime Environment within its Linux environment and then run our code within that Java VM. Our code, therefore, must be compatible with that runtime environment, but we're not restricted to just using the Java language. Scala, Clojure, Kotlin, and more, can all be run on Lambda (see more at "Other JVM Languages and Lambda" on page 224).

There's also an advanced option with Lambda to define your own runtime if neither of these Java versions is sufficient—we discuss this further in "Custom Runtimes" on page 223.

The Lambda platform supplies a few basic libraries with the runtime (e.g., a small subset of the AWS Java library) but any other libraries that your code needs must be supplied with your code itself. You will learn how to do that in "Build and Package" on page 65.

Finally, while Java has the programming construct of *Lambda expressions* (*https:// oreil.ly/nnjwh*), these are unrelated to AWS Lambda functions. You are free to use Java Lambda expressions within your AWS Lambda function if you'd like (since AWS Lambda supports Java 8 and later) or not.

Summary

In this chapter, you learned how serverless computing is the next evolution of the cloud—a way of building applications by relying on services that handle resource management, scaling, and more, transparently and without configuration.

Further, you now understand that functions as a service (FaaS) and backend as a service (BaaS) are the two halves of serverless, with FaaS being the general-purpose computing paradigm within serverless. For more information on serverless in general, we refer you to our free O'Reilly ebook *What Is Serverless?* (*https://oreil.ly/ 5YbLa*)

You also have at least a basic knowledge of Amazon Web Services—one of the world's most popular cloud platforms. You've learned about the vast capacity that AWS has to host our applications and how you access AWS both via the web console and the API/ CLI.

You've been introduced to AWS Lambda—Amazon's FaaS product. We compared "thinking in Lambda" to a traditionally built application, talked about why you may want to use Lambda versus other FaaS implementations, and then gave some examples of applications built using Lambda.

Finally, you saw a quick overview of Java as a Lambda language option.

In Chapter 2 we implement our first Lambda function—get ready for a brave new world!

Exercises

1. Acquire credentials for an AWS account (*https://aws.amazon.com*). The easiest way to do this is by creating a new account. As we mentioned earlier, if you do this, you'll need to supply a credit card number, but everything we do in this book should be covered by the free tier, unless you get very enthusiastic with tests!

   Alternatively you can use an existing AWS account, but if so, we recommend using a "development" account so as not to interfere with any "production" systems.

   We also strongly recommend that whatever access you use grants you full administrative permissions within the account; otherwise, you'll be bogged down by distracting security issues.

2. Log in to the AWS Console (*https://console.aws.amazon.com*). Find the Lambda section—are there any functions there yet?

3. *Extended task*: Look at Amazon's serverless marketing page (*https:// aws.amazon.com/serverless*), specifically where it describes the various services in its "serverless platform." Which of these services fully satisfy the differentiating criteria of a serverless service we described earlier? Which don't, and in what ways are they "mostly" serverless?

CHAPTER 2

Getting Started with AWS Lambda

Chapter 1 provided you with the background for the rest of this book: the cloud, serverless, AWS, and an introduction to what Lambda is, how it works, and what it can be used for. But this is a practical book, for practical people, so in this chapter we're going to roll up our sleeves and deploy some working functions to the cloud.

We'll start by getting you a little more acclimated with the AWS Console, and then we'll deploy and run our first Lambda function. After that we'll get a local development environment ready, and finally we'll build and deploy a locally developed function to Lambda.

 If you're already experienced with AWS, please feel free to skip ahead to "Lambda Hello World (as Quickly as Possible)" on page 22.

Quick Guide to the AWS Console

The first two exercises in Chapter 1 involved acquiring AWS credentials and then logging into the AWS Web Console (*https://console.aws.amazon.com*). If you haven't done that already, you should do that now.

Slightly confusingly, there are three different types of credential that you may have used to log in:

- You may have used the account "root" user, using an email address and password. This is equivalent to using the root user in a Linux system.

- You may have used an "IAM user" and password. In this case you will have also needed to have provided the numeric AWS account ID (or an AWS account alias).

- Finally, you might have used a single sign-on method (e.g., via a Google Apps account).

Are you signed in successfully now? Great! Let's go on a little tour of the AWS world.

 First of all, a quick word of warning/explanation. The AWS Web Console has frequent UX changes, and by the time you read this book, some of the UI may look different than what you see here in the book. We'll do what we can to explain the intent of an example, not just the interactions, so that you'll still be able to follow along when Amazon changes its UI.

Regions

Let's dive in. First let's talk regions. At the top right you'll see the currently selected region (Figure 2-1).

Figure 2-1. Currently selected region

As you learned in Chapter 1, AWS organizes its infrastructure into data centers called *Availability Zones* (AZs) and then clusters AZs into a closely located group known as a *region*. Each region operates semi-autonomously. Right now you're looking at the web console home page for a specific region—in our previous example that's Oregon, otherwise known as the us-west-2 region.

You don't have to use the default region that was selected when you log in—you're free to traverse the globe in search of the right region for you. Click the region name and see the list of regions available to you (Figure 2-2).

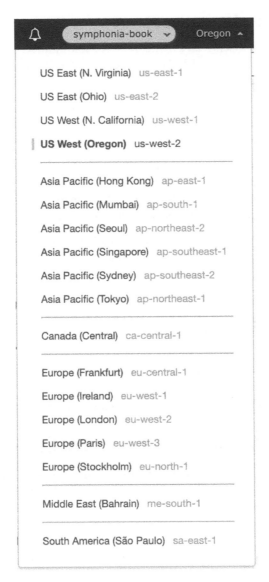

Figure 2-2. Pick a region

For what we're going to be covering in this book, any region should be sufficient. We're going to be defaulting to US West (Oregon) for everything we do, and you may want to use that too as a fallback choice, but feel free to use a region closer to your home if you'd like.

Identity and Access Management

Now let's pick our first service. On the web console home page, either expand all services and find the one named *IAM* or search for *IAM* in the search box, and select it.

IAM stands for *Identity and Access Management*—it's the most fundamental security service within AWS. It's also one of the few AWS services that is not tied to any one region (note the reference to *Global* where your region used to be defined).

IAM lets you create "IAM users," groups, roles, policies, and more. If you're using the AWS account you created for this book (and therefore used the "root" email address user to log in), we recommend creating an IAM user for future work. We'll describe how to do this in "Acquiring credentials for the AWS CLI" on page 28.

Roles are like users, in that they can be used to allow a human, or process, to acquire certain privileges in order to fulfill a task. Unlike users, they don't have a username or password, and instead a role must be *assumed* in order to be used.

One of the things you'll quickly discover is that AWS are sticklers for security. When you create Lambda functions, you *must* specify a role that it is to assume when it is executing. AWS will *not* give it a default role if one isn't specified. We'll see this when we create our first function in a moment.

It's crucial that you have a fundamental understanding of IAM, since aspects like roles and policies are ubiquitous in Lambda development. We give you a thorough grounding of IAM in "Identity and Access Management" on page 78.

Lambda Hello World (as Quickly as Possible)

In this section we're going to deploy and run our first Lambda function. We'll let you in on a little secret—we're going to do this with JavaScript. Shhh—don't tell our editors—we promised this would be a Java book!

The reason for doing this first example in JavaScript is that we can do the whole exercise purely in the web browser, giving us a taste of what's possible in Lambda in just a few minutes.

First, go back to the AWS Web Console home screen, and pick Lambda. If you've never used Lambda in this account before, you'll get a screen that looks something like Figure 2-3.

Figure 2-3. Lambda welcome screen

If Lambda has been used in this account before, the web console will look more like Figure 2-4.

Figure 2-4. Lambda function list

Again, it might look different depending on when you read this due to Amazon's ever-changing UI designs.

Either way, click *Create function*, and then choose *Author from scratch*—there are some other options here for getting started with more complicated functions, but we're going to be doing something very simple right now.

In the name box (see Figure 2-5), type **HelloWorld**, and under *Runtime* click *Node.js 10.x.* Don't worry, we'll be working with Java soon! Now click *Create function.*

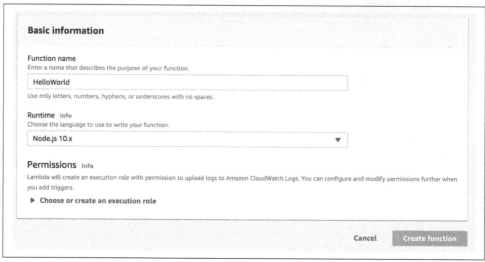

Basic information

Function name
Enter a name that describes the purpose of your function.

HelloWorld

Use only letters, numbers, hyphens, or underscores with no spaces.

Runtime Info
Choose the language to use to write your function.

Node.js 10.x

Permissions Info
Lambda will create an execution role with permission to upload logs to Amazon CloudWatch Logs. You can configure and modify permissions further when you add triggers.

▶ Choose or create an execution role

Cancel   Create function

Figure 2-5. Create HelloWorld function

If after doing this the console expands the Permissions section, select *Create a new role with basic Lambda permissions* in the *Execution role* drop-down, and then click *Create function* again (see Figure 2-6).

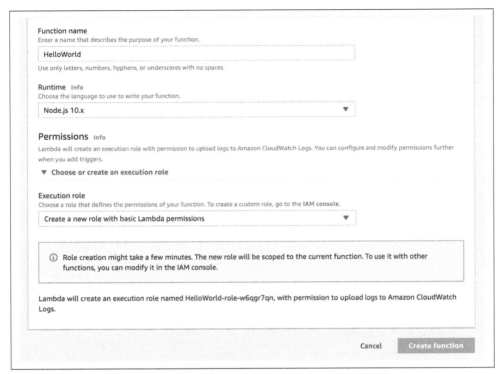

Figure 2-6. Create HelloWorld function, specifying to create a new role

Lambda will create a Lambda function configuration within the Lambda platform and bring you to the main console page for the Lambda function after a short wait.

If you scroll down, you'll see that it's even given the function some default code—that code is perfectly fine for us for now.

Scroll back to the top, and click the *Test* button. This will open a dialog named *Configure test event*—enter **HelloWorldTest** in the *Event name* box, and click *Create*. This will take you back to the Lambda function screen. Now click *Test* again.

This time Lambda will actually execute your function, and there will be a short delay as it instantiates an environment for the code. Then you'll see a box with *Execution result*—it should say that the function succeeded!

Expand the *Details* control, and you'll see the value returned from your function, plus some other diagnostics (see Figure 2-7).

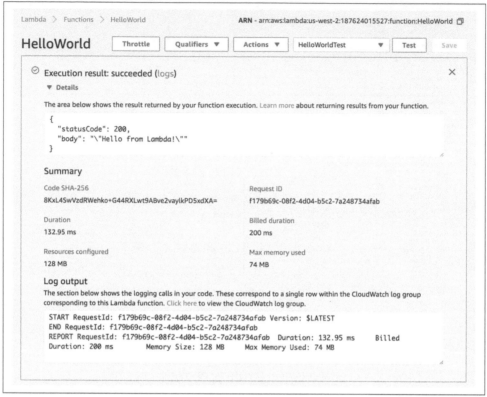

Figure 2-7. HelloWorld executed

Congratulations—you've created and run your first Lambda function!

Setting Up Your Development Environment

Now that you have a little taste of running functions (no servers!), we'll turn to actually building and deploying Java Lambda functions in a way more suited to rapid iteration and automation.

First you need to set up a local development environment.

AWS Command Line Interface

If you've used the AWS CLI before and already have it configured on your machine you can skip ahead.

Installing the AWS CLI

Amazon and AWS are built on APIs. In this classic story of Amazon's API mandate (*https://oreil.ly/AixTf*), we see that "All teams will henceforth expose their data and functionality through service interfaces" and "All service interfaces, without exception, must be designed from the ground up to be externalizable." What this means is that almost anything that we can do through the AWS Web Console UI we can also do using the AWS API and CLI.

The AWS API is a large collection of HTTP endpoints that we can call to perform actions within AWS. While calling the API directly is perfectly supported, it's also a little laborious due to things like authentication/request signing, correct serialization, etc. For this reason, AWS gives us two tools to make things easier—SDKs and the CLI.

Software development kits (SDKs) are libraries that AWS provides that we can use within our code to call the AWS APIs, smoothing some of the tricky or repetitive points of doing so, for example authentication. We use the SDKs later in the book— "Example: Building a Serverless API" on page 92 looks at this subject in depth.

For now though, we're going to use the AWS CLI. The CLI is a tool you can use from a terminal—it wraps the AWS API, so almost anything available through the API is also accessible via the CLI.

You can use the CLI on macOS, Windows, and Linux; however, all the examples and suggestions we give are for macOS. If you use a different operating system for your development machine, then you should combine the instructions here with whatever is specified in the AWS CLI documentation.

Follow these instructions to install the CLI (*https://oreil.ly/84dGt*). If you use a Mac and Homebrew (*https://brew.sh*), installing the CLI is as simple as running `brew install awscli`.

To validate your install of the CLI, run `aws --version` from a terminal prompt. It should return something similar to the following:

```
$ aws --version
aws-cli/1.15.30 Python/3.6.5 Darwin/17.6.0 botocore/1.10.30
```

The precise output will depend on your operating system, among other factors.

A Quick Note on Operating Systems

We developed this book using the Mac operating system (specifically macOS 10.14 Mojave), and all examples were tested with this OS.

Linux users should be able to use all the examples we give without any changes.

Windows users will need to modify the examples related to running commands from a terminal in a number of places, in the following ways:

- Where we use an example starting with a $ (e.g., the one immediately preceding this section: $ aws --version), you should run the command that follows after the $ in your machine's terminal/command prompt.
- Single quotes (') can often be substituted by double quotes (").
- Double quotes (") can be escaped with backslashes like this: \".
- For variable substitution (where in the examples we say, e.g., $CF_BUCKET) use the form %CF_BUCKET%.
- Instead of the cat command, use the type command.
- The backslashes used to indicate multiline commands in the examples should be removed—instead, make one long line and execute that at the command prompt.

Acquiring credentials for the AWS CLI

The credentials that you use with the AWS CLI are *different* from those that you used to log in to the AWS Web Console. For the CLI, you need two values: an *Access Key ID* along with its *Secret Access Key*. If you already have these values, feel free to skip ahead to the next section.

The Access Key ID and Secret Access Key pair are credentials that are assigned to an *IAM user*. It's also possible to assign a key and secret to the account root user associated with an email address, but AWS strongly advises against doing this for security reasons, and so do we.

If you don't already have an IAM user (because you logged in with the root user, or because you used SSO), you'll need to create an IAM user. To do this, go to the IAM console in the AWS Web Console that we visited earlier in this chapter. Click on *Users* and double-check that there isn't a user on that screen for you (see Figure 2-8).

Figure 2-8. IAM user list

If you do in fact need to create a user, click *Add user*. On the first screen, give your user a name and select both *Programmatic access* and *AWS Management Console access*. Then select *Custom password* and enter a new password—this will be the password for logging in to the AWS Web Console with this new user, should you wish to do so. Deselect *Password reset* (see Figure 2-9). Then click *Next: Permissions*.

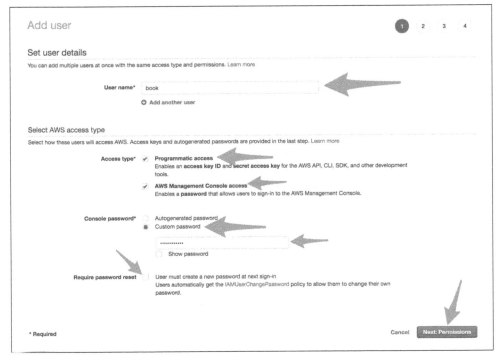

Figure 2-9. Add IAM user

On the next screen, select *Attach existing policies directly* and select *Administrator Access* (see Figure 2-10). For the sake of learning Lambda, having a user with full permissions is going to make our lives much easier. You should not do this for real production accounts.

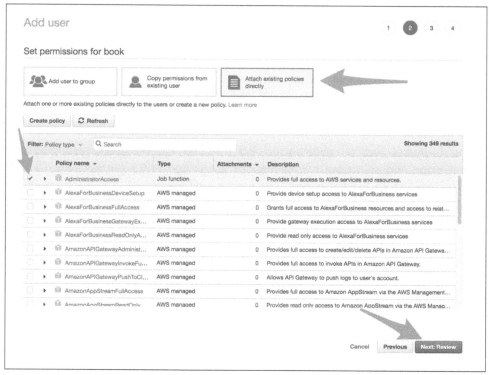

Figure 2-10. Add IAM user permissions

Click *Next: Tags* and on the screen after that *Next: Review.*

On the next screen, check that the details correspond to what we just described and click *Create user.*

On the final screen you'll be given the programmatic security credentials for your new user! Copy the Access Key ID and the Secret Access Key (after revealing it) to a note (keep it secure), or download the provided CSV file. Finally, click *Close.*

If you already had an IAM user, but no programmatic credentials, or you lose the credentials for the account you just created, go back to the User list in the IAM console, select the user, and then choose the *Security credentials* tab. You'll be able to create a new Access Key (and associated Secret Access Key ID) from there.

Configuring the AWS CLI

Now it's time to configure the CLI. From a terminal run **aws configure**. For the first two fields, paste the values you copied from the previous section. For your default region name, type the region code that corresponds to your chosen AWS region. You'll see the region code in the drop-down in the web console (these mappings can also be found in the AWS documentation (*https://oreil.ly/sV10t*)). Because we've picked *Oregon* for our examples in the web console, we'll use us-west-2 for the examples at our terminal. Finally, for the default output format, type **json**.

 If you've already configured a different AWS account in the CLI and are adding a new one for this book, you'll need to create a different profile; otherwise the preceding instructions will replace your existing credentials. Use the --profile option of aws config ure, and see more details in the AWS documentation (*https:// oreil.ly/Aj5y5*).

To confirm your values, run **aws configure** again, and you'll see your settings, something like the following:

```
$ aws configure
AWS Access Key ID [********************]:
AWS Secret Access Key [********************]:
Default region name [us-west-2]:
Default output format [json]:
```

A good way to quickly validate your AWS profile is to run the command **aws iam get-user**, which should result in something that looks like the following, where User Name is the name of the correct IAM user:

```
$ aws iam get-user
{
  "User": {
    "Path": "/",
    "UserName": "book",
    "UserId": "AIDA111111111111111111",
    "Arn": "arn:aws:iam::181111111111:user/book",
    "CreateDate": "2019-10-21T20:27:05Z"
  }
}
```

If you need more help, visit the documentation (*https://oreil.ly/JMtUt*).

Java Setup

Now that you have a local AWS environment, it's time to get set up with Java.

Java Versions and AWS Lambda

During almost all of the time we were writing this book, the only Java Runtime supported by AWS Lambda was Java 8. Because of this, all of the examples in this book assume Java 8, and we used the Java 8 Runtime and SDK for developing all of the code examples.

Just as we were finishing our final edits AWS announced Lambda support for Java 11. Because this announcement came right before we finished the book, we haven't had the chance to make any changes related to Java 11.

Our initial understanding of Java 11 support in Lambda, however, is that there are no breaking changes with respect to the Java 8 Lambda runtime. This means you should be able to use Java 9, 10, and 11 features in your Java code if you choose the Java 11 Runtime and that everything else in this book still holds true—you just may want to update the code to use newer Java capabilities!

As we learn more about the Java 11 Lambda runtime, we'll be updating our blog (*https://blog.symphonia.io*), so please check in to see what we discover.

AWS Lambda supports Java 8 and Java 11, and it's strongly recommended that you have the same major version of the Java SE Development Kit available locally as you are configuring your Lambda functions for. Most operating systems support having multiple versions of Java installed.

If you don't already have Java installed, then you have at least a couple of options:

- One is AWS's own distribution of Java—Corretto. Corretto, in AWS's words is, "a no-cost, multiplatform, production-ready distribution of the Open Java Development Kit (OpenJDK)." See "What Is Amazon Corretto 8?"" (*https://oreil.ly/9AYfs*) for Java 8 or "What Is Amazon Corretto 11?" (*https://oreil.ly/SB2-J*) for Java 11 for details of installing Corretto.

- Another option is Oracle's own distribution (*https://oreil.ly/WnBD8*); however, this now comes with licensing caveats that may be an issue for your use.

At this time, the difference as far as Lambda developers are concerned between these two options is mostly a legal, rather than technical, one. However, we expect AWS to transition all of their Java environments to Corretto where they haven't done so already, so if in doubt we recommend Lambda developers pick the Corretto Java SDK.

To validate your Java environment, run **`java -version`** from a terminal, and you should see something like the following:

```
$ java -version
openjdk version "1.8.0_232"
OpenJDK Runtime Environment Corretto-8.232.09.1 (build 1.8.0_232-b09)
OpenJDK 64-Bit Server VM Corretto-8.232.09.1 (build 25.232-b09, mixed mode)
```

The precise build version of Java doesn't matter (although it's always prudent to keep up-to-date with security patches), but it *is* important that you have the correct base version.

We also use Maven—the build and packaging tool. If you've already installed Maven, make sure it's somewhat up-to-date. If you haven't installed Maven and use a Mac, then we recommend using Homebrew to install it—run `brew install maven`. Otherwise, see the Maven home page (*https://maven.apache.org*) for installation instructions.

Open a terminal and run `mvn -v` to validate your environment. You should see some output that starts with something like the following:

```
$ mvn -v
Apache Maven 3.6.0 (97c98ec64a1fdfee77...
Maven home: /usr/local/Cellar/maven/3.6.0/libexec
Java version: 1.8.0_232, vendor: Amazon.com Inc., runtime: /Library/Java...
Default locale: en_US, platform encoding: UTF-8
OS name: "mac os x", version: "10.14.6", arch: "x86_64", family: "mac"
```

Any 3.x version of Maven will be fine for our needs in this book.

Finally, you should be comfortable creating Java projects that use Maven in your development editor of choice. We use the free version of IntelliJ IDEA (*https://oreil.ly/RWtqv*), but you should feel free to use whatever editor you want.

AWS SAM CLI Installation

The final tool you need to install is the AWS SAM CLI. SAM stands for Serverless Application Model, and we explore it later in "CloudFormation and the Serverless Application Model" on page 74. For now all you need to know is that the SAM CLI layers on top of the regular AWS CLI to give us some useful extra tools.

To install SAM, refer to the comprehensive instructions (*https://oreil.ly/slxxA*). If you're in a hurry, you can skip the elements of the documentation that refer to Docker since we won't use those, at least not initially!

 We use some features of SAM CLI that were introduced in late 2019, so make sure to update it if you're using an earlier version.

Lambda Hello World (the Proper Way)

With our development environment ready, it's time to create and deploy a Lambda function written in Java.

Creating Your First Java Lambda Project

There's some "boilerplate code" necessary in building and deploying a Lambda function in an automated way. We're going to go through all the complexities over the course of this book, but to get you up and running quickly, we've created a template to speed things up.

First, go to a terminal and run the following command:

```
$ sam init --location gh:symphoniacloud/sam-init-HelloWorldLambdaJava
```

This will ask you for a `project_name` value, and for now just hit Enter to use the default.

The command will then generate a project directory. Change into that directory, and take a look. You'll see the following files:

README.md
: Some instructions on how to build and deploy the project

pom.xml
: A Maven project file

template.yaml
: A SAM template file—used for deploying the project to AWS

src/main/java/book/HelloWorld.java
: The source code for a Lambda function

Now open the project in your IDE/editor of choice. If you're using Jetbrains IntelliJ IDEA, you can do that by running the following:

```
$ idea pom.xml
```

Within the *pom.xml* file itself, change the `<groupId>` to be more appropriate for yourself, if you'd like.

Now take a look at Example 2-1, which shows the *src/main/java/book/Hello-World.java* file.

Example 2-1. Hello World Lambda (in Java)

```
package book;

public class HelloWorld {
  public String handler(String s) {
    return "Hello, " + s;
  }
}
```

This class represents an entire Java Lambda function. Small, isn't it? Don't worry too much about the whats and whys; we'll get to them before too long. For now, let's build our Lambda deployment artifact.

Building Hello World

We deploy code to the Lambda platform by uploading a ZIP file, or in the Java world we can also deploy a JAR file (a JAR is just a ZIP with some embedded metadata). For now we're going to create an *uberjar*—a JAR that contains all of our code, plus all the classpath dependencies our code needs that aren't in the JVM environment we'll be running on.

The template project that you've just created is set up to create an uberjar for you. We're not going to examine that now because in Chapter 4 we'll go much deeper into a better method of producing a Lambda ZIP file ("Assembling a ZIP File" on page 67).

To build the JAR file, from your project's working directory, run `mvn package`. This should complete successfully with the following lines near the end:

```
[INFO] ---------------------------------------------------------------
[INFO] BUILD SUCCESS
[INFO] ---------------------------------------------------------------
```

It should also create our uberjar. Run `jar tf target/lambda.jar` to list the contents of the JAR file. The output should include book/HelloWorld.class, which is our application code, embedded within the artifact.

Creating the Lambda Function

Earlier in the chapter we walked you through creating a Lambda function via the web console. Now we're going to do the same thing from the terminal. We're going to use two further commands using `sam` to do this.

Before we do that, however, we need to create or identify a *staging bucket* within the S3 AWS Service where we can store temporary build artifacts. If you followed the AWS instructions for installing the SAM CLI or already know that you have one of these buckets available from your current AWS account, feel free to use it. Otherwise you can create one using the following command, substituting your own name for bucketname. Note that S3 bucket names need to be globally unique, across all AWS accounts, so you may need to try a few to get one that's available:

```
$ aws s3 mb s3://bucketname
```

Once you've done this successfully, note this bucket name—we'll be using it a lot throughout the rest of the book and will refer to it as $CF_BUCKET.

 Wherever you see $CF_BUCKET from now on, use the bucket name that you just created. Why CF? That stands for *CloudFormation*, which we'll explain in Chapter 4.

Alternatively, if you're more shell-script-savvy, assign this bucket name to a shell variable named CF_BUCKET, and then you can verbatim use the references to $CF_BUCKET.

With the S3 bucket ready, we can create our Lambda function. Run the following (after running mvn **package**):

```
$ sam deploy \
  --s3-bucket $CF_BUCKET \
  --stack-name HelloWorldLambdaJava \
  --capabilities CAPABILITY_IAM
```

Again, don't worry too much for now what this all means—we'll explain it later. If this worked correctly, the console output should end with the following (although your region may be different):

```
Successfully created/updated stack–HelloWorldLambdaJava in us-west-2
```

This means that your function is deployed and ready to run, so let's do that.

Running the Lambda function

Go back to the Functions list in the Lambda web console, and you should now see two functions listed: the original HelloWorld and a new one with a name that will be something like HelloWorldLambdaJava-HelloWorldLambda-YF5M2KZHXZF5. If you don't see the new Java one, make sure you have your regions in sync between the terminal and the web console.

Click through to the new function and take a look at the configuration screen. You'll see that the source code is no longer available since the function was created with a compiled artifact.

To test this function, we need to create a new test event. Click *Test* again, and on the *Configure test event* screen (Figure 2-11), give the event name `HelloWorldJavaEvent`. In the actual event body section, enter the following:

```
"Java World!"
```

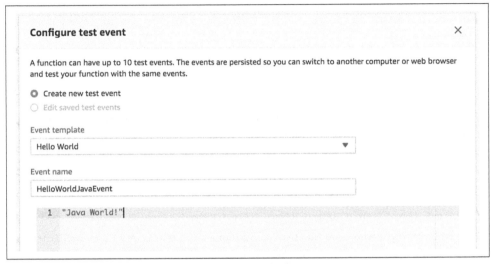

Figure 2-11. Configure test event for Java Lambda function

Click *Create* to save the test event.

This should take you back to the main Lambda screen, with the new test event selected (if it isn't, select it manually). Click *Test*, and your Lambda function will be executed! (See Figure 2-12.)

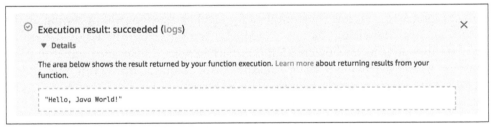

Figure 2-12. Result for Hello World in Java

> ## Tearing Down Resources
>
> In this book, almost every example we give will be deployed using CloudFormation—either directly or indirectly using SAM. We talk in detail about CloudFormation in Chapter 4 (see "CloudFormation and the Serverless Application Model" on page 74), but one important aspect we want to discuss now is how you can clean up any examples.
>
> When you run `sam deploy`, it creates or updates a CloudFormation *stack*—a set of resources that has a name, which you've seen already with the `--stack-name` parameter of `sam deploy`.
>
> When you want to clean up your AWS account after trying an example, the simplest method is to find the corresponding CloudFormation stack in the AWS Web Console (in the CloudFormation section) and delete the stack using the *Delete* button.
>
> Alternatively, you can tear down the stack from the command line. For example, to tear down the `HelloWorldLambdaJava` stack, run the following:
>
> ```
> $ aws cloudformation delete-stack --stack-name HelloWorldLambdaJava
> ```
>
> The only example where we don't use CloudFormation is the very first one earlier in this chapter—the `HelloWorld` JavaScript function—which can be deleted using the Lambda section of the AWS Web Console.

Summary

In this chapter, you learned how to sign in to the AWS Web Console and pick a region. Then you created and ran your first Lambda function, via the web console.

You also prepared your local environment for Lambda development by setting up the AWS CLI, Java, Maven, and the AWS SAM CLI. You learned the basics of developing Lambda functions in Java by creating a project in your development environment, building it, and deploying it using Amazon's SAM tooling. Finally, you now understand how to perform simple testing of Lambda functions by simulating events using the web console's test event mechanism.

In the next chapter, we'll start taking a look at how Lambda works, and the ways that impacts how you write Lambda code.

Exercises

1. If you haven't run through the step-by-step descriptions in this chapter, then it's worth doing that now since it's a good way to validate your environment.

2. Create a new version of the Java Lambda function with slightly different code, by using a different `stack-name` value at `sam deploy` time. Note how you can select between these functions in the web console.

CHAPTER 3

Programming AWS Lambda Functions

This chapter is about digging into what it means to build Lambda functions—what do they look like, how do you configure how they run, and how do you specify your own environmental configuration. You'll learn about these topics by examining core concepts for Lambda execution environments, input and output, timeout, memory and CPU, and finally, how Lambda uses environment variables for application configuration.

To start, let's take a look at how Lambda functions are executed. Grab your hiking boots—it's time to explore.

Core Concepts: Runtime Model, Invocation

In Chapter 2, you created a Java class, uploaded it to the Lambda service somewhere in the nebulous "cloud," and magically were able to execute that code. You didn't have to consider operating systems, containers, startup scripts, deployment of the code to an actual host, or JVM settings. Nor did you think about any of those pesky "servers." So how did your code execute?

To understand this, you need to first understand the basics of the Lambda execution environment, as shown in Figure 3-1.

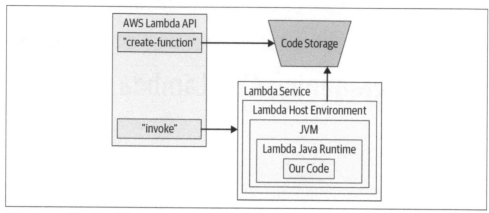

Figure 3-1. The Lambda execution environment

The Lambda Execution Environment

As we mentioned in Chapter 2 (see "Installing the AWS CLI" on page 27), both AWS management and function operations (often referred to as the *control plane* and *data plane*, respectively) make extensive use of APIs. Lambda is no different and offers an API both for management of functions and for execution of functions.

A function is executed, or *invoked*, whenever the invoke command of the AWS Lambda API is called. This happens at the following times:

- When a function is triggered by an event source
- When you use the test harness in the web console
- When you call the Lambda API invoke command yourself, typically via the CLI or SDK, from your own code or scripts

Invoking a function for the first time will start the following chain of activity that will end in your code being executed.

First, the Lambda service will create a host Linux environment—a lightweight micro-virtual machine. You typically won't need to worry about the precise nature of what type of environment it is (which kernel, what distribution, etc.), but if you do care, Amazon makes that information public. But don't rely on it staying constant—Amazon can and does make frequent changes to the OS of Lambda functions, often for your own benefit, including automatic security patches.

Once the host environment has been created, then Lambda will start a language runtime within it—in our case a Java virtual machine. At the time of this writing, the JVM version will always be Java 8 or Java 11. You must supply Lambda with code compatible with the version of Java that you choose. The JVM is started with a set of environment flags that we can't change.

You may have noticed when we wrote our code that there was no "main" method—the top-level Java application is Amazon's own Java application server, which we'll refer to as the *Lambda Java Runtime*; that's the next component to be started. The runtime is responsible for top-level error handling, logging, and more.

Of course, the Lambda Java Runtime's primary concern is executing our code. The final steps of the invocation chain are (a) to load our Java classes and (b) to call the handler method that we specified during deployment.

Invocation Types

Great—our code is alive! What happens next?

To explore this, let's start using the AWS CLI. In Chapter 2 we used the higher-level SAM CLI tool—the AWS CLI is a little closer to the guts of the AWS machine. Specifically, we're going to use a command in the AWS CLI for calling Lambda functions: `aws lambda invoke`.

Assuming you ran the examples in Chapter 2, let's start with a small update. Open the *template.yaml* file (which we'll refer to as the *SAM template* occasionally from now on), and within the properties section, add a new property named `FunctionName` with the value `HelloWorldJava` so that the resource section looks as follows:

```
HelloWorldLambda:
  Type: AWS::Serverless::Function
  Properties:
    FunctionName: HelloWorldJava
    Runtime: java8
    MemorySize: 512
    Handler: book.HelloWorld::handler
    CodeUri: target/lambda.jar
```

Run the **sam deploy** command from Chapter 2 again. This should complete after a couple of minutes. If you go back to the Lambda console, you'll see your strangely named Java function has now been renamed to `HelloWorldJava`. In most real-use cases, we like using the generated names that AWS provides, but when we're learning about Lambda, it's nice to be able to refer to functions with more succinct names.

> To use the Java 11 runtime instead of Java 8, simply change the `Run time:` property in your SAM template from `java8` to `java11`.

Let's get back to invocation. From the terminal, run the following command:

```
$ aws lambda invoke \
  --invocation-type RequestResponse \
  --function-name HelloWorldJava \
  --payload \"world\" outputfile.txt
```

This should return the following:

```
{
  "StatusCode": 200,
  "ExecutedVersion": "$LATEST"
}
```

You can tell that everything was OK because `StatusCode` was `200`.

You can also see what the Lambda function returned by executing the following:

```
$ cat outputfile.txt && echo
"Hello, world"
```

When we executed the `invoke` command, the Lambda function was first instantiated, as we described in the previous section. With instantiation complete, the Lambda Java Runtime, itself within the JVM, then called our Lambda function with the data that we passed in the `payload` parameter—in this case the string `"world"`.

Our code then ran. As a reminder, here it is:

```
public String handler(String s) {
  return "Hello, " + s;
}
```

It takes our input (`"world"`), and returns `"Hello, world"`.

There's an important but subtle point here. When we called `invoke`, we specified `--invocation-type RequestResponse`—this means that we are calling the function *synchronously* (i.e., the Lambda runtime calls our code and waits for the result). We explained this in "What Does a Lambda Application Look Like?" on page 13. *Synchronous behavior* is useful for scenarios like web APIs.

Because we called the function synchronously, the Lambda runtime was able to return the response to our terminal, and this is what was saved to *outputfile.txt*.

Now let's invoke the function slightly differently:

```
$ aws lambda invoke \
  --invocation-type Event \
  --function-name HelloWorldJava \
  --payload \"world\" outputfile.txt
```

Notice that we've changed the `--invocation-type` flag to `Event`. The result is now as follows:

```
{
  "StatusCode": 202
}
```

`StatusCode` is 202, not 200. 202 means *Accepted* in HTTP terms. If you take a look at *outputfile.txt*, you'll see that it's empty.

This time we have called the function *asynchronously*. The Lambda runtime calls our code precisely as before, but it does not wait for, or use, the value returned by our code—that value returned by our code is discarded. The point of using asynchronous execution is that we can perform a "side effect" on some other function or service. In the asynchronous example in "What Does a Lambda Application Look Like?" on page 13, the side effect was to upload a file to Amazon's S3 service—a new, resized, version of a photo.

As you start using Lambda, you'll discover that most classes of Lambda function use asynchronous invocation, embracing the idea that Lambda is an *event-driven platform*. We'll explore this further later in the book when we start examining "Lambda Event Sources" on page 86.

We used the same code in the previous two examples; however, if you know that your Lambda function will never be used synchronously, you don't need to return a value —the method can have a `void` return type. Let's see an example of that.

First, change your function's method to the following:

```
public void handler(String s) {
  System.out.println("Hello, " + s);
}
```

Notice that we've changed the return type to `void` and are now writing a message to `System.out`.

Now we need to rebuild and redeploy our code. To do this, run the same two commands you did in Chapter 2:

- `mvn package`
- `sam deploy...`

where ... refers to the same arguments you used before. You're going to be running these commands often enough that you'll probably want to put them in a script.

Now invoke the code again with the `Event` invocation type, and you should receive another `"StatusCode": 202` response. But where does that message to `System.out` go? To understand that, we'll take a quick look at logging.

You now know enough about the mvn, sam, and aws commands to run the remaining examples in this chapter. If you get into a weird state, go to *CloudFormation* in the AWS Web Console, delete the HelloWorldLambdaJava stack, and deploy again.

Introduction to Logging

The Lambda runtime captures anything written by our function to either the standard output or standard error process streams. In Java terms, these correspond to System.out and System.err. Once the Lambda runtime has caught this data, it sends it to CloudWatch Logs. If you're new to AWS, this will need a little more explanation!

CloudWatch Logs consists of a few components. The principal one is a log capturing service. It's cheap, dependable, easy to use and handles all the scale you can throw at it.

Once CloudWatch Logs has captured log messages, there are a few ways that you can view or process them. The simplest way is to use the CloudWatch Logs log viewer in the AWS Web Console.

There are various ways to get to this, but for now open up your Lambda function's page in the AWS Web Console (as we showed in "Running the Lambda function" on page 36). If you click the Monitoring tab of that page, you should be able to see a *View logs in CloudWatch* button—click that, as shown in Figure 3-2.

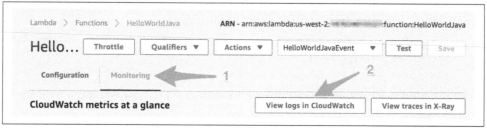

Figure 3-2. Access Lambda logs

What you'll see next will depend a little on how the CloudWatch console is working, but if you're not already seeing log output, then click the blue *Search Log Group* button and scroll down to the most recent log lines. You should then be able to see something like in Figure 3-3.

```
START RequestId: 52b522bc-a261-11e8-b336-7dd1098d0cdc Version: $LATEST
Hello, world
END RequestId: 52b522bc-a261-11e8-b336-7dd1098d0cdc
REPORT RequestId: 52b522bc-a261-11e8-b336-7dd1098d0cdc Duration: 32.79 ms Bille
```

Figure 3-3. Lambda logs

Notice there on the second line is the output we wrote from our Lambda function.

No good, self-respecting Java programmer does real production logging using `System.out.println`, though—logging frameworks give far more flexibility and control over logging behavior. We dig into logging practices in detail in "Logging" on page 157.

Input, Output

When a Lambda function is executed, it is always passed an input argument, typically referred to as an *event*. Within the Lambda execution environment, this event is specifically always a JSON value, and in our examples so far we've been handcrafting a string—by itself valid JSON.

In real use cases, the input to the Lambda function will be a JSON object that represents an event from some other component or system. For example, it may be a representation of the details of an HTTP request, or some metadata of an image uploaded to the S3 storage service. Again, we look in detail at tying event sources to Lambda functions later in the book—see "Lambda Event Sources" on page 86.

The JSON that we create in our test events, or that comes from event sources, is passed to the Lambda Java Runtime. In most use cases, the Lambda Java Runtime will automatically *deserialize* this JSON payload for us, and we have several options of how to guide this.

As you saw in the previous section, when we invoke a function synchronously, we can return a useful value to the environment. The Lambda Java Runtime will automatically *serialize* this return value to JSON for us.

How the Java Runtime performs this serialization and deserialization depends on types we specify within the function signature, so it's time we took a deeper look at what makes a Lambda function statically valid.

Lambda Function Method Signatures

Valid Java Lambda methods must fit one of the following four signatures:

- *output-type handler-name*(*input-type* input)
- *output-type handler-name*(*input-type* input, Context context)
- void *handler-name*(InputStream is, OutputStream os)
- void *handler-name*(InputStream is, OutputStream os, Context context)

where:

- *output-type* can be void, a Java primitive, or a JSON-serializable type.
- *input-type* is a Java primitive, or a JSON-serializable type.
- Context refers to com.amazonaws.services.lambda.runtime.Context (we describe this more later in the chapter).
- InputStream and OutputStream refer to the types with those names in the java.io package.
- *handler-name* can be any valid Java method name, and we refer to it in our application's configuration.

Java Lambda methods can be either instance methods or static methods, but must be public.

A class containing a Lambda function cannot be abstract and must have a no-argument constructor—either the default constructor (i.e., no constructor specified) or an explicit no-argument constructor. The main reason to consider using a constructor at all is for caching data between Lambda calls, which is an advanced topic that we'll get to later in the book—see "Caching" on page 214.

Beyond those limitations, there are no static typing requirements of a Java Lambda function. You are not required to implement any interfaces or base classes, although you may do so if you desire. AWS provides a RequestHandler interface if you want to be very explicit about the type of your Lambda classes, but we have never found a need to make use of this. Also, you can if you like extend your own classes, subject to the constructor rules, but again we find this is rarely a useful ability.

You may have multiple Lambda functions defined in one class with different names, but we don't usually recommend this style. Since two different Lambda functions never run in the same execution environment, we find it makes it clearer for subsequent engineers when we cleanly separate the code for each function.

Lambda functions, statically, are simple in comparison with some other application frameworks. The first two signatures listed earlier are the most common for Java Lambdas, and we'll look at those next.

Configuring the Handler Function in the SAM Template

So far we've made only one change to the SAM template file—*template.yaml*—to change the function's name. Before we go too much further, we need to look at another property in that file: Handler.

Open the *template.yaml* file, and you'll see that Handler is currently set to book.Hello World::handler. What this means is that for this Lambda function, the Lambda platform will attempt to find a method named handler in a class named HelloWorld in the package named book.

If you create a new class named Cow in a package named old.macdonald.farm, and you have a method named moomoo that is your Lambda function, then you would set Handler instead to old.macdonald.farm.Cow::moomoo.

With this information, you're all set to create some new Lambda handlers!

Basic Types

Example 3-1 shows a class with three different Lambda handler functions (yes, we just said a moment ago that we don't tend to use multiple Lambda functions per class in real use—we're doing so here for brevity!)

Example 3-1. Basic type serialization and deserialization

```
package book;

public class StringIntegerBooleanLambda {
  public void handlerString(String s) {
    System.out.println("Hello, " + s);
  }

  public boolean handlerBoolean(boolean input) {
    return !input;
  }

  public boolean handlerInt(int input) {
    return input > 100;
  }
}
```

To try this code, add the new class `StringIntegerBooleanLambda` to your source tree, change the `Handler` in the *template.yaml* file (e.g., to `book.StringIntegerBoolean` `Lambda::handlerString`), and then run your package and deploy commands.

The first of these functions is the same as we described in the previous section. We can test this method by invoking it with the JSON object `"world"`, and since it had a void return type, it is meant for asynchronous usage.

 From here on in you should assume that when we say to invoke a function in an example, we mean you should invoke it *synchronously* unless we specify otherwise. You can do this either using the `--invocation-type RequestResponse` flag when invoking from a terminal or using the *Test* functionality in the AWS Web Console.

The second function can be invoked with a Boolean—any of the JSON values `true`, `false`, `"true"`, or `"false"`—and it will also return a Boolean, the inverse of the input in this case.

The final function takes an integer (either a JSON integer or a number in a JSON string, e.g., 5 or `"5"`) and returns a Boolean.

In the second and third examples we're using a primitive type, but you may use boxed types if you prefer. For example, you are free to use `java.lang.Integer` instead of plain `int` if you like.

What's happening in all of these cases is that the Lambda Java Runtime is deserializing the JSON input to a simple type on our behalf. If the event that is passed can't be deserialized to the specified parameter type, you'll get a failure, with a message that starts as follows:

```
An error occurred during JSON parsing: java.lang.RuntimeException
```

Strings, integers, and Booleans are the only basic types that are explicitly documented as being supported, but with some experimentation we see other basic types, such as doubles and floats, are also included.

Lists and Maps

JSON also includes arrays and objects/properties (see Example 3-2). The Lambda Java Runtime will automatically deserialize those to Java `Lists` and `Maps`, respectively, and will also serialize output `Lists` and `Maps` to JSON arrays and objects.

Example 3-2. List and Map serialization and deserialization

```java
package book;

import java.util.ArrayList;
import java.util.HashMap;
import java.util.List;
import java.util.Map;
import java.util.stream.IntStream;

public class ListMapLambda {
  public List<Integer> handlerList(List<Integer> input) {
    List<Integer> newList = new ArrayList<>();
    input.forEach(x -> newList.add(100 + x));
    return newList;
  }

  public Map<String,String> handlerMap(Map<String,String> input) {
    Map<String, String> newMap = new HashMap<>();
    input.forEach((k, v) -> newMap.put("New Map -> " + k, v));
    return newMap;
  }

  public Map<String,Map<String, Integer>>
    handlerNestedCollection(List<Map<String, Integer>> input) {
    Map<String, Map<String, Integer>> newMap = new HashMap<>();
    IntStream.range(0, input.size())
          .forEach(i -> newMap.put("Nested at position " + i, input.get(i)));
    return newMap;
  }
}
```

Invoking the function `handlerList()` with the JSON array `[ 1, 2, 3 ]` returns `[ 101, 102, 103 ]`. Invoking the function `handlerMap()` with the JSON object `{ "a" : "x", "b" : "y"}` returns `{ "New Map → a" : "x", "New Map → b" : "y" }`.

Furthermore, you can use nested collections as you would expect; for example, invoking `handlerNestedCollection()` with

```
[
  { "m" : 1, "n" : 2 },
  { "x" : 8, "y" : 9 }
]
```

returns

```
{
  "Nested at position 0": { "m" : 1, "n" : 2},
  "Nested at position 1": { "x": 8, "y" : 9}
}
```

Finally, you can also just use `java.lang.Object` as the type of the input parameter. While not often useful in production (unless you don't care about the input argument's value, which is sometimes a valid use), this can be handy at development time if you don't know the precise format of an event. For example, you can use `.get Class()` on the argument to find out what type it really is, print out the `.toString()` value, etc. We'll show you a better way of getting the JSON structure of an event a little later in this chapter.

POJOs and Ecosystem Types

The previous input types work well for very fairly simple inputs. An alternative for more complex types is to use the Lambda Java Runtime's automatic POJO (Plain Old Java Object) serialization. Example 3-3 shows an example where we use this for both input and output.

Example 3-3. POJO serialization and deserialization

```
package book;

public class PojoLambda {
  public PojoResponse handlerPojo(PojoInput input) {
    return new PojoResponse("Input was " + input.getA());
  }

  public static class PojoInput {
    private String a;

    public String getA() {
      return a;
    }

    public void setA(String a) {
      this.a = a;
    }
  }

  public static class PojoResponse {
    private final String b;

    PojoResponse(String b) {
      this.b = b;
    }

    public String getB() {
```

```
        return b;
    }
  }
}
```

Obviously this is a very simple case, but it shows POJO serialization in action. We can execute this Lambda with the input `{ "a" : "Hello Lambda" }`, and it returns `{ "b" : "Input was Hello Lambda" }`. Let's look a little more closely at the code.

First of all, we have our handler function, `handlerPojo()`. This takes as input the type `PojoInput`, which is a POJO class we've defined. POJO input classes can be static nested classes, as we've written here, or regular (outer) classes. The important thing is that they need to have an empty constructor and have field setters that follow the naming of the expected fields to be deserialized from the input JSON. If no JSON field is found with the same name as a setter, then the POJO field will be left null. Input POJO objects need to be mutable since the runtime will modify them after they've been instantiated.

Our handler function interrogates the POJO object and creates a new instance of the `PojoResponse` class, which we pass back to the Lambda runtime. The Lambda runtime serializes it to JSON by reflecting over all the `get…` methods. There are fewer limitations on POJO output classes—since they are not created or mutated by the Lambda runtime, you are free to construct them as you please and free to make them immutable. And like input classes, POJO output classes can be static nested classes or regular (outer) classes.

For both POJO input and output classes, you can nest further POJO classes, using the same rules, to serialize/deserialize nested JSON objects. Further, you can mix up POJOs and the collection types we discussed (`Lists` and `Maps`) in your input and output.

The example we gave previously follows most of the documentation you'll see online: using a *JavaBean* convention for fields. However, if you don't want to use setters in your input class or getters in your output class, you're free to also use public fields. For instance, Example 3-4 shows another example.

Example 3-4. POJO serialization and deserialization alternative definition

```
package book;

public class PojoLambda {
  public PojoResponse handlerPojo(PojoInput input) {
    return new PojoResponse("Input was " + input.c);
  }

  public static class PojoInput {
    public String c;
```

```
    }

  public static class PojoResponse {
    public final String d;

    PojoResponse(String d) {
      this.d = d;
    }
  }
}
```

We can execute this Lambda with the input `{ "c" : "Hello Lambda" }`, and it returns `{ "d" : "Input was Hello Lambda" }`.

One of the main uses for POJO input deserialization is when you tie your Lambda function to one of the AWS ecosystem Lambda event sources. Here's an example of a handler function that would process the event of an object being uploaded to the S3 storage service:

```
public void handler(S3Event input) {
  // …
}
```

`S3Event` is a type that you can access from an AWS library dependency—we discuss this more in "Example: Building a Serverless Data Pipeline" on page 111. You're also free to build your own POJO classes to handle AWS events.

Streams

The input/output types we've covered so far will be useful for you in many, and possibly all, of your use of Lambda in the real world. But what if you have a fairly dynamic and/or complicated structure that you can't, or don't want to, use any of the previous deserialization methods for?

The answer is to use option 3 or 4 of the valid signature list, making use of `java.io.InputStream` for the event parameter. This gives you access to the raw bytes passed to your Lambda function.

The signature for a Lambda using an `InputStream` is a little different in that it always has a `void` return type. If you take an `InputStream` as a parameter, you must also take a `java.io.OutputStream` as the second parameter. To return a result from such a handler function, you need to write to the `OutputStream`.

Example 3-5 shows a handler that can process streams.

Example 3-5. Using streams as handler parameters

```
package book;
```

```
import java.io.IOException;
import java.io.InputStream;
import java.io.OutputStream;

public class StreamLambda {
  public void handlerStream(InputStream inputStream, OutputStream outputStream)
    throws IOException {
    int letter;
    while((letter = inputStream.read()) != -1)
    {
      outputStream.write(Character.toUpperCase(letter));
    }
  }
}
```

If we execute this handler with the input "Hello World", it will write "HELLO WORLD" to the output stream, which becomes the function's result.

You may well want to use your own JSON manipulation code if you're using an Input Stream, but we'll leave that as an exercise to the reader. You should also practice good stream hygiene—error checking, closing, etc.

For more on this subject, see the official documentation on using streams in handler functions (*https://oreil.ly/oXm39*).

One particularly handy use of this type of Lambda function is at development time when you don't know the structure of the event you are coding for. Example 3-6 will log the received event to CloudWatch Logs so you can see what it is.

Example 3-6. Log received event to CloudWatch Logs

```
package book;

import java.io.InputStream;
import java.io.OutputStream;

public class WhatIsMyLambdaEvent {
  public void handler(InputStream is, OutputStream os) {
    java.util.Scanner s = new java.util.Scanner(is).useDelimiter("\\A");
    System.out.println(s.hasNext() ? s.next() : "No input detected");
  }
}
```

Context

So far we've covered signature formats 1 and 3 of our earlier list, but what of 2 and 4? What's that Context object about?

In all of our examples so far, the only input we've taken for a Lambda handler function is that of the event that occurred. But that's not the only information the handler can receive when it wants to do some processing. Additionally, you can add a `com.amazonaws.services.lambda.runtime.Context` parameter to the end of any handler parameter list, and the runtime will pass in an interesting object that you can use. Let's look at an example (Example 3-7).

Example 3-7. Examining the Context object

```java
package book;

import com.amazonaws.services.lambda.runtime.Context;

import java.util.HashMap;
import java.util.Map;

public class ContextLambda {
  public Map<String,Object> handler (Object input, Context context) {
    Map<String, Object> toReturn = new HashMap<>();
    toReturn.put("getMemoryLimitInMB", context.getMemoryLimitInMB() + "");
    toReturn.put("getFunctionName",context.getFunctionName());
    toReturn.put("getFunctionVersion",context.getFunctionVersion());
    toReturn.put("getInvokedFunctionArn",context.getInvokedFunctionArn());
    toReturn.put("getAwsRequestId",context.getAwsRequestId());
    toReturn.put("getLogStreamName",context.getLogStreamName());
    toReturn.put("getLogGroupName",context.getLogGroupName());
    toReturn.put("getClientContext",context.getClientContext());
    toReturn.put("getIdentity",context.getIdentity());
    toReturn.put("getRemainingTimeInMillis",
                  context.getRemainingTimeInMillis() + "");
    return toReturn;
  }
}
```

This is the first full example where we need to use a type outside of the Java standard library. We'll look in more detail at dependencies and packaging in the next chapter, but for now add the following section anywhere under the root element of your *pom.xml* file:

```xml
<dependencies>
  <dependency>
    <groupId>com.amazonaws</groupId>
    <artifactId>aws-lambda-java-core</artifactId>
    <version>1.2.0</version>
    <scope>provided</scope>
  </dependency>
</dependencies>
```

When you run `mvn package` now, it will compile your code using the core Lambda library provided by AWS, enabling you to use the `Context` interface.

The `Context` object gives us information about the current Lambda invocation. We can use this information during the processing of a Lambda event. When we invoke the example (passing anything as an input event—it won't be used), we'll get something like the following as a result:

```
{
  "getFunctionName": "ContextLambda",
  "getLogStreamName": "2019/07/24/[$LATEST]0f1b1111111111111111111111111111",
  "getInvokedFunctionArn":
    "arn:aws:lambda:us-west-2:181111111111:function:ContextLambda",
  "getIdentity": {
    "identityId": "",
    "identityPoolId": ""
  },
  "getRemainingTimeInMillis": "2967",
  "getLogGroupName": "/aws/lambda/ContextLambda",
  "getLogger": {},
  "getFunctionVersion": "$LATEST",
  "getMemoryLimitInMB": "512",
  "getClientContext": null,
  "getAwsRequestId": "2108d0a2-a271-11e8-8e33-cdbf63de49d2"
}
```

All the different `Context` fields are described in the AWS documentation (*https:// oreil.ly/oE2hP*).

Most of these fields will stay the same whenever you call them during the processing of a particular event, but `getRemainingTimeInMillis()` is a notable exception. It's related to *timeout*, which is what we look at next.

Timeout

Lambda functions are subject to a configurable timeout. You are able to specify this timeout when you create the function, or you can update it later in the function's configuration.

At the time of this writing, the *maximum* timeout is 15 minutes. That means the longest a single invocation of a Lambda function can run is 15 minutes. This restriction is one that AWS may increase in the future, and they've done so before—for a long time the maximum timeout was 5 minutes.

In our examples so far we haven't specified a timeout setting, so it defaults to 3 seconds. That means if our function doesn't finish executing within 3 seconds, then the Lambda Java Runtime will abort it. You'll see an example of this in a moment.

In the previous section, we looked at the `Context` object. Calling `context.getRemai ningTimeInMillis()` will tell you how much time to run you have left at any given point during execution before the function is aborted by the runtime. Subsequent calls will give an updated duration. This is useful if you are writing a fairly long-lived Lambda and want to save any state before the timeout occurs.

One question you may be asking yourself—why not always configure the timeout to the maximum of 900 seconds? As we'll explore further in the next section, Lambda costs are based significantly on how long functions run—if your function should only ever run for at most 10 seconds, then you don't want a billion invocations taking 90 times that long, since you'll be charged 90 times as much as you want to be.

The timeout does *not* include the time our function is being instantiated—in other words, the timeout period is not started during the *cold start* of a function. Or, to be even more precise, the timeout applies only to the time from when Lambda calls our handler method. We discuss cold starts further in "Cold Starts" on page 201.

The timeout maximum of 15 minutes is a significant constraint for Lambda functions —if you are writing functionality that needs more than 15 minutes, you'll need to either break it up into multiple, orchestrated, Lambda functions, or not use Lambda at all.

Enough theory, let's look at timeouts in action.

Example 3-8 shows a Lambda function that will query the remaining time and then eventually fail due to timeout.

Example 3-8. Looking at timeout with Context.getRemainingTimeInMillis()

```
package book;

import com.amazonaws.services.lambda.runtime.Context;

public class TimeoutLambda {
  public void handler (Object input, Context context) throws InterruptedException {
    while(true) {
      Thread.sleep(100);
      System.out.println("Context.getRemainingTimeInMillis() : " +
        context.getRemainingTimeInMillis());
    }
  }
}
```

Update your *template.yaml* file, adding a new property named Timeout to the Proper ties section of your function. Set the value to be 2—this says that the function's time-out is now two seconds. Also, remember to update your Handler property.

Then run your package and deploy steps as usual.

If we execute this using the test functionality in the web console, it will fail with the message "Task timed out after 2.00 seconds." The log output will be as follows:

```
START RequestId: 6127fe67-a406-11e8-9030-69649c02a345 Version: $LATEST
Context.getRemainingTimeInMillis() : 1857
Context.getRemainingTimeInMillis() : 1756
... Cut for brevity ...
Context.getRemainingTimeInMillis() : 252
Context.getRemainingTimeInMillis() : 152
Context.getRemainingTimeInMillis() : 51
END RequestId: 6127fe67-a406-11e8-9030-69649c02a345
REPORT RequestId: 6127fe67-a406-11e8-9030-69649c02a345  Duration: 2001.52 ms
  Billed Duration: 2000 ms  Memory Size: 512 MB Max Memory Used: 51 MB
2019-07-24T21:22:30.076Z 444e6ae0-9217-4cd2-8568-7585ca3fafee
  Task timed out after 2.00 seconds
```

Here we can see the `getRemainingTimeInMillis()` method being queried as we'd expect and then the function finally failing as Lambda's timeout occurs.

Memory and CPU

Lambda functions do not have infinite amounts of RAM, and in fact every function is configured with a `memory-size` setting. The setting defaults to 128MB, but this is rarely enough for a production Java Lambda function, so you should treat `memory-size` as something you actively think about for every function.

`memory-size` can be as small as 64MB, although for Java Lambda functions you should probably use at least 256MB. `memory-size` must be a multiple of 64MB.

A very important thing to know is that the `memory-size` setting is not just for how much RAM your function can use—*it also specifies how much CPU power you get*. In fact, a Lambda function's CPU power scales linearly from 64MB up to 1792MB. Therefore a Lambda function configured with 1024MB of RAM has twice the CPU power of one with 512MB of RAM.

A Lambda function with 1792MB RAM gets a full virtual CPU core—larger RAM settings than that enable fractions of a second virtual core. This is worth knowing if your code is not multithreaded at all—you may not see a CPU improvement for memory settings higher than 1792MB in such a case.

We discuss how the Lambda execution environment interacts with multiple threads in "Lambda and Threading" on page 197.

But why should you care about this—why not always just set `memory-size` to its maximum of 3008MB? The reason is cost. AWS charges for Lambda functions by two primary factors:

- How long a function runs, rounded up to the nearest 100 ms
- How much memory a function is specified to use

In other words, given the same execution duration, a Lambda function that has 2GB of RAM costs twice as much to execute as one with 1GB of RAM. Or, one with 512MB of RAM costs 17% of one with 3008MB. This, at scale, could be a big difference.

Surely that means you should always use the smallest amount of memory possible then? No, that's not always the best choice. Since a function with twice as much memory of a smaller function also has twice the CPU power, it might take half the time to execute, meaning the cost is the same, and it gets its work done more quickly.

Right-sizing Lambda functions is something of an art. We recommend you stick with somewhere between 512MB and 1GB to start with and then start tuning as your functions get bigger or as you need to scale them.

How Expensive Is Lambda?

Some people, when they first hear about Lambda, assume that it's great for small tasks —things that don't run very frequently—but is too expensive for "grown up" applications that service real-time multiuser applications. How much truth is there to this? Let's take a look at a couple of examples.

First, let's think back to the photo resizer (see "File processing" on page 15). Let's say that we set that function to use 1.5GB RAM, it takes on average 10 seconds to run, and it processes 10,000 photos per day. Lambda pricing consists of two parts—*request* pricing, which is \$0.20 per million requests, and *duration* pricing, which is \$0.0000166667 per gigabyte-second. Therefore we need to calculate both parts to estimate cost for our photo resizer:

- The request cost is \$0.20 × .01 = \$0.002/day, or \$0.06/month.
- The duration cost is 10 (seconds/invocation) × 10,000 (invocations) × 1.5 (GB) × \$0.0000166667 = \$2.50/day, or \$75/month.

Obviously the duration cost is the vast majority here.

\$75/month is about the same cost as a "m5.large" EC2 instance—which is \$70/month. An m5.large EC2 instance is the smallest size VM in the m5 "general purpose" family; it has 8GB RAM and two CPUs, so it would likely be about right as an alternative to host our photo resizer. However, Lambda has significant benefits as a solution, even though the costs appear at first glance about the same:

- Lambda doesn't require the operations cost of managing an EC2 instance—there's no need to think about operating system patches, user management, etc. Therefore our total cost of ownership (TCO) is lower for Lambda.

- Lambda already manages the "event driven" nature of the application, so we don't need to build that into the version we would run on a regular server.

- Lambda will auto-scale without effort and so will handle, without concern, any spikes in traffic. A server-based solution may become overloaded or need to be built to include buffering. In fact, the more "spikey" your application's load, the more cost effective Lambda is as a solution.

- Lambda is already highly available across AZs—to guarantee that availability with a server-based solution, we would need to *double or triple our costs* for two or three zones of availability.

Now let's look back to our web API (see Figure 1-5). Let's say we set the web API Lambda functions to use 512MB RAM and each invocation takes no more than 100 ms to run. Let's say the API processes on average 10 requests per second (864,000 requests/day) but can peak up to 100 requests per second.

- The request cost is $0.20 \times 0.864 = \$0.17$/day, or $5.18/month.
- The duration cost is $0.1 \times 864,000 \times 0.5 \times \$0.0000166667 = \$0.72$/day, or $21.60/month.

In other words, we need to spend $27/month to handle 10 requests/second average, and this system could happily could peak to 10x that rate, without breaking a sweat (or increasing the costs).

Now neither of these components by themselves is gargantuan in size, but they aren't trivial either. For many applications, these are not unrealistic performance needs and so we can see that Lambda is often going to be a cost-efficient choice of platform.

The pricing example here assumes using Lambda in its regular, "on-demand" mode. Lambda has alternative pricing when using Provisioned Concurrency, which we describe in "Provisioned Concurrency" on page 208.

Environment Variables

The previous two sections were all about Lambda's own system configuration—what if you want to use configuration for your own application?

We can specify *environment variables* for our Lambda functions. This allows us to alter how our function runs in different contexts for the same code. It's very typical, for example, to specify connection settings for external processes, or secure configuration, through environment variables.

Let's try this. Example 3-9 shows a function that reads from the environment using Java's standard method for doing so.

Example 3-9. Using an environment variable

```
package book;

public class EnvVarLambda {
  public void handler(Object event) {
    String databaseUrl = System.getenv("DATABASE_URL");
    if (databaseUrl == null || databaseUrl.isEmpty())
      System.out.println("DATABASE_URL is not set");
    else
      System.out.println("DATABASE_URL is set to: " + databaseUrl);
  }
}
```

Update the *template.yaml* file to point to this new class and perform the package and deploy process.

If we run this function (using any test input we like), the log output will include the following:

```
DATABASE_URL is not set
```

Now update the *template.yaml* file again so that the HelloWorldLambda section looks as follows (careful with your YAML tabbing!):

```
HelloWorldLambda:
    Type: AWS::Serverless::Function
    Properties:
      FunctionName: HelloWorldJava
      Runtime: java8
      MemorySize: 512
      Handler: book.EnvVarLambda::handler
      CodeUri: target/lambda.jar
      Environment:
        Variables:
          DATABASE_URL: my-database-url
```

After packaging and deploying, if we test the function now, the log output includes this instead:

```
DATABASE_URL is set to: my-database-url
```

We are free to update the environment configuration as much as we would like.

When using environment variables, you often want to store sensitive data, for example access keys to remote services. There are a number of ways of doing this in a secure way with Lambda, and they are explained in Amazon's documentation.

Summary

The programming model for AWS Lambda is significantly different from other models that you may be used to.

In this chapter, you explored what it means to program Lambda functions—what the runtime environment is, how functions are invoked, and the different ways you can get data in and out of functions.

Then you learned some aspects of configuration for Lambda functions—timeout and memory—and what those settings mean. Finally, you saw how you can apply your own application configuration through environment variables.

Now that you know how to program Lambda functions, in the next chapter we will examine Lambda operations—packaging, deployment, security, monitoring, and more.

Exercises

1. Take some time to work through the step-by-step descriptions in this chapter—Lambda is very different than how you may have built and run Java applications in the past.

2. Try logging something using `System.err`—the standard error stream—instead of `System.out`. Does the log output appear any differently to `System.out`? Does it change the result of calling the function, either asynchronously or synchronously?

3. Deliberately call a function with invalid input to see the parsing exception described earlier: `An error occurred during JSON parsing`. Where do you see this error? How does it impact the result of calling the function, either asynchronously or synchronously?

4. Try building your own POJO types and calling Lambda with JSON versions of them. Do you prefer the *JavaBean* style, or public fields?

5. Try using the `StreamLambda` described earlier that outputs the entire input event with one of the provided test event template objects in the Lambda web console.

6. Try converting one of your classes to use a static handler method, rather than an instance method, to confirm that it works just as well.

Operating AWS Lambda Functions

This chapter will introduce a more advanced method of building and packaging Java-based AWS Lambda functions. We'll also go into more detail on the serverless-oriented version of AWS's infrastructure-as-code tool, SAM, which you first used in Chapter 2. Finally, we'll go over how Lambda functions and serverless applications are affected by AWS's security model and how to use SAM to automatically enforce a least-privilege security model for our serverless application.

Before proceeding, we recommend that if you haven't done so already that you download this book's code examples (*https://oreil.ly/t0Bgg*).

Build and Package

The Lambda platform expects all user-provided code to be in the form of a ZIP (*https://oreil.ly/aECWk*) archive file. Depending on which runtime you're using and your actual business logic, that ZIP file may consist of source code, or code and libraries, or, in the case of Java, compiled byte code (class files) and libraries.

In the Java ecosystem, we often package our code into JAR (Java ARchive) files, to be run via the `java -jar` command, or to be used as libraries by other applications. It turns out that a JAR file is simply a ZIP file with some additional metadata. The Lambda platform doesn't perform any special handling of JAR files—it treats them as ZIP files, just as it does for the other Lambda language runtimes.

Using a tool like Maven, we can specify the other libraries that our code depends on and have Maven download the right versions of those libraries (and any transitive dependencies that they might have), compile our code into Java class files, and package everything up into a single JAR file (often called an *uberjar*).

Uberjars

Despite using the uberjar approach in Chapters 2 and 3, there are a few problems with it that are worth calling out before we go any further.

First, the uberjar approach unpacks and then overlays libraries on top of each other in the target uberjar file. In the following example, Library A contains a class file and a properties file. Library B contains a different class file and a properties file with the same name as the properties file from Library A.

```
$ jar tf LibraryA.jar
book/
book/important.properties
book/A.class

$ jar tf LibraryB.jar
book/
book/important.properties
book/B.class
```

If these JAR files were used to create an uberjar (as we did in prior chapters), the result would contain two class files and one properties file—but the properties file from which source JAR?

```
$ jar tf uberjar.jar
book/
book/important.properties # Which properties file is this?
book/A.class
book/B.class
```

Because the JAR files are unpacked and overlaid, only one of those properties files will make it into the final uberjar, and it can be difficult to know which one will win without delving into the dark arts of Maven resource transformers.

The second major issue with the uberjar approach is oriented around creating a JAR file—the fact that JAR files are also ZIP files that can be used by the Lambda runtime is incidental from the perspective of the Maven build process. Two specific issues arise from this JAR versus ZIP situation. One is that any JAR-specific metadata is unused (and in fact, ignored) by the Lambda runtime. Things like a `Main-Class` attribute in a *MANIFEST.MF* file—a piece of metadata common to JAR files—are meaningless in the context of a Lambda function.

Furthermore, the JAR creation process itself introduces a certain amount of non-determinism into the build process. For example, tool versions and build timestamps are recorded in *MANIFEST.MF* and *pom.properties* files—and that makes it impossible to reproducibly build the same JAR file from the same source code every time. This nonreproducibility wreaks havoc on downstream caching, deployment, and security processes, so we want to avoid it when possible.

Since we're not actually interested in the JAR-ness of an uberjar file, it makes sense for us to consider not using the uberjar process at all. Of course, the uberjar process itself isn't necessarily the only source of nondeterminism in our build process, but we'll deal with the rest of it later.

Despite these drawbacks, the uberjar process is simpler to configure and use for simple cases, especially when a Lambda function has few (or no) third-party dependencies. This was the case in the examples in Chapters 2 and 3, which is why we used the uberjar technique up until this point, but for any real-world use of Java and Lambda of any significant scale, we recommend the ZIP file approach that we describe next.

Assembling a ZIP File

So, in the Java world, our alternative to using an uberjar file is to fall back to a trusty old ZIP file. In this scenario, the archive layout is going to be a little different, but we'll see how a careful approach can avoid the issues with the uberjar and give us an artifact that the Lambda platform can use. We'll discuss how to achieve this using Maven, but of course you should feel free to translate this method to your preferred build tool—the outcome is more important than the process itself.

Starting Fresh with sam init

If you want to create a new project using the ideas we discuss in this chapter—packaging and deploying reproducible ZIP artifacts—then you can use a different version of the sam init template we introduced in Chapter 2. Run the following, and it will generate a version with the updated *pom.xml* and *template.yaml* files, along with the *lambda-zip.xml* assembly descriptor file that we'll be using later in the chapter:

```
$ sam init \
  --location \
  gh:symphoniacloud/sam-init-HelloWorldLambdaJava-zip
```

To make a more interesting example, first we'll add a dependency on the AWS SDK for DynamoDB to our Maven build for the Lambda function from "Lambda Hello World (the Proper Way)" on page 34.

Add a dependencies section to the *pom.xml* file:

```
<dependencies>
  <dependency>
    <groupId>com.amazonaws</groupId>
    <artifactId>aws-java-sdk-dynamodb</artifactId>
    <version>1.11.319</version>
  </dependency>
</dependencies>
```

With that dependency added, here's what the desired ZIP file layout looks like for our simple Lambda function and dependencies:

```
$ zipinfo -1 target/lambda.zip
META-INF/
book/
book/HelloWorld.class
lib/
lib/aws-java-sdk-core-1.11.319.jar
lib/aws-java-sdk-dynamodb-1.11.319.jar
lib/aws-java-sdk-kms-1.11.319.jar
lib/aws-java-sdk-s3-1.11.319.jar
lib/commons-codec-1.10.jar
lib/commons-logging-1.1.3.jar
lib/httpclient-4.5.5.jar
lib/httpcore-4.4.9.jar
lib/ion-java-1.0.2.jar
lib/jackson-annotations-2.6.0.jar
lib/jackson-core-2.6.7.jar
lib/jackson-databind-2.6.7.1.jar
lib/jackson-dataformat-cbor-2.6.7.jar
lib/jmespath-java-1.11.319.jar
lib/joda-time-2.8.1.jar
```

In addition to our application code (*book/HelloWorld.class*), we see a *lib* directory full of JAR files, one for the AWS DynamoDB SDK, and one for each of its transitive dependencies.

We can build that ZIP output using the Maven Assembly plug-in. This plug-in allows us to add some special behavior to a specific part of the Maven build (in this case, the package phase where the results of the Java compilation process are packaged up alongside other resources into a set of output files).

First, we've configured the Maven Assembly plug-in in the *pom.xml* file for the project, in the build section:

```
<build>
  <plugins>
    <plugin>
      <artifactId>maven-assembly-plugin</artifactId>
      <version>3.1.1</version>
      <executions>
        <execution>
          <phase>package</phase>
          <goals>
            <goal>single</goal>
          </goals>
        </execution>
      </executions>
      <configuration>
        <appendAssemblyId>false</appendAssemblyId>
        <descriptors>
```

```
            <descriptor>src/assembly/lambda-zip.xml</descriptor>
          </descriptors>
          <finalName>lambda</finalName>
        </configuration>
      </plugin>
    </plugins>
  </build>
```

The two most important parts of this configuration are the assembly `descriptor`, which is a path to another XML file in our project, and the `finalName`, which instructs the plug-in to name our output file *lambda.zip* instead of something else. We'll see later how picking a simple `finalName` will aid in rapid iteration of our project, especially after we start using Maven submodules.

Most of the configuration for our ZIP file is actually located in the assembly `descriptor` file, which was referenced in the *pom.xml* file earlier. This `assembly` configuration is a description of exactly which contents to include in our output file:

```
<assembly>
  <id>lambda-zip</id> ❶
  <formats>
    <format>zip</format> ❷
  </formats>
  <includeBaseDirectory>false</includeBaseDirectory> ❸
  <dependencySets>
    <dependencySet> ❹
      <includes>
        <include>${project.groupId}:${project.artifactId}</include>
      </includes>
      <unpack>true</unpack>
      <unpackOptions>
        <excludes>
          <exclude>META-INF/MANIFEST.MF</exclude>
          <exclude>META-INF/maven/**</exclude>
        </excludes>
      </unpackOptions>
    </dependencySet>
    <dependencySet> ❺
      <useProjectArtifact>false</useProjectArtifact>
      <unpack>false</unpack>
      <scope>runtime</scope>
      <outputDirectory>lib</outputDirectory> ❻
    </dependencySet>
  </dependencySets>
</assembly>
```

❶ We've given the assembly a unique name, `lambda-zip`.

❷ The output format itself will be of type `zip`.

❸ The output file will not have a base directory—this means that when extracted, our ZIP file's contents will be unpacked into the current directory rather than into a new subdirectory.

❹ The first `dependencySet` section explicitly includes our application code, by referencing the project's `groupId` and `artifactId` properties. When we start using Maven submodules, this will need to be altered. Our application code will be "unpacked." That is, it won't be contained in a JAR file; rather, it will just be a normal directory structure and Java *.class* files. We've also explicitly excluded the unnecessary *META-INF* directory.

❺ The second `dependencySet` section handles our application's dependencies. We exclude the project's artifact (as it was handled in the first `dependencySet` section). We only include dependencies that are in the `runtime` scope. We don't unpack the dependencies; rather, we just leave them packaged as JAR files.

❻ Finally, instead of including all of the JAR files in the root of our output file, we'll put them all into a *lib* directory.

So how does this complicated new Maven configuration help us avoid the issues with uberjars?

First, we've stripped out some of the unnecessary META-INF information. You'll notice we've been a bit selective—there are some cases where having META-INF information (like "services") is still valuable, so we don't want to get rid of it completely.

Second, we've included all of our dependencies, but as individual JAR files in a *lib* directory. This avoids the file and path overwriting issue completely. Each dependency JAR remains self-contained. According to the AWS Lambda best practices documentation (*https://oreil.ly/euF1U*), this approach also pays some performance dividends in that it's faster for the Lambda platform to unpack a ZIP file and faster for the JVM to load classes from JAR files.

---

io.symphonia/lambda-packaging

Rather than copy and paste the `lambda-zip` assembly descriptor into all of your projects, we have built a prepackaged descriptor that is available on Maven Central. Just use the following configuration in the `build` section of your *pom.xml* file:

```
<plugin>
  <artifactId>maven-assembly-plugin</artifactId>
  <version>3.1.1</version>
  <dependencies>
    <dependency>
```

```
            <groupId>io.symphonia</groupId>
            <artifactId>lambda-packaging</artifactId>
            <version>1.0.0</version>
        </dependency>
    </dependencies>
    <executions>
        <execution>
            <id>make-assembly</id>
            <phase>package</phase>
            <goals>
                <goal>single</goal>
            </goals>
        </execution>
    </executions>
    <configuration>
        <appendAssemblyId>false</appendAssemblyId>
        <descriptorRefs>
            <descriptorRef>lambda-zip</descriptorRef>
        </descriptorRefs>
        <finalName>lambda</finalName>
    </configuration>
</plugin>
```

Reproducible Builds

When our source code or dependencies change, we expect the contents of the deployment package (the uberjar or ZIP file) to change too (after running our build and packaging process). However, when our source code and dependencies don't change, the contents of the deployment package should remain the same even if the build and packaging process is executed again. The output of the build should be reproducible (e.g., deterministic). This is important because downstream processes (like deployment pipelines) are often triggered based on whether a deployment package has changed as indicated by the MD5 hash of the contents, and we want to avoid triggering those processes unnecessarily.

Even though we've eliminated the autogenerated *MANIFEST.MF* and *pom.properties* files using the `lambda-zip` assembly descriptor, we still haven't removed all of the potential sources of nondeterminism in the build process. For example, when we build our application code (e.g., `HelloWorld`), the timestamp on the compiled Java class files may change. These altered timestamps are propagated into the ZIP file, and then the hash of the ZIP file's contents changes even though the source code didn't.

Fortunately, a simple Maven plug-in exists to strip these sources of nondeterminism from our build process. The `reproducible-build-maven-plugin` can be executed during the build process and will render our output ZIP file completely deterministic. It can be configured as a `plugin` in the `build` section of our *pom.xml* file:

```xml
<plugin>
  <groupId>io.github.zlika</groupId>
  <artifactId>reproducible-build-maven-plugin</artifactId>
  <version>0.10</version>
  <executions>
    <execution>
      <phase>package</phase>
      <goals>
        <goal>strip-jar</goal>
      </goals>
    </execution>
  </executions>
</plugin>
```

Now, when we rebuild our deployment packages multiple times using the same unchanged source code, the hash is always the same. You'll see how this affects the deployment process in the next section.

Deploy

There are many options for deploying Lambda code. Before we dive in, however, it's worth clarifying what we mean by *deploy*. In this case, we're simply talking about updating the code or configuration for a particular Lambda function, or a group of Lambda functions and related AWS resources, through the use of APIs or other services. We're not extending the definition to include deployment orchestration (like AWS CodeDeploy).

In no particular order, the methods of deploying Lambda code are as follows:

- AWS Lambda web console
- AWS CloudFormation/Serverless Application Model (SAM)
- AWS CLI (which uses the AWS API)
- AWS Cloud Development Kit (CDK)
- Other AWS-developed frameworks, like Amplify and Chalice
- Third-party frameworks targeting serverless components that build primarily on top of CloudFormation, like the Serverless Framework
- Third-party tools and frameworks targeting serverless components that build primarily on top of the AWS API, like Claudia.js and `lambda-maven-plugin` from Maven
- General-purpose third-party infrastructure tools, like Ansible or Terraform

In this book, we'll address the first two (and indeed have already touched upon the AWS Lambda web console and SAM in Chapters 2 and 3). We also use the AWS CLI, although not as a deployment tool. With a solid understanding of those methods, you should be able to evaluate the other options and decide whether one of them is a better fit for your environment and use case.

Infrastructure as Code

When we interact with AWS via the web console or the CLI, we're creating, updating, and destroying infrastructure manually. For example, if we create a Lambda function using the AWS Web Console, the next time we want to create a Lambda function with the same parameters, we still have to perform the same manual actions via the web console. This same characteristic applies to the CLI as well.

For initial development and experimentation, this is a reasonable approach. However, when our projects begin building momentum, this manual approach to infrastructure management will turn into a roadblock. A well-proven way to address this issue is called *infrastructure as code*.

Rather than manually interacting with AWS via the web console or CLI, we can declaratively specify our desired infrastructure in a JSON or YAML file and submit that file to AWS's infrastructure-as-code service: CloudFormation. The CloudFormation service takes our input file and makes the necessary changes to AWS infrastructure on our behalf, taking into account resource dependencies, the current state of previously deployed versions of our app, and the idiosyncrasies and specific requirements of the various AWS services. A set of AWS resources created from a CloudFormation template file is called a *stack*.

CloudFormation is AWS's proprietary infrastructure-as-code service, but it's not the only option in this area. Other popular choices that work with AWS are Terraform, Ansible, and Chef. Each service has its own configuration languages and patterns, but all achieve essentially the same outcome—cloud infrastructure provisioned from configuration files.

A key benefit of using configuration files (rather than pointing and clicking in the console) is that those files, which represent our application infrastructure, can be version-controlled alongside our application source code. We can see a complete timeline of changes to our infrastructure, using the same version-control tools we use for the other pieces of our application. Furthermore, we can incorporate those configuration files into our continuous deployment pipelines, so when we make changes to our application infrastructure, those changes can be rolled out safely using industry-standard tools, alongside our application code.

CloudFormation and the Serverless Application Model

While there are obvious benefits to an infrastructure-as-code approach, CloudFormation itself has a reputation for being verbose, unwieldy, and inflexible. Configuration files for even the simplest application architectures can easily run into the hundreds or thousands of lines of JSON or YAML. When dealing with an existing CloudFormation stack of that size, there's an understandable temptation to fall back to using the AWS Web Console or CLI.

Fortunately, as AWS serverless developers, we have the good fortune to be able to use a different "flavor" of CloudFormation called the Serverless Application Model (SAM), which we used in Chapters 2 and 3. This is essentially a superset of CloudFormation, which allows us to use some special resource types and shortcuts to represent common serverless components and application architectures. It also includes some special CLI commands to ease development, testing, and deployment.

Here's the SAM template we first used in "Creating the Lambda Function" on page 35, updated to use our new ZIP deployment package (note that the `CodeUri` suffix has changed from `.jar` to `.zip`):

```
AWSTemplateFormatVersion: 2010-09-09
Transform: AWS::Serverless-2016-10-31
Description: Chapter 4

Resources:
  HelloWorldLambda:
    Type: AWS::Serverless::Function
    Properties:
      Runtime: java8
      MemorySize: 512
      Handler: book.HelloWorld::handler
      CodeUri: target/lambda.zip
```

We can deploy the new ZIP-based Lambda function using the same SAM command you learned in Chapter 2:

```
$ sam deploy \
  --s3-bucket $CF_BUCKET \
  --stack-name chapter4-sam \
  --capabilities CAPABILITY_IAM
```

`sam deploy` starts by uploading our deployment package to S3, but only if the contents of that package have changed. Earlier in the chapter, we spent some time setting up a reproducible build so that operations like this upload process don't have to execute if nothing has actually changed.

Behind the scenes `sam deploy` also creates a modified version of our template (also stored in S3) to reference the newly uploaded S3 locations of our artifact(s), rather than the local ones. This step is necessary because CloudFormation requires any referenced artifacts within a template to be available in S3 at deployment time.

 The files that `s3 deploy` stores in S3 should be considered merely staging versions as part of a deployment process, rather than application artifacts to be kept. Because of this, we recommend that you set a "Lifecycle Policy" on your SAM S3 bucket, if it isn't being used for anything else, that will automatically delete the deployment artifacts after a period of time—we usually set it to a week.

After the upload step, the `sam deploy` command creates a new CloudFormation stack if one doesn't already exist with the provided name in this AWS account and region. If the stack already exists, the `sam deploy` command will create a CloudFormation *change set*, which lists which resources will be created, updated, or deleted *before* taking action. The `sam deploy` command will then apply the change set to update the CloudFormation stack.

Listing the stack resources, we can see that not only did CloudFormation create our Lambda function, but it also created the supporting IAM roles and policies (which we'll explore later) without our having to specify them explicitly:

```
$ aws cloudformation list-stack-resources --stack-name chapter4-sam
{
  "StackResourceSummaries": [
    {
      "LogicalResourceId": "HelloWorldLambda",
      "PhysicalResourceId": "chapter4-sam-HelloWorldLambda-1HP15K6524D2E",
      "ResourceType": "AWS::Lambda::Function",
      "LastUpdatedTimestamp": "2019-07-26T19:16:34.424Z",
      "ResourceStatus": "CREATE_COMPLETE",
      "DriftInformation": {
        "StackResourceDriftStatus": "NOT_CHECKED"
      }
    },
    {
      "LogicalResourceId": "HelloWorldLambdaRole",
      "PhysicalResourceId":
        "chapter4-sam-HelloWorldLambdaRole-1KV86CI9RCXY0",
      "ResourceType": "AWS::IAM::Role",
      "LastUpdatedTimestamp": "2019-07-26T19:16:30.287Z",
      "ResourceStatus": "CREATE_COMPLETE",
      "DriftInformation": {
        "StackResourceDriftStatus": "NOT_CHECKED"
      }
    }
  ]
}
```

In addition to Lambda functions, SAM includes resource types for DynamoDB tables (`AWS::Serverless::SimpleTable`) and API Gateways (`AWS::Serverless::Api`). These resource types are focused on popular use cases and may not be usable for all application architectures. However, because SAM is a superset of CloudFormation, we can use plain old CloudFormation resource types in our SAM templates. That means we can mix and match serverless and "normal" AWS components in our architectures, gaining the benefits of both approaches, and the idempotent CLI semantics of SAM's `sam deploy` command. You'll see examples of combining SAM and Cloud-Formation resources in one template in Chapter 5.

Security

Security permeates every aspect of AWS. As you learned in Chapter 2, we must deal with AWS's security layer, called Identity and Access Management (IAM), from the very beginning. However, rather than gloss over the details by simply running everything with the broadest, least-secure set of IAM permissions possible, we're going to dive a little deeper in this section and explain how access to the Lambda platform is controlled by IAM, how that affects our functions' interactions with other AWS resources, and how SAM makes it a bit easier to build secure applications.

Necessary Complexity

It would be undeniably easier for us to build applications in AWS if we didn't have to worry about IAM at all. Why do we need it, and why does AWS require it? To answer those questions, let's imagine how the AWS ecosystem might work without IAM.

Without IAM, our Lambda functions could access any other AWS resource, like a DynamoDB table or S3 bucket. This is simple to reason about—if a resource exists, we can use it. Of course, with no restrictions in place, we could even access resources in other AWS accounts, and those other accounts could access our resources!

This world of "open access" might be convenient for developers, but unfortunately it's a nightmare for security and privacy. If we want to limit access to our applications and data, we need a system to enforce those limitations. In AWS, IAM is that system.

IAM controls access to AWS services by limiting who can perform certain actions against a set of resources. The *who* in this case is an IAM principal, which is a user or role. The actions and resources are defined in an IAM policy. As you might imagine, IAM introduces a tremendous amount of complexity into our AWS applications, especially when we're using many different serverless components and resources that each has its own action and resource specifications.

But understanding IAM and using it correctly are critical to building serverless applications, as we'll see in this chapter.

The Principle of Least Privilege

Unlike in a traditional monolithic application, a serverless application could potentially have hundreds of individual AWS components, each with different behavior and access to different pieces of information. If we simply applied the broadest security permissions possible, then every component would have access to every other component and piece of information in our AWS account. Every gap we leave in a security policy is an opportunity for information to leak or be lost or be altered or for our application's behavior to be changed. And, if a single component is compromised, the entire AWS account (and any other applications deployed in it) is at risk as well.

We can address this risk by applying the principle of "least privilege" to our security model. In a nutshell, this principle states that every application and indeed every component of an application should have the least possible access it needs to perform its function. For example, let's consider a Lambda function that reads from a DynamoDB table. The broadest possible permissions would allow that Lambda function to read, write, or otherwise interact with every other component and piece of information in the AWS account. It could read from S3 buckets, create new Lambda functions, or even launch EC2 instances. If the Lambda code had a bug or vulnerability (in parsing user input, for example), its behavior could be altered to do those things, and it wouldn't be constrained by its IAM role.

The principle of least privilege, applied to this particular Lambda function, would lead to an IAM role that allows the function to only access the DynamoDB service. Going a step further, we might only allow the function to read data from DynamoDB and remove its ability to write data or to create or delete tables. We can go even further in this case and restrict the function's read-only access to the single DynamoDB table it requires. Taken to the logical extreme, we can even restrict which items in the table the function can read, based on the user who has executed the function in the first place.

Having applied the principle of least privilege to our Lambda function, we've now limited its access to only the specific resources that it needs to perform its job. If the Lambda function was compromised or hacked in some way, its security policy would still constrain it to reading specific items from a single DynamoDB table. That said, the principle of least privilege is not only applicable to preventing compromises. It's also an effective means of limiting the "blast radius" of bugs in your application code.

Let's consider a situation in which our Lambda function has a bug that, for example, uses the wrong value to delete data. In a wide-open security model, that bug could result in the Lambda function deleting data for the wrong user! However, because we've limited the "blast radius" of bugs by applying the principle of least privilege for our Lambda function, this particular issue will result in it simply doing nothing or throwing an error.

> ### The Control Plane and the Data Plane
>
> As we briefly mentioned in Chapter 3 (Figure 3-1), the Lambda service is split into the control plane and the data plane. The control plane manages Lambda functions and provides APIs like CreateFunction, DeleteFunction, and UpdateFunctionCode. The control plane also manages integrations with other AWS services. Invocation of a Lambda function is handled by the data plane, which provides the Invoke and InvokeAsync APIs.
>
> When considering how IAM is integrated with Lambda, it's important to understand which plane is involved.

Identity and Access Management

A working knowledge of IAM is critical to successfully building any kind of application on AWS, and as we discussed in the previous section, effectively applying the principle of least privilege is even more important when building a serverless application. IAM is a complex, multifaceted service, and we're not going to come close to covering all of it here. Rather, in this section, we're just going to dive into IAM from the perspective of building serverless applications. Where IAM most commonly and frequently comes into play for serverless applications is in execution roles, in the policies attached to those roles, and in policies attached to specific AWS resources.

Roles and policies

An IAM role is an identity that can be assumed by an AWS component (like a Lambda function). A role differs from an IAM user in that a role is assumable by anyone (or anything) who needs it, and a role doesn't have long-term access credentials. With that in mind, we can define an IAM role as an assumable identity, with an attached set of permissions.

The phrase *assumable identity* might make it sound like anyone or anything can assume an IAM role. If that were the case, then using roles wouldn't really provide any benefit because there would be no restrictions on assuming a role and therefore no restrictions on what actions any given user or component could undertake. Fortunately, IAM roles are not assumable by just anyone. When building a role, we must specify who (or what) can assume that role. For example, if we're building a role for use by a Lambda function, we must explicitly grant the Lambda service (in this case the data plane) permission to assume that role, by specifying the following "trust relationship":

```
{
  "Version": "2012-10-17",
  "Statement": [
    {
```

```
      "Effect": "Allow",
      "Principal": {
        "Service": "lambda.amazonaws.com"
      },
      "Action": "sts:AssumeRole"
    }
  ]
}
```

This statement specifies an effect (`Allow`), which applies to an action (`sts:Assume Role`). Most important, however, it specifies a principal, which is the identity that is allowed to assume the role. In this case, we're allowing the Lambda service's data plane (`lambda.amazonaws.com`) to assume this role. If we tried to use this role with a different service, like EC2 or ECS, it wouldn't work unless we changed the principal.

Now that we've established who can assume the role, we need to add permissions. IAM roles don't inherently have any permissions to access resources or perform actions. Also, IAM's default behavior is to deny permission, unless that permission is explicitly allowed in a policy. Those permissions are contained in policies, which state permissions using the following constructs:

- An *effect* (like `Allow` or `Deny`)
- A set of *actions*, which are generally namespaced to a specific AWS service (like `logs:PutLogEvents`)
- A set of *resources*, which are generally Amazon Resource Names (ARNs) that define specific AWS components. Different services support varying levels of specificity for resources. For example, DynamoDB policies can apply down to the level of a table.

Here's an example policy that allows a set of actions against the "logs" service (aka CloudWatch Logs) and doesn't restrict those actions to any particular "logs" resource:

```
{
  "Version": "2012-10-17",
  "Statement": [
    {
      "Effect": "Allow",
      "Action": [
        "logs:CreateLogGroup",
        "logs:CreateLogStream",
        "logs:PutLogEvents"
      ],
      "Resource": "*"
    }
  ]
}
```

We established earlier who can assume the role (the Lambda service's data plane, as specified by the principal identifier `lambda.amazonaws.com`) and what permissions the role has. By itself, however, this role isn't used until it's attached to a Lambda function, which we would need to explicitly configure. That is, we need to tell the Lambda service to use this role when executing a particular Lambda function.

Lambda resource policies

As if the world of security and IAM weren't complex enough, AWS also occasionally uses IAM policies applied to resources (rather than identities) to control actions and access. Resource policies invert control compared to an identity-based IAM policy: a resource policy states what other principals can do to the resource in question. In particular, this is useful for allowing principals in different accounts access to certain resources (like Lambda functions or S3 buckets).

A Lambda function invocation resource policy consists of a series of statements, each of which specifies a principal, a list of actions, and a list of resources. These policies are used by the Lambda data plane to determine whether to allow a caller (e.g., a principal) to successfully invoke a function. Here's an example Lambda resource policy (also called a *function policy*) that allows the API Gateway service to invoke a particular function:

```
{
  "Version": "2012-10-17",
  "Id": "default",
  "Statement": [
    {
      "Sid": "Stmt001",
      "Effect": "Allow",
      "Principal": {
        "Service": "apigateway.amazonaws.com"
      },
      "Action": "lambda:invokeFunction",
      "Resource":
        "arn:aws:lambda:us-east-1:555555555555:function:MyLambda",
      "Condition": {
        "ArnLike": {
          "AWS:SourceArn": "arn:aws:execute-api:us-east-1:
            555555555555:xxx/*/GET/locations"
        }
      }
    }
  ]
}
```

In this policy, we've also added a condition, which more specifically limits the allowed source of the action to only API Gateway deployments with an ID of "xxx" that include the "/GET/locations" path. Conditions are service-specific and depend on what information the caller makes available.

Let's work through the scenario in which API Gateway invokes a Lambda function, using Figure 4-1.

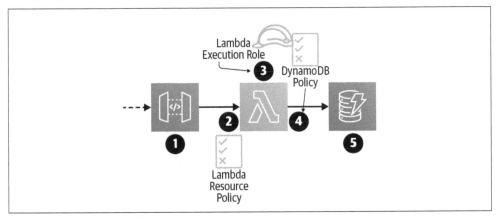

Figure 4-1. Overview of Lambda and IAM security

1. Did the caller have permission to call the API? For this scenario, we'll assume the answer is yes. Please see the API Gateway documentation (*https://oreil.ly/Sb6N2*) for more information.

2. The API Gateway API is attempting to invoke the Lambda function. Does the Lambda service allow this? This is controlled by a Lambda function invocation resource policy.

3. What permissions should the Lambda function code have when it executes? This is controlled by the Lambda execution role, and that role is assumed through a trust relationship with the Lambda service.

4. The Lambda code is trying to put an item into a DynamoDB table. Can it do that? This is controlled by a permission, which comes from an IAM policy attached to the Lambda execution role.

5. DynamoDB doesn't use resource policies, so calls from anyone (including Lambda functions) are permitted, as long as their role (e.g., the Lambda execution role) permits it.

SAM IAM

Unfortunately, the complexity of IAM puts its effective use somewhat at odds with a rapid prototyping workflow. Throw a serverless application architecture into the mix, and it's no wonder so many Lambda execution roles have completely open policies, allowing all forms of access to every resource in the AWS account. Even though it's easy to agree that the principle of least privilege provides valuable benefits, when faced with the somewhat daunting task of implementing it using IAM for dozens or hundreds of AWS resources, many otherwise conscientious engineers choose to forgo security for simplicity.

Autogenerated execution roles and resource policies.   Fortunately, the Serverless Application Model addresses this issue in a few different ways. In the simplest of cases, it will automatically create the appropriate Lambda execution roles and function policies, based on the various functions and event sources configured in the SAM infrastructure template. This neatly handles permissions for executing Lambda functions and allowing them to be invoked by other AWS services.

For example, if you configured a single Lambda function with no triggers, SAM will automatically generate a Lambda execution role for that function, which would allow it to write to CloudWatch Logs. If you then added an API Gateway trigger to that Lambda function, SAM will generate a Lambda function invocation resource policy, which allows the Lambda function to be invoked by the API Gateway platform. This will make our lives a little easier in the next chapter!

Common policy templates.   Of course, if your Lambda function needs to interact with other AWS services in code (for example, to write to a DynamoDB table), it will likely require additional permissions. For these situations, SAM provides a selection of common IAM policy templates that allow us to concisely specify permissions and resources. Those templates are then expanded during the SAM deployment process and become fully specified IAM policy statements. Here we've added a DynamoDB table to our SAM template. We've used a SAM policy template to allow our Lambda function to perform create, read, update, and delete actions (aka CRUD) against that DynamoDB table.

```
AWSTemplateFormatVersion: 2010-09-09
Transform: AWS::Serverless-2016-10-31
Description: Chapter 4

Resources:

  HelloWorldLambda:
    Type: AWS::Serverless::Function
    Properties:
      Runtime: java8
      MemorySize: 512
      Handler: book.HelloWorld::handler
      CodeUri: target/lambda.zip
      Policies:
        - DynamoDBCrudPolicy:
          TableName: !Ref HelloWorldTable  ❶

  HelloWorldTable:
    Type: AWS::Serverless::SimpleTable
```

❶ Here we've used the CloudFormation Intrinsic Function `Ref` (*https://oreil.ly/ ScQ9Q*), which allows us to use the logical ID of a resource (in this case `Hello WorldTable`) as a placeholder for the physical ID of the resource (which would be something like `stack-name-HelloWorldTable-ABC123DEF`). The CloudFormation service will resolve logical IDs to physical IDs when a stack is created or updated.

Summary

In this chapter, we covered building and packaging Lambda code and dependencies in a reproducible, deterministic way. We started to use AWS's SAM to specify our infrastructure (e.g., our Lambda function and later a DynamoDB table) as YAML code—we'll explore this much further in Chapter 5. We then explored the two different kinds of IAM constructs that affect Lambda functions: execution roles and resource policies. Finally, using SAM instead of raw CloudFormation meant that we didn't have to add very much additional YAML code to apply the principle of least privilege to the IAM roles and policies for our Lambda function.

We now have nearly all the basic building blocks in place to create complete applications using Lambda and associated tools. In Chapter 5 we'll show how to tie Lambda functions to event sources and then build two example applications.

Exercises

1. Deliberately misconfigure the Lambda function in this chapter by setting the `Han dler` property to `book.HelloWorld::foo`. What happens when the function is deployed? What happens when you invoke the function?

2. Read the IAM reference guide (*https://oreil.ly/nBdd9*) to learn which AWS services (and actions) can have granular IAM permissions.

3. If you'd like an extra challenge, replace `AWS::Serverless::Function` with `AWS::Lambda::Function` in the *template.yaml* file. What other changes do you have to make for CloudFormation to deploy your function? If you get stuck, you can look at the post-transform template (for the original stack) via the CloudFormation web console.

Building Serverless Applications

So far we've talked a lot about Lambda functions—how to program them, how to package and deploy them, how to process input and output, etc. One important aspect to Lambda, however, that we haven't covered much so far, is that Lambda functions are rarely invoked directly from code we write in a different system. Instead, for the *vast majority* of usages of Lambda, we configure an *event source*, or *trigger*, that is *another AWS service*, and let AWS invoke our Lambda function for us.

We looked at a couple of examples of this in "What Does a Lambda Application Look Like?" on page 13:

- To implement an HTTP API, we configure AWS API Gateway as the event source.
- To implement file processing, we configure S3 as the event source.

There are many different AWS services that directly integrate with Lambda, and even more that integrate indirectly. This means that we can build *serverless applications*, using Lambda as the compute platform, that can perform a vast range of tasks.

In this chapter, we look at how to tie event sources to Lambda and then explore how to build specific types of application with this technique. Along the way, you'll learn more about how to architect, build, package, and deploy Lambda-based applications, building on our knowledge from the previous chapter.

If you haven't done so already, you'll likely want to download the example source code (*https://oreil.ly/8DQe_*) before trying any of the examples in this chapter.

Lambda Event Sources

As you just learned, the typical usage pattern for Lambda is to tie a function to an event source. In this section, we describe the workflow to follow when you build a Lambda function to integrate with a particular upstream service.

Writing Code to Work with Input and Output for Event Sources

When programming a Lambda function to respond to a particular event source, the first thing you'll typically want to do is understand the format of events that your Lambda function will receive.

The SAM CLI tool that we've already used has an interesting command to help with this exercise—sam local generate-event. If you run this command, sam lists all the services it can generate stub events for, which you can then examine and use to drive your code. For example, part of the output for sam local generate-event looks like this:

```
Commands:
  alexa-skills-kit
  alexa-smart-home
  apigateway
  batch
  cloudformation
  cloudfront
  cloudwatch
  codecommit
  codepipeline
```

Let's say we're interested in building a serverless HTTP API. In this case, we use AWS API Gateway as our upstream event source. If we run sam local generate-event apigateway the output includes the following:

```
Commands:
  authorizer  Generates an Amazon API Gateway Authorizer Event
  aws-proxy   Generates an Amazon API Gateway AWS Proxy Event
```

It turns out that API Gateway can integrate with Lambda in multiple ways. The one we typically want from this list is the aws-proxy event, where API Gateway acts as a proxy server in front of a Lambda function, so let's give that a try.

```
$ sam local generate-event apigateway aws-proxy

{
  "body": "eyJ0ZXN0IjoiYm9keSJ9",
  "resource": "/{proxy+}",
  "path": "/path/to/resource",
  "httpMethod": "POST",
  "isBase64Encoded": true,
  "queryStringParameters": {
```

```
    "foo": "bar"
  },
  ....
```

This JSON object is a fully baked sample of a typical event a Lambda function receives from API Gateway. In other words, when you set up API Gateway as a trigger for your Lambda function, the event argument that is passed to the Lambda function has this structure.

This sample event doesn't necessarily help you with the *semantics* of the integration with API Gateway, but it does give you the shape of the event that your Lambda function receives, which in turn gives you a solid start to writing your code. You can use this JSON object as inspiration, or you can take it a step further and actually embed it in a test—more on that in Chapter 6!

Using the AWS Toolkit

We focus in this book on using the SAM CLI tool to provide various interactions with AWS's serverless services. However, AWS also provides some IDE plug-ins for this purpose, for Jetbrains IntelliJ, Eclipse, VS Code, and more.

The IntelliJ Toolkit pictured in Figure 5-1 is introduced on its own page (*https://aws.amazon.com/intellij*) on the AWS website. It offers a good number of features for Lambda developers.

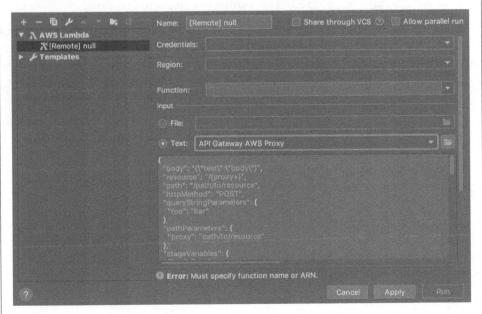

Figure 5-1. AWS IntelliJ Toolkit

At the time of this writing, we think that most of these features have a few restrictions that limit its use, but it is worth exploring, and for some of you it might fit well in your workflow.

One feature that we particularly like is the *Run (Invoke) the Remote Version of a Function* tool. There's a couple of reasons we like this:

- It offers the same event templates offered by `sam local generate-event` (see Figure 5-1).
- It provides quick access to Lambda logs as you invoke the function running on AWS—this can occasionally be a frustrating thing to do otherwise.

The Toolkit also offers features to build and deploy Lambda functions/serverless applications, but there are some restrictions here on how your code can be packaged. At the time of writing, for example, the Toolkit doesn't support our recommended workflow for multimodule projects, which we explore later in this chapter.

Finally, the Toolkit enables local debugging of a Lambda function within a "platform-like" environment, which can be useful to an extent, but again you'll need to be able to work in the constraints of how the tool packages applications.

Because you now know the format of the data that your Lambda function receives, you are able to create a handler signature to process this format. Remember "POJOs and Ecosystem Types" on page 52? That's going to come into play now.

One option you have in setting up your handler is to create your own POJO input type that fits the structure of the inbound event but only creates fields for the properties you care about. For instance, if you cared only about the `path` and `queryString Parameters` properties of the aws-proxy event, you could create a POJO as follows:

```
package book.api;

import java.util.Map;

public class APIGatewayEvent {
  public String path;
  public Map<String, String> queryStringParameters;
}
```

A second option is to use a library of types that AWS provides in a Java library precisely for this purpose—the "AWS Lambda Java Events Library." If you use this library, refer to the documentation (*https://oreil.ly/5DMvp*) and look to find the latest versions in Maven Central (*https://oreil.ly/8WvbA*).

If you want to use this library to handle aws-proxy events, then you need to first include a library in your Maven dependencies. Add the `<dependencies>` section to the root of your *pom.xml* file if it isn't already there. Otherwise, add this <depend ency> subsection to the preexisting <dependencies> section:

```
<dependencies>
  <dependency>
    <groupId>com.amazonaws</groupId>
    <artifactId>aws-lambda-java-events</artifactId>
    <version>2.2.6</version>
  </dependency>
</dependencies>
```

With that update made, we can use the `APIGatewayProxyRequestEvent` class (*https:// oreil.ly/S1y95*) as our input POJO.

Now we have a class to represent the event that our Lambda function is going to receive. Next, let's look at how to perform the same activity for the event that will be our function's response. As you know from "Input, Output" on page 47, this is where POJOs come into play again.

The SAM CLI can't help us this time, so alternatively you can look up the AWS documentation (*https://oreil.ly/RnyUg*) to find valid output event structures and generate your own output POJO type, or you can use the AWS Lambda Java Events Library again. This time, use the `APIGatewayProxyResponseEvent` class if responding to an API Gateway proxy event (see "API Gateway Proxy Events" on page 96).

Let's say that you want to build your own POJO class and want to return just an HTTP Status code and a body in the HTTP response. In that case, your POJO might look as follows:

```
package book.api;

public class APIGatewayResponse {
  public final int statusCode;
  public final String body;

  public APIGatewayResponse(int statusCode, String body) {
    this.statusCode = statusCode;
    this.body = body;
  }
}
```

Whether you use the AWS-provided POJO types or code them yourself is not a particularly clear-cut choice. At the present time, we default to using the AWS library for a couple of reasons:

- While in the past the library has lagged behind significantly with what's actually available in the Lambda platform, these days AWS does a decent job keeping it up-to-date.

- Similarly, this library used to bring in a huge number of SDK dependencies, and so would significantly increase the size of your artifact. This is much improved now, and the base JAR (which is sufficient for quite a few event sources, including API Gateway and SNS) is less than 100KB.

That said, coding your own POJOs is a perfectly reasonable approach—it means your deployed artifact will be even smaller, it reduces the number of library dependencies your code has (including transitive dependencies), and it adds a succinctness to your code, aiding maintainability later. In this chapter, we give examples of both approaches.

Once your basic Lambda function is coded, it's time to move on to the next step—configuring the event source for deployment.

Configuring a Lambda Event Source

Just as there are multiple ways of deploying and configuring a Lambda function (remember that long list of deployment tools from "Deploy" on page 72?), there are multiple ways of configuring an event source. However, since in this book we are using SAM to deploy our code, it makes sense, as much as possible, to use SAM to configure our event sources too.

Let's continue our API Gateway example. The simplest way of defining an API Gateway event source in SAM is to update your Lambda function definition in your *template.yaml* as follows:

```
HelloAPIWorldLambda:
  Type: AWS::Serverless::Function
  Properties:
    Runtime: java8
    MemorySize: 512
    Handler: book.HelloWorldAPI::handler
    CodeUri: target/lambda.zip
    Events:
      MyApi:
        Type: Api
        Properties:
          Path: /foo
          Method: get
```

Take a look at the Events key—that's where the magic happens. What SAM does in this case is create a whole bunch of resources, including a globally accessible API endpoint (which we get to later in the chapter), but part of what it also does is configure API Gateway to trigger your Lambda function.

SAM can directly configure many different event sources (*https://oreil.ly/s_4W2*). However, if it doesn't do enough for your requirements, you can always drop down to lower-level CloudFormation resources.

Understanding Different Event Source Semantics

Back in Chapter 1 we described that Lambda functions can be invoked in two ways—synchronously and asynchronously—and showed how those different invocation types were used in different scenarios.

Unsurprisingly, that means there are at least two different kinds of event source—those, like API Gateway, that invoke a Lambda function synchronously and wait for the reply ("synchronous event sources"), and others that invoke a Lambda function asynchronously, and don't wait for the reply ("asynchronous event sources").

In the case of the former group, your Lambda function needs to return the appropriate type of response, just like we did with the API Gateway earlier. For the latter group, your handler function can have a return type of void, showing that you don't return a response.

It would be convenient to say, in fact, that *all* event sources fit into one of these two kinds, but unfortunately there's a slight complication—there's a third kind, and that's Stream/queue event sources, such as:

- Kinesis Data Streams
- DynamoDB Streams
- Simple Queue Service (SQS)

In all three of these cases, we configure the Lambda *platform* to reach out to the upstream service to *poll* for events, as opposed to all the other event sources where we configure a Lambda trigger directly from the upstream service to *push* events to Lambda.

This reversal for stream/queue sources has no impact on the Lambda handler programming model—the method signature is precisely the same. For example, here is the format of a Lambda handler event for SQS (note the array of Records):

```
{
  "Records": [
    {
      "messageId": "19dd0b57-b21e-4ac1-bd88-01bbb068cb78",
      "receiptHandle": "MessageReceiptHandle",
      "body": "Hello from SQS!",
      "attributes": {
        "ApproximateReceiveCount": "1",
        "SentTimestamp": "1523232000000",
        "SenderId": "123456789012",
        "ApproximateFirstReceiveTimestamp": "1523232000001"
      },
      "messageAttributes": {},
      "md5OfBody": "7b270e59b47ff90a553787216d55d91d",
      "eventSource": "aws:sqs",
```

```
        "eventSourceARN": "arn:aws:sqs:us-east-1:123456789012:MyQueue",
        "awsRegion": "us-east-1"
      }
    ]
  }
```

Table 5-1. Lambda event source types

Event Source Type	Event Sources
Synchronous	API Gateway, Amazon CloudFront (Lambda@Edge), Elastic Load Balancing (Application Load Balancer), Cognito, Lex, Alexa, Kinesis Data Firehose
Asynchronous	S3, SNS, Amazon SES, CloudFormation, CloudWatch Logs, CloudWatch Events, CodeCommit, Config
Stream/Queue	Kinesis Data Streams, DynamoDB Streams, Simple Queue Service (SQS)

Stream/queue event sources are also a little different when it comes to error handling (see "Error Handling" on page 183). But for now, we know enough about event sources to explore a couple of detailed examples. Let's dig into our serverless HTTP API.

Example: Building a Serverless API

In Chapter 1, we briefly discussed how Lambda can be used as part of a web API. In this section, we will show how this is built.

Behavior

This application allows a client to upload weather data to an API, and then allows other clients to retrieve that data (Figure 5-2).

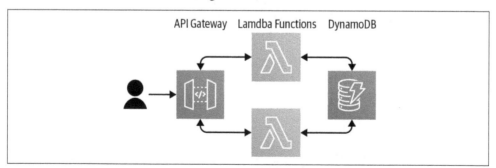

Figure 5-2. Web API using AWS Lambda

The write path consists of making an HTTP POST request to the endpoint /events, with the following JSON data structure in the body of the request:

```
{
    "locationName":"Brooklyn, NY",
    "temperature":91,
    "timestamp":1564428897,
    "latitude": 40.70,
    "longitude": -73.99
}
```

The read path consists of making a GET request to the endpoint /locations, which returns the latest weather data for each location that we've saved data for. The format of this data is a JSON list of objects in the same format as the write path. An optional query string parameter limit can be added to the GET request to specify a maximum number of records to return.

Architecture

We use AWS API Gateway to implement all of the HTTP elements of this application. The read path and write path are implemented using two different Lambda functions. These are triggered by API Gateway. We store our data in a DynamoDB table. DynamoDB is Amazon's "NoSQL" database service. It's a great fit for many serverless systems because:

- It offers the same "lightweight operations" model as Lambda—we configure the table structure we want and Amazon handles all runtime considerations.
- It can be used in a full "on-demand" scaling mode that scales up and down in reaction to actual usage, just like Lambda does.

Because DynamoDB is a NoSQL technology, it isn't the right choice for all applications, but it's definitely a quick way to get started.

For our DynamoDB table in this example, we declare a primary key named location Name and use "on-demand" capacity control.

We treat all of these resources—an API Gateway definition, two Lambda functions, and a DynamoDB table as one unified "serverless application." We treat the code, configuration, and infrastructure definitions as one, collectively deployed, unit. This is not a particularly new idea just for serverless, though—encapsulating a database within a service is a fairly common idea of microservice architecture.

Apart from adding a useful grouping, using the idea of a serverless application also helps solve a concern that some people have when they consider how many Lambda functions they might have in their organization—it's tough enough herding hundreds of microservices, but a company may end up with thousands or tens of thousands of Lambda functions. How can we manage all of those functions? By namespaceing functions within a serverless application, and by tagging or locating the deployed versions of those applications by their environment/stage, we can start bringing some order to the chaos. This concept of a serverless application is not just a design-time consideration—AWS actually supports it directly (see "Deployment" on page 107).

Which Flavor of API Gateway?

AWS API Gateway was launched in July 2015, using the terminology of a "REST API" very much at its core (REST referring to the "representational state transfer" (*https://oreil.ly/FdDze*) style of building applications). Over the years since its launch, AWS has added a lot of features to API Gateway—security, request and response mapping, rate limiting, and more.

At the time of writing, AWS has just launched, currently as a beta release, *API Gateway HTTP APIs* (*https://oreil.ly/fOd1n*). This is a different "flavor" of API Gateway that doesn't have as many features as the "REST API" version—it's missing things like rate limiting and request/response mapping, for instance—but it does come with approximately 70% cost savings and better (lower latency) performance. Also note that while AWS names this "HTTP APIs," the "traditional" REST APIs variant still implements the HTTP protocol. AWS's choice of names for various things still continues to baffle us.

The reason that AWS has introduced HTTP APIs is that it has found that many customers don't use most of the features of API Gateway. Many people instead just want a simple way of exposing Lambda functions to the public internet, with a minimum amount of complexity. HTTP APIs gives these people that, with a nice reduction in cost.

Looking at the beta version of HTTP APIs, we see that from a programming model point of view very little is different versus REST APIs. The changes are mostly architectural—what the service can and can't do—but that of course has an impact on what code you may need to write. For example, the current version of HTTP APIs doesn't support custom/Lambda authorizers, but instead you could implement this feature within your Lambda handler code.

It also appears that, if you're using SAM at least, there's not very much different for the deployment template of a REST API versus an HTTP API—for simple use cases at least, but remember, that's what the HTTP API variant is built for.

In this book, we *only* use the REST API version of API Gateway. We recommend you:

- Don't use an HTTP API if it's still in beta.
- Otherwise, use an HTTP API if its limited feature set is sufficient for your needs, knowing that you can migrate to the full REST API version later if necessary.

AWS goes into more detail on this choice in the API Gateway documentation (*https://oreil.ly/GmksV*).

Lambda Code

At this point in the book we don't discuss error checking or testing —we've done that for clarity of example. Don't worry—both of these important subjects are addressed later in the book!

We mentioned earlier that one of the first things you need to do when implementing an application using Lambda is to understand the format of the events that your Lambda function will receive, and the format of the response your Lambda function should return (if any).

We already examined the API Gateway proxy types earlier. In this weather API, we write our own classes for POJO serialization and deserialization, rather than using the AWS-supplied library. Examples 5-1 and 5-2 are sufficient for our needs for both Lambda functions.

Example 5-1. For deserializing API requests

```
package book.api;

import java.util.HashMap;
import java.util.Map;

public class ApiGatewayRequest {
  public String body;
  public Map<String, String> queryStringParameters = new HashMap<>();
}
```

Example 5-2. For serializing API responses

```
package book.api;

public class ApiGatewayResponse {
  public Integer statusCode;
  public String body;

  public ApiGatewayResponse(Integer statusCode, String body) {
    this.statusCode = statusCode;
    this.body = body;
  }
}
```

We wouldn't actually recommend this approach in general—see earlier about whether or not to use the AWS POJO type library ("Writing Code to Work with Input and Output for Event Sources" on page 86)—but we wanted to show examples of both approaches. The second example in this chapter uses the AWS Library. When you build your own production implementation of an HTTP API with Lambda, you can substitute the `APIGatewayProxyRequestEvent` and `APIGatewayProxyResponseEvent` classes in the `com.amazonaws.services.lambda.runtime.events` package for these DIY classes.

Now let's look in detail at the code necessary to implement this application. We start with the write path.

API Gateway Proxy Events

You may have noticed that we keep using phrases like *API Gateway proxy* throughout this chapter. This is because there are two different ways of triggering Lambda from API Gateway for HTTP requests.

API Gateway Lambda proxy integration (*https://oreil.ly/kaTa0*) is the type we use in this serverless API example. *Integration* is the API Gateway term for connecting to a backend service—which can be Lambda, or other types of service too. A Lambda proxy integration is an integration where API Gateway converts the whole original HTTP request into a JSON form, passes this to the Lambda function, and then converts the Lambda's JSON response into an HTTP response. The *proxy* here means that API Gateway isn't doing any custom mapping to the request or response.

API Gateway "Lambda custom integrations" (*https://oreil.ly/niw8d*), on the other hand, have specific mapping templates for both the request path and the response path. This is done by giving API Gateway these mapping templates when the API is configured. With this type of integration, the structure of the JSON that is passed to the backing Lambda function will depend on the contents of the mapping template, which is why you don't see an option for these types of events in `sam local generate-event`.

The benefit of Lambda custom integrations is that the event objects passed to, and returned from, the Lambda function are significantly less complicated, and in fact the Lambda function doesn't need to understand the details of the HTTP protocol at all. For example, the status code can be set in the response template, and the Lambda function doesn't need to know its 200 s from its 418 s (*https://oreil.ly/Iy3fi*).

The drawback of Lambda custom integrations is that all that logic that does need to know about HTTP requests and responses has to go into a Velocity template (*https://oreil.ly/d1NlX*)—these are brittle and tricky to develop and unit test.

These drawbacks are so significant that we recommend in almost all circumstances that you use the "Lambda proxy" integration type when integrating Lambda with API Gateway. If necessary, you can pull some of the HTTP request/response wrangling into shared code to reduce the burden on individual Lambda functions, but either way it's typically a lot easier and cleaner to define that in code, rather than in mapping templates.

Two further quick points about using API Gateway with Lambda. We're only going to mention them here so that you're aware of them:

- API Gateway has another meaning of the word proxy, and that's when it's used in the phrase *proxy resource*. Here *proxy* is used to say that the path that is being defined is partly or wholly a wildcard, e.g. */foo/{proxy}* will map both the request paths /foo/sheep and /foo/cheese to the same integration. You may use proxy *resources* combined with proxy *integrations* but you aren't required to.

- API Gateway has another way it can call Lambda—for authorizing requests *before* passing to a backend resource (which may itself be any of the API Gateway integration types). You'll see that referred to by the "authorizer" event source type when calling sam local generate-event apigateway with no other arguments.

For more information about using API Gateway and Lambda in this way, see the AWS documentation (*https://oreil.ly/PWoi_*).

Uploading weather data with WeatherEventLambda

We know that the rough skeleton of our code to process uploaded data is going to be the following:

```
package book.api;

public class WeatherEventLambda {
  public ApiGatewayResponse handler(ApiGatewayRequest request) {
    // process request

    // send response
    return new ApiGatewayResponse(200, ..).;
  }
}
```

The first thing we need to do is capture the input of our event. Lambda deserialization starts this work for us, and the structure of the ApiGatewayRequest object that is passed to our function is as follows:

```
{
  "body": "{\"locationName\":\"Brooklyn, NY\", \"temperature\":91,...",
  "queryStringParameters": {}
}
```

We don't care about the queryStringParameters field in this Lambda function—that will be used in the querying function—so we can ignore that for now.

That body field, though, is a little tricky—the JSON object uploaded by the client is still serialized as a string value. That's because Lambda only deserialized the event that API Gateway created; it also can't deserialize the "next level in" of the weather data.

No matter, we can perform our own deserialization for body, and one way we can do that is to use the Jackson library (*https://github.com/FasterXML/jackson*).

Once we've deserialized the weather data, we're ready to save it to the database. Example 5-3 shows the full code for the Lambda function—you may also want to open up the example code in the *chapter5-api* directory.

Example 5-3. WeatherEventLambda handler class

```java
package book.api;

import com.amazonaws.services.dynamodbv2.AmazonDynamoDBClientBuilder;
import com.amazonaws.services.dynamodbv2.document.DynamoDB;
import com.amazonaws.services.dynamodbv2.document.Item;
import com.amazonaws.services.dynamodbv2.document.Table;
import com.fasterxml.jackson.databind.DeserializationFeature;
import com.fasterxml.jackson.databind.ObjectMapper;

import java.io.IOException;

public class WeatherEventLambda {
  private final ObjectMapper objectMapper =
      new ObjectMapper()
          .configure(
              DeserializationFeature.FAIL_ON_UNKNOWN_PROPERTIES,
              false);
  private final DynamoDB dynamoDB = new DynamoDB(
      AmazonDynamoDBClientBuilder.defaultClient());
  private final String tableName = System.getenv("LOCATIONS_TABLE");

  public ApiGatewayResponse handler(ApiGatewayRequest request)
    throws IOException {

    final WeatherEvent weatherEvent = objectMapper.readValue(
        request.body,
        WeatherEvent.class);

    final Table table = dynamoDB.getTable(tableName);
    final Item item = new Item()
        .withPrimaryKey("locationName", weatherEvent.locationName)
        .withDouble("temperature", weatherEvent.temperature)
        .withLong("timestamp", weatherEvent.timestamp)
        .withDouble("longitude", weatherEvent.longitude)
        .withDouble("latitude", weatherEvent.latitude);
    table.putItem(item);

    return new ApiGatewayResponse(200, weatherEvent.locationName);
  }
}
```

First you can see we create a few instance variables outside of the handler function. We talk about why we do that in "Scaling" on page 193, but the summary is that the Lambda platform typically uses the same instance of a Lambda function several times (although never concurrently), so we can optimize performance a little by only creating certain things once for the lifetime of the Lambda function instance.

The first instance variable is Jackson's ObjectMapper, and the second is the DynamoDB SDK. The third and final instance variable is the table name within DynamoDB that we want to use. The precise value of that comes from our infrastructure template, so we use an environment variable to configure our Lambda function, just as we discussed in "Environment Variables" on page 61.

The remainder of the class is our Lambda handler function. First of all, you can see the signature, with the types that you'd expect given the event source that we're dealing with. One slight addition here, though, is that our Lambda handler declares that it may throw an exception—this is completely valid, and we discuss error handling more in "Error Handling" on page 183.

The first line of the handler deserializes the weather event embedded within the body field of the original HTTP request. WeatherEvent is defined in Example 5-4 in its own class.

Example 5-4. WeatherEvent class

```
package book.api;

public class WeatherEvent {
    public String locationName;
    public Double temperature;
    public Long timestamp;
    public Double longitude;
    public Double latitude;

    public WeatherEvent() {
    }

    public WeatherEvent(String locationName, Double temperature,
            Long timestamp, Double longitude, Double latitude) {

        this.locationName = locationName;
        this.temperature = temperature;
        this.timestamp = timestamp;
        this.longitude = longitude;
        this.latitude = latitude;
    }
}
```

In this case, Jackson uses the no-argument constructor, and populates the fields of the object based on the value passed in the body field of the original Lambda event.

Now we've captured our full weather event, we can save this to the database. We're not going to go into detail of how to use DynamoDB here, but you can see from the code that:

- We use the environment variable of the table name to connect to our desired table.
- We use the DynamoDB Java SDK's "Document model" to save data to the table, using the location name as the primary key.

Finally, we need to return a response. Since we got this far, we assume (for now!) that everything worked successfully, in which case returning an HTTP 200 ("OK") response is the right thing to do, and to make it clearer to the client what we actually did, we return the location name that was saved.

That's all the code that we need to handle the write path of our API. Now let's look at the read path.

Reading weather data with WeatherQueryLambda

As you'd expect, `WeatherQueryLambda` is similar to `WeatherEventLambda`, but reversed. Example 5-5 shows the code.

Example 5-5. WeatherQueryLambda handler class

```
package book.api;

import com.amazonaws.services.dynamodbv2.AmazonDynamoDB;
import com.amazonaws.services.dynamodbv2.AmazonDynamoDBClientBuilder;
import com.amazonaws.services.dynamodbv2.model.ScanRequest;
import com.amazonaws.services.dynamodbv2.model.ScanResult;
import com.fasterxml.jackson.databind.ObjectMapper;

import java.io.IOException;
import java.util.List;
import java.util.stream.Collectors;

public class WeatherQueryLambda {
  private final ObjectMapper objectMapper = new ObjectMapper();
  private final AmazonDynamoDB dynamoDB =
      AmazonDynamoDBClientBuilder.defaultClient();
  private final String tableName = System.getenv("LOCATIONS_TABLE");

  private static final String DEFAULT_LIMIT = "50";

  public ApiGatewayResponse handler(ApiGatewayRequest request)
```

```
        throws IOException {

    final String limitParam = request.queryStringParameters == null
        ? DEFAULT_LIMIT
        : request.queryStringParameters.getOrDefault(
            "limit", DEFAULT_LIMIT);
    final int limit = Integer.parseInt(limitParam);

    final ScanRequest scanRequest = new ScanRequest()
        .withTableName(tableName)
        .withLimit(limit);
    final ScanResult scanResult = dynamoDB.scan(scanRequest);

    final List<WeatherEvent> events = scanResult.getItems().stream()
        .map(item -> new WeatherEvent(
            item.get("locationName").getS(),
            Double.parseDouble(item.get("temperature").getN()),
            Long.parseLong(item.get("timestamp").getN()),
            Double.parseDouble(item.get("longitude").getN()),
            Double.parseDouble(item.get("latitude").getN())
        ))
        .collect(Collectors.toList());

    final String json = objectMapper.writeValueAsString(events);

    return new ApiGatewayResponse(200, json);
  }
}
```

We see a similar set of instance variables. The DynamoDB one is slightly different because of the DynamoDB SDK's API, but the Jackson one is the same, and again we capture the environment variable that specifies the table name.

In the WeatherEventLambda handler, we cared about the input event's body field. This time we care about the queryStringParameters field, and specifically the limit parameter, if it's set. If it is set, we use it. Otherwise, we default to 50 as the maximum number of records we want to retrieve from DynamoDB.

The next couple of statements read the data from DynamoDB, and after those, we convert the DynamoDB results back into WeatherEvent objects. With the weather events captured, we use Jackson again to create a JSON string response to return to the client.

Finally, we send our API response—again setting 200 OK as the status code, but this time putting the useful response in the body field.

And that's it for code! With very little code, even with the verbosity of Java, we have a full HTTP API that reads and writes values to a database. But, of course, our code isn't all there is to defining the app. As we saw in Chapter 4, we also need to build and package our code. And we actually need to define our infrastructure too.

Serverless Without Lambda

Even though there is very little code in this serverless API example, the entire application as it stands could actually be implemented with zero lines of code. This is not some strange wizardry, but in fact is due to another type of API Gateway integration.

As we mentioned earlier, API Gateway can integrate with Lambda (in two different ways). That said, it can also integrate with any other HTTP application, acting more like a traditional reverse proxy, or it can also integrate directly with another AWS service. In either of these other cases, you supply mapping templates to map requests to the underlying service and map responses from the underlying service.

With this capability, we could implement our weather API by integrating API Gateway directly with DynamoDB, mapping between HTTP formats and the underlying storage format using mapping templates. This is described further on AWS's blog (*https://oreil.ly/CNtzT*). With this solution, no Lambda functions are required, and therefore no code is required.

An immediate follow-on question to this is, "Just because you can directly integrate API Gateway with a AWS Service, does it mean you should?" There are differing opinions on this in the serverless community. One school of thought is that this kind of "Lambda-less" application is better because:

- It requires no code, and is therefore easier to maintain and safer.
- Since we don't call Lambda, and API Gateway's pricing is based on a "per-request" model (no matter how complicated the definition of the request), then it's cheaper to use the "Lambda-less" solution.

On the other hand, "pro-Lambda" people argue:

- It's a lot easier to maintain and test mapping code in Lambda, than it is to do the same with Velocity mapping templates.
- Therefore, any money you save on Lambda invocations will be wiped out by the time you spend getting your templates right.

Which group is correct? As is so often the case, "it depends." Our own take is to default to the code approach, with Lambda. However, if a particular element of your application is simple enough to create easily with mapping templates, and if the expected throughput is high enough that you'd see real cost savings if you don't call Lambda, then use the Lambda-free approach.

The client-facing part is API Gateway in both solutions, so you can change your mind about architecture down the road without impacting clients.

We look at building and packaging next.

Build and Package Using the AWS SDK BOM

In Chapter 4 we showed how to build and package a Lambda application using Maven. In this example, we're going to use the ZIP format that we described there, so we need a *pom.xml* file, and an assembly description file. The latter of those is no different to what we've seen before, so we ignore that here.

Let's take a quick look at the *pom.xml* file, cut down a little for brevity:

Example 5-6. Partial Maven POM file for HTTP API

```
<project>
  <dependencyManagement>
    <dependencies>
      <dependency>
        <groupId>com.amazonaws</groupId>
        <artifactId>aws-java-sdk-bom</artifactId>
        <version>1.11.600</version>
        <type>pom</type>
        <scope>import</scope>
      </dependency>
    </dependencies>
  </dependencyManagement>

  <dependencies>
    <dependency>
      <groupId>com.amazonaws</groupId>
      <artifactId>aws-lambda-java-core</artifactId>
      <version>1.2.0</version>
      <scope>provided</scope>
    </dependency>
    <dependency>
      <groupId>com.amazonaws</groupId>
      <artifactId>aws-java-sdk-dynamodb</artifactId>
    </dependency>
    <dependency>
      <groupId>com.fasterxml.jackson.core</groupId>
      <artifactId>jackson-databind</artifactId>
      <version>2.10.1</version>
    </dependency>
  </dependencies>

  <!-- Other sections would follow -->
</project>
```

An element that we've added here since Chapter 4 is the `<dependencyManagement>` section. In this tag we reference a dependency named `aws-java-sdk-bom`. This useful element is a feature of Maven known as a "bill of materials" (BOM), and in essence it groups all the version dependencies for a set of libraries. We use it here so that any

AWS Java SDK dependencies that we use are guaranteed to be in sync with each other with respect to versions.

In this particular project, we actually use only one AWS Java SDK library—aws-java-sdk-dynamodb—and so using the BOM is less necessary for this example. But many Lambda applications use multiple AWS SDKs, so it's useful to start off on solid footing.

You can also see that we don't define the version for aws-java-sdk-dynamodb in the <dependency> section, because it uses the version defined in the BOM. We do still have to declare the version of aws-lambda-java-core because that's not part of the AWS Java SDK, and therefore not in the BOM—you can tell because it doesn't have "sdk" in its name. You can read more about the AWS Java SDK BOM in this blog article (*https://oreil.ly/V1x9x*).

In this example, we collect the code for both of our different Lambda functions into one zipped package. In the next example later in this chapter, we show how you can break this package up into individual artifacts.

With the dependency updates defined, we can build and package our application, using mvn package as usual.

Infrastructure

The one element we still need to define is our infrastructure template.

So far in this book we've only defined Lambda resources. Now we need to define our API Gateway, and our database. How do we do that? Example 5-7 shows the *template.yaml*.

Example 5-7. SAM template for HTTP API

```
AWSTemplateFormatVersion: 2010-09-09
Transform: AWS::Serverless-2016-10-31
Description: chapter5-api

Globals:
  Function:
    Runtime: java8
    MemorySize: 512
    Timeout: 25
    Environment:
      Variables:
        LOCATIONS_TABLE: !Ref LocationsTable
  Api:
    OpenApiVersion: '3.0.1'

Resources:
```

```
LocationsTable:
  Type: AWS::Serverless::SimpleTable
  Properties:
    PrimaryKey:
      Name: locationName
      Type: String

WeatherEventLambda:
  Type: AWS::Serverless::Function
  Properties:
    CodeUri: target/lambda.zip
    Handler: book.api.WeatherEventLambda::handler
    Policies:
      - DynamoDBCrudPolicy:
          TableName: !Ref LocationsTable
    Events:
      ApiEvents:
        Type: Api
        Properties:
          Path: /events
          Method: POST

WeatherQueryLambda:
  Type: AWS::Serverless::Function
  Properties:
    CodeUri: target/lambda.zip
    Handler: book.api.WeatherQueryLambda::handler
    Policies:
      - DynamoDBReadPolicy:
          TableName: !Ref LocationsTable
    Events:
      ApiEvents:
        Type: Api
        Properties:
          Path: /locations
          Method: GET
```

Let's go through this from the top.

First of all we have our CloudFormation and SAM headers—these are no different to what we've seen before.

Next is a new top-level section named Globals. Globals is a code-optimizing feature of SAM that allows us to define some of the properties common to all the resources of the same type in an application. We mostly use it here to define a few properties common to both of the Lambda functions that we declare later in the file. We've already seen Runtime, MemorySize, and Timeout, but the way we've declared LOCA TIONS_TABLE in the Environment key, with the !Ref string, is new—we will come back to that in a moment. Note that not all properties from a function definition work within the `Globals` section, which is why you don't see `CodeUri` defined within the `Globals`.

Finally, in the `Globals` section is a small configuration of the API Gateway settings to use the most up-to-date version of SAM's API configuration.

Then we move into the rest of the template, which consists of `Resources` elements.

The first one is new—it's of type `AWS::Serverless::SimpleTable`. This is SAM's way of defining DynamoDB databases. It works for simple configurations, which is fine for us in this example.

Note that what we're doing here isn't merely pointing to a database that already exists —we're actually declaring that we want CloudFormation to create a database for us, and managing it in the same stack of components as our Lambda functions, etc. All we do is specify what we want the primary key field to be named, and AWS does everything else to manage the table on our behalf.

We don't even give the table a physical name—CloudFormation generates a unique name for us based on the name of the stack, the logical name of the table, `LocationsTable`, plus some randomly generated uniqueness. That's all well and good, but if we don't know the name of the table, how are we meant to use it from our Lambda functions?

That's where the `!Ref LocationsTable` value that we saw earlier comes in. CloudFormation substitutes that string for the physical name of the DynamoDB table, and so our Lambda functions have an environment variable pointing them to the correct location.

Moving on from the DynamoDB table, we see the definitions of our two Lambda functions. These elements contain a lot of ideas we've covered already. We saw the `Policies` section in Chapter 4—note how we're embracing the principle of least privilege here by:

- Only giving our functions access to one specific DynamoDB table (see `!Ref` being used again)
- Only giving the Lambda function that is querying data read-only access (by declaring the `DynamoDBReadPolicy` policy)

We also see the `Events` section in each Lambda function that we covered briefly earlier in this chapter. As we mentioned then, what's happening here is that SAM is defining an implicit API Gateway, and then is attaching our Lambda functions to that Gateway with the `Path` and `Method` properties defined in the `Events` sections.

In many real-life scenarios, the implicit API Gateway configuration won't be quite enough for your needs, and in that case you can define either an explicit SAM API

Gateway resource (using a resource of type `AWS::Serverless::Api`), or the underlying CloudFormation API Gateway resource types. If you use the first of these options, you can add a `RestApiId` property to the API `Event` property of your Lambda functions to tie them to your self-defined API.

You can also use Swagger/Open API as part of the CloudFormation/SAM definition of your API Gateway. That way you'll get better documentation, plus the opportunity for some amount of "no code required" input validation—but definitely don't rely on Swagger/API Gateway as a complete input validator. Also there are certain aspects to API Gateway's configuration that can be defined only using AWS's own OpenAPI extensions (*https://oreil.ly/Cq-_T*). We could write an entire mini-book just on this area, though, so we'll leave you to go explore the AWS documentation for yourself if that's what you need!

This is all a little theoretical, but fortunately we've finished looking at the template, so it's time to deploy and test our application!

Deployment

 As is, the API in this example is publicly accessible on the internet. While this is OK for experimentation (since the full API name isn't easily discoverable), it's not something you want to leave around forever since anyone can read and write to this API. In a production scenario you would want to add some amount of security at least around the write path, but that's beyond the scope of what we're going to cover here.

To deploy the application, use precisely the same incantation of `sam deploy` that you've done already (if you need to refresh your memory, take a look at "CloudFormation and the Serverless Application Model" on page 74). The only thing you may want to change is the `stack-name` so that you deploy this to a new stack (e.g., `Chapter FiveApi`).

Once SAM and CloudFormation have completed, you'll have deployed a new stack to CloudFormation. We can see this in the CloudFormation section of the AWS Web Console (Figure 5-3).

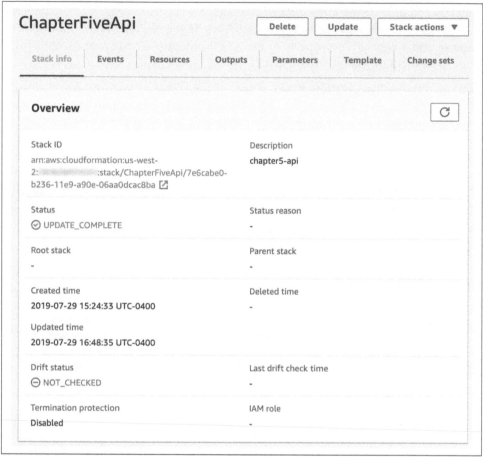

Figure 5-3. CloudFormation stack for HTTP API

CloudFormation is a little low level, though, and so usefully AWS also provides a way of viewing this deployment in a view called *Serverless Application*, just as we designed earlier in "Architecture" on page 112. You can access this view via the Applications tab of the Lambda console (Figure 5-4).

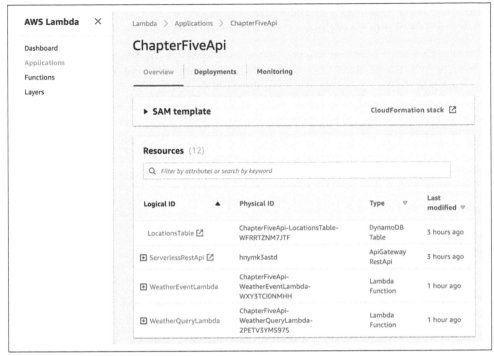

Figure 5-4. Serverless Application view for HTTP API

In this view you can see the DynamoDB table, the API Gateway (referred to as a *RestAPI* in AWS terms), and our two Lambda functions. If you click any of these resources, you are taken to the correct service console, and into that resource—try it out for the *ServerlessRestApi* resource. This puts you in the API Gateway console. Click *Stages* on the left and then *Prod*—you should see something like Figure 5-5.

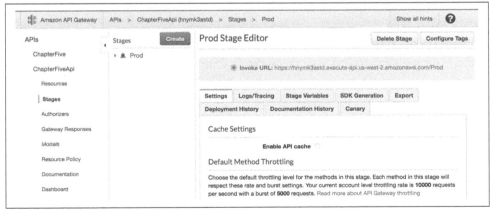

Figure 5-5. API Gateway view for HTTP API

The *Invoke URL* value is the publicly accessible URL for your API—make a note of it since you'll need it in a moment.

You can also see in the *Serverless Application* view that the physical names for the resources have the partially generated/partially random structure we discussed earlier. For example, in this case, our DynamoDB table is actually named *ChapterFiveApi-LocationsTable-WFRRTZNM7JTF*. And sure enough, if we look in the Lambda console at either of the two functions for this application, we can see that the LOCATIONS_TABLE environment variable is correctly set to this value (Figure 5-6).

LOCATIONS_TABLE	ChapterFiveApi-LocationsTable-WFRRTZNM7JTF	Remove

Figure 5-6. API Gateway view for HTTP API

Finally, let's test our deployment by calling both API routes. To do this, you need that URL from a moment ago.

First, let's send some data. The base of the URL is the one from the API Gateway console, but we append /events. We can call our API using curl, for example, as follows (substitute in your URL):

```
$ curl -d '{"locationName":"Brooklyn, NY", "temperature":91,
  "timestamp":1564428897, "latitude": 40.70, "longitude": -73.99}' \
  -H "Content-Type: application/json" \
  -X POST https://hnymk3astd.execute-api.us-west-2.amazonaws.com/Prod/events

Brooklyn, NY

$ curl -d '{"locationName":"Oxford, UK", "temperature":64,
  "timestamp":1564428898, "latitude": 51.75, "longitude": -1.25}' \
  -H "Content-Type: application/json" \
  -X POST https://hnymk3astd.execute-api.us-west-2.amazonaws.com/Prod/events

Oxford, UK
```

This has saved two new events to DynamoDB. You can prove that to yourself by clicking on the DynamoDB table from the Serverless Application console, and then clicking on the *Items* tab once you're in the DynamoDB console (Figure 5-7).

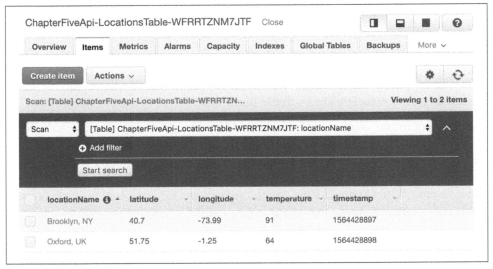

Figure 5-7. DynamoDB table for HTTP API

And now we can use the final part of our application—reading from the API. We can use curl for that again, adding `/locations` to the API Gateway console URL, for example:

```
$ curl https://hnymk3astd.execute-api.us-west-2.amazonaws.com/Prod/locations

[{"locationName":"Oxford, UK","temperature":64.0,"timestamp":1564428898,
  "longitude":-1.25,"latitude":51.75},
  {"locationName":"Brooklyn, NY","temperature":91.0,
  "timestamp":1564428897,"longitude":-73.99,"latitude":40.7}]
```

As expected, this returns the list of locations that we've stored weather for.

Congratulations! You've built your first full serverless application! While it has only one simple feature, think of all the *nonfunctional* capabilities it has—it auto-scales up to handle a vast load and then back down when not in use, it's fault-tolerant across multiple availability zones, it has infrastructure that is automatically updated to include critical security patches, and it has a whole lot more besides.

Now let's look at a different type of application, using a couple of other different AWS services.

Example: Building a Serverless Data Pipeline

In Chapter 1 we listed two use cases for Lambda ("What Does a Lambda Application Look Like?" on page 13). The first was an HTTP API that we just described in more detail—an example of synchronous usage of Lambda. The second use case was file processing—uploading a file to S3 and then using Lambda to do something with that file.

In this example, we're building on that second idea to create a *data pipeline*. A data pipeline is a pattern where we chain together multiple asynchronous stages and branches of processing data. It's a popular pattern where the scalability of cloud resources gives a real-time alternative to batch systems.

Another important element of this example is that we're going to change the build and packaging phases of our application to create isolated output artifacts for each Lambda function. As the amount of code in your Lambda functions grows—both that which is specific to the function and that which is imported as libraries—then deployment and startup will slow down. Breaking up the packaged artifacts is a valuable technique to mitigate that.

Let's get started.

Behavior

This example is going to be another take on the weather event system we started in the previous example. This time an application will upload a list of "weather events" in a JSON file to S3. A data pipeline will then process this file, and for now the side effect will merely be logging the events to AWS CloudWatch Logs (Figure 5-8).

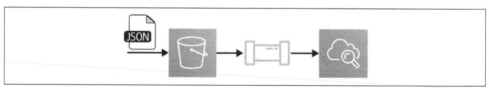

Figure 5-8. Data pipeline example behavior

Architecture

What we've just shown is the *behavior* of this application—the *architecture* has a few more details (Figure 5-9).

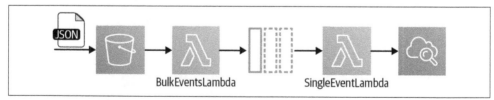

Figure 5-9. Data pipeline example architecture

We start this application with an S3 bucket. The act of uploading a file, or in S3 terms an *object*, to S3 will (asynchronously) trigger a Lambda function. This first function

(BulkEventsLambda) will read the JSON list of weather events, separate them out into individual events, and then publish each one onto a SNS topic. This in turn will trigger (asynchronously again) a second Lambda function (SingleEventLambda) which will then process each weather event. In our case, this will simply mean logging the event.

This architecture is obviously far too complicated just for logging the contents of an uploaded file! However, the important aspect of the example is that it provides a "walking skeleton" of an application that has a complete, deployable, multistage data pipeline. You could then use this as a starting point for adding interesting processing logic.

All of these components are treated as one collectively deployed serverless application, just as we did in the HTTP API example.

Now we'll dig in further to each of these stages of the architecture.

S3

S3 is one of the oldest services in AWS, as we described in "The Cloud Grows" on page 3. While it's often used in the application architecture of systems, it's commonplace too when deploying and operating AWS applications—we've used S3 a number of times in this book already when deploying our Lambda-based applications.

More than that, however, we think that S3 is one of the earliest examples of a serverless BaaS product, at least on AWS. If we look back to Chapter 1 at the factors that "differentiate" serverless, we can see it ticks all the boxes:

Does not require managing a long-lived host or application instance
Yes—we have no "file servers" or otherwise to manage when we use S3.

Self auto-scales and auto-provisions, dependent on load
Yes, we never have to manually configure how much capacity we want with S3—it auto-scales both for total storage, and for traffic.

Has costs that are based on precise usage, up from and down to zero usage
Yes! If you have an empty bucket, you don't pay anything. Alternatively, your cost will be dependent on the amount of bytes stored, amount of traffic, and your storage class (see next point).

Has performance capabilities defined in terms other than host size/count
Yes, again! S3's performance capabilities are the storage class you choose—how quickly you need to access data. The more quickly you want to be able to access your data, the more you'll pay.

Has implicit high availability

And yes. S3 replicates data across AZs within a region. If one AZ has a problem, you'll still be able to access all of your data.

Because S3 is serverless, it is a great partner to Lambda, especially because of their similar scaling capabilities. Further, S3 directly integrates with Lambda by allowing Lambda functions to be triggered whenever data changes in an S3 bucket. This way of reacting to changes automatically in S3 in an event-driven manner, rather than having to poll S3 to look for changes from a long-running traditional process, is cleaner, easier to understand, and more efficient from an infrastructure costs point of view.

All of the non-Lambda services we use in these two examples—API Gateway, DynamoDB, S3, and SNS—are serverless BaaS services within the AWS ecosystem.

For now we won't provide an "upload client" to S3 in the example, and instead will use AWS tools to handle uploading. In a real application you may choose to allow your end user client to upload directly to S3 by means of a "Signed URL"—this is a "pure" serverless approach since you are not only not running servers, you're in fact pushing behavior to the client that you may otherwise have implemented in a server-side application.

Lambda functions

When you see the code for the Lambda functions a little later, you won't come across anything new given everything you've already learned. The only real difference to what we did in the first example is that these functions won't need to return any values since they are invoked asynchronously.

One question that might be on your mind, though, is why do we separate out processing for each event to a separately invoked Lambda function? This pattern is what we often call *fan-out*. Alternatively, it's the "map" part of a "map-reduce" system, and there are a couple of reasons for using it with Lambda.

The first reason is to introduce parallelism. Each SNS message will trigger a new invocation of our `SingleEventLambda` function. For each invocation of a Lambda function, if the previous invocation is not complete, then the Lambda platform will automatically create a new instance of the Lambda function, and call that instead. In the case of our example app, if you upload a file of one hundred events, and each event individually took at least a few seconds to process, then Lambda would create one hundred instances of `SingleEventLambda`, and process each weather event in parallel (Figure 5-10).

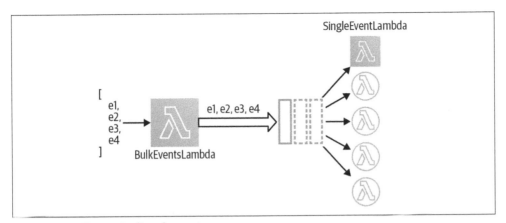

Figure 5-10. Data pipeline fan-out

This scaling aspect of Lambda is hugely valuable, and we'll be discussing it further in Chapter 8 ("Scaling" on page 193).

The second reason for introducing fan-out is if each individual event takes a long time to process—say a few minutes. In this case, processing one hundred weather events would take longer than the maximum 15-minute timeout we have with Lambda, but putting each event into its own Lambda invocation means we may be able to avoid a timeout concern.

There are other ways of solving Lambda's timeout restriction. One alternative (which is somewhat dangerous—see the following warning!) is to use a recursive call in a Lambda function. In Chapter 3 ("Timeout" on page 57), we saw that we could use the `getRemainingTimeInMillis()` method of the `Context` object passed to a Lambda handler to keep track of how long a function has left until it times out. A strategy of using this value is to asynchronously directly invoke the same Lambda function that's currently running, but only with the remaining data to be processed.

This is a better choice than "fan-out" if your data needs to be processed linearly.

 Be careful when calling Lambda functions recursively since it's easy to have runaway scenarios where either (a) you never stop and/or (b) you scale out your function hundreds or thousands of instances wide. Either of these can seriously impact your AWS bill! Because of reason (b), we recommend in the very rare case where a recursive Lambda call makes sense that you use a low "reserved concurrency" configuration (see "Reserved concurrency" on page 196).

SNS

SNS is one of AWS's messaging services. On one hand, SNS offers a simple publish-subscribe message bus (*https://oreil.ly/D5jdc*); on another, it provides the capability to send *SMS* text messages, and similar human-targeted messages. For our example, we only care about the first of these!

SNS is another serverless service. You are responsible for asking AWS to create a Topic, and then AWS handles all the scaling and operations of that Topic behind the scenes.

It's simple to publish a message with a string as its contents to a Topic using the SNS SDK, as we'll see later. There are also multiple subscription types for SNS, but we (not surprisingly) are only going to use the Lambda subscription type in this example. The way this works is that when a message is published to a Topic, all subscribers for that Topic will be sent the message. In the case of Lambda, the Lambda platform will receive the message, and then asynchronously invoke the Lambda function we've associated with the subscription.

In the case of our example, we want a Lambda function to be asynchronously invoked for each weather event in an uploaded file. We could have just directly called the `Invoke` method of the Lambda SDK to directly (but asynchronously) invoke `Single EventLambda` from `BatchEventsLambda`, but instead we used SNS as an intermediary —why?

This is because we want to reduce the structural coupling between the two Lambda functions. We want `BatchEventsLambda` to know that its responsibility is splitting up a batch of weather events, but we don't necessarily want it to be involved with what happens to those weather events next. If we decide later to evolve our architecture so that each event is processed by multiple consumers, or perhaps we substitute the AWS Step Functions service (*https://oreil.ly/LWX1e*) for `SingleEventLambda`, then the code for `BatchEventsLambda` doesn't need to change.

Finally, we chose SNS because of its simplicity and ubiquity within Lambda applications. AWS offers a number of other messaging systems—SQS, Kinesis, and Event Bridge are some examples, and you can even use S3 if you like! Which service you choose really comes down to the specific requirements of your application, and the various capabilities of each service. Picking the right messaging service for an application can be a little tricky, so it's worthwhile to do appropriate research.

Lambda Code

Our code consists of three classes.

The first is the same `WeatherEvent` as we had in the first example, but copied into a new package, for reasons that will become clearer later.

Processing the batch with BulkEventsLambda

The next class is our `BulkEventsLambda` code.

As we've discussed already the first thing to do is understand the format of the input event.

If we run `sam local generate-event s3`, we see that S3 can generate events for both "puts" (creates and updates) and "deletes." We care about the former, and the example event looks as follows (trimmed a little for conciseness):

```json
{
  "Records": [
    {
      "eventSource": "aws:s3",
      "awsRegion": "us-east-1",
      "eventTime": "1970-01-01T00:00:00.000Z",
      "eventName": "ObjectCreated:Put",
      "s3": {
        "bucket": {
          "name": "example-bucket",
          "arn": "arn:aws:s3:::example-bucket"
        },
        "object": {
          "key": "test/key",
          "size": 1024
        }
      }
    }
  ]
}
```

The first thing to notice is that the event contains an array of `Records`. In fact, S3 will only ever send an array with exactly one element in it, but it's good practice to code defensively for this if it's easy to do so.

The next thing to notice is that we are told what object has caused this event— `test/key` in bucket `example-bucket`. It's important to remember that S3 isn't actually a file system, even though we often treat it as such. It's actually a key-value store where it just so happens that we might consider the key as if it were a path in a file system with directories.

The final thing to notice is that we don't receive the contents of the uploaded object— we're only told the *location* of the object. In our example application, we want the contents, so we need to load the object from S3 ourselves.

In this example, we're going to use the `S3Event` class from the `aws-lambda-java-events` library as our input event POJO. This class references other types from the `aws-java-sdk-s3` SDK library, so we need that in our library dependencies too. That's

OK, though, from the perspective of wanting to minimize library dependencies, since we make direct calls to the S3 SDK anyway in this class.

An S3Event object, and its fields, includes everything we need for the input event, and since this function is asynchronous, there is no return type. That means we're done with the POJO definition phase and can move on to writing code.

We're leaving the package and import lines out of Example 5-8 because there are a lot of them, but if you're interested in seeing them, please download the sample code for the book.

Example 5-8. BulkEventsLambda.java

```java
public class BulkEventsLambda {
  private final ObjectMapper objectMapper =
      new ObjectMapper()
          .configure(
              DeserializationFeature.FAIL_ON_UNKNOWN_PROPERTIES,
              false);
  private final AmazonSNS sns = AmazonSNSClientBuilder.defaultClient();
  private final AmazonS3 s3 = AmazonS3ClientBuilder.defaultClient();
  private final String snsTopic = System.getenv("FAN_OUT_TOPIC");

  public void handler(S3Event event) {
    event.getRecords().forEach(this::processS3EventRecord);
  }

  private void processS3EventRecord(
      S3EventNotification.S3EventNotificationRecord record) {

    final List<WeatherEvent> weatherEvents = readWeatherEventsFromS3(
        record.getS3().getBucket().getName(),
        record.getS3().getObject().getKey());

    weatherEvents.stream()
        .map(this::weatherEventToSnsMessage)
        .forEach(message -> sns.publish(snsTopic, message));

    System.out.println("Published " + weatherEvents.size()
            + " weather events to SNS");
  }

  private List<WeatherEvent> readWeatherEventsFromS3(String bucket, String key) {
    try {
      final S3ObjectInputStream s3is =
          s3.getObject(bucket, key).getObjectContent();
      final WeatherEvent[] weatherEvents =
          objectMapper.readValue(s3is, WeatherEvent[].class);
      s3is.close();
      return Arrays.asList(weatherEvents);
```

```
      } catch (IOException e) {
        throw new RuntimeException(e);
      }
    }

    private String weatherEventToSnsMessage(WeatherEvent weatherEvent) {
      try {
        return objectMapper.writeValueAsString(weatherEvent);
      } catch (JsonProcessingException e) {
        throw new RuntimeException(e);
      }
    }
  }
}
```

The handler method loops over each record in the S3Event. We know that there should only ever be one, but we'll be safe with this code if that's not the case.

The requirements for the remainder of the code are fairly simple:

1. Read uploaded JSON object from S3.
2. Deserialize the JSON object into a list of WeatherEvent objects.
3. For each WeatherEvent object serialize it back into JSON…
4. …and then publish it to SNS.

If you look at the code, you'll see all of these expressed. We use Jackson for serialization/deserialization just as we did in the first example. We use the AWS SDK twice— once to read from S3 (s3.getObject()) and once to publish to SNS (sns.pub lish()). While these are different SDKs, each requiring their own library dependency, they feel broadly the same to use as the DynamoDB SDK did in the previous example.

One thing that's interesting to notice is that just like in the first example we never give any credentials when creating our connections to the AWS SDKs: when we call defaultClient() on AmazonSNSClientBuilder and AmazonS3ClientBuilder, there is no username or password. This works because the Java AWS SDKs, in the context of running within Lambda, by default use the Lambda execution role that we configure for the Lambda (and which we discussed in "Identity and Access Management" on page 78). That means there aren't any passwords that can leak from our source code!

Processing an individual weather event with SingleEventLambda

On to our final class. You should be getting the hang of this by now, so let's zoom through it!

First of all, the input event. Running sam local generate-event sns notification gives us the following, and again this is trimmed a little:

```json
{
  "Records": [
    {
      "EventSubscriptionArn": "arn:aws:sns:us-east-1::ExampleTopic",
      "Sns": {
        "Type": "Notification",
        "MessageId": "95df01b4-ee98-5cb9-9903-4c221d41eb5e",
        "TopicArn": "arn:aws:sns:us-east-1:123456789012:ExampleTopic",
        "Subject": "example subject",
        "Message": "example message",
        "Timestamp": "1970-01-01T00:00:00.000Z",
      }
    }
  ]
}
```

Similar to S3, our input event consists of a single-element list of `Records`. Within a `Record`, and the `Sns` object within that, are a number of fields. The one we care about in this example is `Message`, but SNS messages also offer a `Subject` field.

We use the `aws-lambda-java-events` library again, as we did with `BulkEvents` `Lambda`, but this time we want to use the `SNSEvent` class. `SNSEvent` doesn't require any other AWS SDK classes, so there's no need to add any further libraries to our Maven dependencies.

And again, this is an asynchronous event type, so there's no return type to worry about.

On to the code (see Example 5-9)! Again, we leave out the `package` and `import` statements here, but they're in the book's downloadable code if you'd like to see them.

Example 5-9. SingleEventLambda Handler Class

```java
public class SingleEventLambda {
  private final ObjectMapper objectMapper =
      new ObjectMapper()
          .configure(
              DeserializationFeature.FAIL_ON_UNKNOWN_PROPERTIES,
              false);

  public void handler(SNSEvent event) {
    event.getRecords().forEach(this::processSNSRecord);
  }

  private void processSNSRecord(SNSEvent.SNSRecord snsRecord) {
    try {
      final WeatherEvent weatherEvent = objectMapper.readValue(
          snsRecord.getSNS().getMessage(),
          WeatherEvent.class);
      System.out.println("Received weather event:");
      System.out.println(weatherEvent);
    } catch (IOException e) {
      throw new RuntimeException(e);
    }
  }
}
```

This time our code is simpler:

1. Code defensively again for multiple `SNSRecord` events (even though there should only be one).

2. Deserialize the `WeatherEvent` from the SNS event.

3. Log the `WeatherEvent` (we'll look more at logging in Chapter 7).

This time there are no references to SDKs because the input event included all the data we cared about.

Build and Package Using Multiple Modules and Isolated Artifacts

With all of the code written, it's time to build and package our application.

From a process point of view, nothing is different with this example from what we've covered before—we'll run `mvn package` before running `sam deploy`.

However, there's a big structural difference to this example—we create separate ZIP file artifacts for each Lambda function. Each ZIP file includes the classes for only one Lambda handler and the library dependencies it needs.

While doing this for an application of this size is somewhat unnecessary, as your applications get bigger, it's valuable to consider breaking up the artifacts for a few reasons:

- Cold start time will be reduced (we'll talk more about cold starts in "Cold Starts" on page 201).
- Deployment time from local machines will typically be reduced since only the artifacts relating to changed functions will be uploaded for each deployment, assuming the use of the reproducible build plug-in we covered in Chapter 4 ("Reproducible Builds" on page 71).
- You may need to do so to avoid Lambda's artifact size limitation.

The final point relates to the 250MB size limit of (uncompressed) function artifacts in Lambda. If you have 10 Lambda functions, all with different dependencies, and their combined (uncompressed) artifact size is more than 250MB, you'll need to break up your artifact for each function to make deployment even possible.

So how do we implement this?

One way to think about it is that we're effectively building a very small monorepo (*https://oreil.ly/p8jk_*) for our serverless application. You can think of it, perhaps, as a "serverless application MiniMono." Regular monorepos consist of multiple projects in one repo; our MiniMono will consist of multiple Maven modules in one Maven project. While Maven has its shortcomings, it does work very well as a way of declaring dependencies between multiple components, and their dependencies on external libraries. And IntelliJ does a great job of interpreting multimodule Maven projects.

Getting multimodule Maven projects working correctly is a little fiddly, so we'll go step-by-step through it here. We strongly recommend that you download the sample code and open it up in IntelliJ, since it's likely to make more sense to you that way.

The top-level project

Our top-level *pom.xml* file is going to look a little like Example 5-10. We've cut out some of it to give clarity to the explanation.

Example 5-10. Parent project pom.xml for data pipeline app

```xml
<project>
  <groupId>my.groupId</groupId>
  <artifactId>chapter5-Data-Pipeline</artifactId>
  <version>1.0-SNAPSHOT</version>
  <packaging>pom</packaging>

  <modules>
    <module>common-code</module>
    <module>bulk-events-stage</module>
    <module>single-event-stage</module>
  </modules>

  <dependencyManagement>
    <dependencies>
      <dependency>
        <groupId>com.amazonaws</groupId>
        <artifactId>aws-java-sdk-bom</artifactId>
        <version>1.11.600</version>
        <type>pom</type>
        <scope>import</scope>
      </dependency>
      <dependency>
        <groupId>com.amazonaws</groupId>
        <artifactId>aws-lambda-java-events</artifactId>
        <version>2.2.6</version>
      </dependency>
      <!-- etc -->
    </dependencies>
  </dependencyManagement>

  <build>
    <pluginManagement>
      <plugins>
        <plugin>
          <artifactId>maven-assembly-plugin</artifactId>
          <version>3.1.1</version>
          <executions>
            <execution>
              <id>001-make-assembly</id>
              <phase>package</phase>
              <goals>
                <goal>single</goal>
              </goals>
            </execution>
          </executions>
```

```
        <configuration>
          <appendAssemblyId>false</appendAssemblyId>
          <descriptors>
            <descriptor>src/assembly/lambda-zip.xml</descriptor>
          </descriptors>
          <finalName>lambda</finalName>
        </configuration>
      </plugin>
      <plugin>
        <groupId>io.github.zlika</groupId>
        <artifactId>reproducible-build-maven-plugin</artifactId>
        <version>0.10</version>
        <executions>
          <execution>
            <id>002-strip-jar</id>
            <phase>package</phase>
            <goals>
              <goal>strip-jar</goal>
            </goals>
          </execution>
        </executions>
        <configuration>
          <outputDirectory>${project.build.directory}</outputDirectory>
        </configuration>
      </plugin>
    </plugins>
  </pluginManagement>
  </build>
</project>
```

There are a few takeaways here:

- We add the `<packaging>pom</packaging>` tag at the top level—this is declaring that this is a multimodule project.

- We include the list of modules in the `<modules>` section.

- Note that we don't declare any inter-module dependencies at this point.

- All of our external dependencies (not just the AWS SDK BOM) move into the `<dependencyManagement>` section. It makes life easier to declare all the dependencies across the entire project here, and it guarantees that dependency versions are common across the whole project, but you don't have too.

- We'll see in a moment that modules will declare which of these external dependencies they need.

- Notice that we've still got the AWS SDK BOM that we talked about in the first example. We move our build plug-in definitions into a `<pluginManagement>` section so that they can be used by the modules.

- The configuration for the assembly plug-in remains at *src/assembly/lambda-zip.xml*, or you can use the version we've created for you in Maven Central.

- There's a whole bunch of other "Maven magic" detail here that we won't go into!

With our top-level project in place, we can now create our modules.

The modules

We create one subdirectory for each module, named the same as each element of the module list in the project *pom.xml*.

Within each module subdirectory we create a new *pom.xml*. We'll start with the most simple one for *common-code*, which allows us to write code that is shared by both Lambda artifacts. In our example, it contains the WeatherEvent class.

Again, all of these Maven examples are slightly trimmed, so please refer to the book source code for the complete versions.

Example 5-11. Module pom.xml for common-code

```
<project>
  <parent>
    <groupId>my.groupId</groupId>
    <artifactId>chapter5-Data-Pipeline</artifactId>
    <version>1.0-SNAPSHOT</version>
  </parent>

  <artifactId>common-code</artifactId>

  <build>
    <plugins>
      <plugin>
        <artifactId>reproducible-build-maven-plugin</artifactId>
        <groupId>io.github.zlika</groupId>
      </plugin>
    </plugins>
  </build>
</project>
```

We declare our parent, our module's artifactId (which for the sake of sanity should be the same as the module name), and then we declare which build plug-ins we want to use. For this module we're just creating a regular JAR file, of just the code in the module itself. That means we don't need to assemble a ZIP file, but we do still want to make use of the reproducible build plug-in. The configuration for the plug-in comes from our definition in the <pluginManagement> section of the parent bom.

Notice that there's no <dependencies> section because this module doesn't have any dependencies at this time.

Next, in the *bulk-events-stage* subdirectory we create the *pom.xml* as shown in Example 5-12.

Example 5-12. Module pom.xml for bulk-events-stage

```xml
<project>
  <parent>
    <groupId>my.groupId</groupId>
    <artifactId>chapter5-Data-Pipeline</artifactId>
    <version>1.0-SNAPSHOT</version>
  </parent>

  <artifactId>bulk-events-stage</artifactId>

  <dependencies>
    <dependency>
      <groupId>my.groupId</groupId>
      <artifactId>common-code</artifactId>
      <version>${project.parent.version}</version>
    </dependency>
    <dependency>
      <groupId>com.amazonaws</groupId>
      <artifactId>aws-lambda-java-events</artifactId>
    </dependency>
    <!-- etc. -->
  </dependencies>

  <build>
    <plugins>
      <plugin>
        <artifactId>maven-assembly-plugin</artifactId>
      </plugin>
      <plugin>
        <artifactId>reproducible-build-maven-plugin</artifactId>
        <groupId>io.github.zlika</groupId>
      </plugin>
    </plugins>
  </build>
</project>
```

The `<parent>` section is the same as for *common-code*, and `<artifactId>` follows the same rule as before.

This time we do have dependencies. The first one is how we declare an inter-module dependency, in this case to the *common-code* module. Notice that we pick up the version from the parent module. Then we declare all of our external dependencies. Notice that there aren't any versions for these—the versions come from the `<dependency-management>` section in the parent *pom.xml* (or, transitively, from the AWS SDK BOM).

And finally in the `<build>` section we declare our build plug-ins. This time we need to create a ZIP file (which will be the ZIP file just for the `BulkEventsLambda` function), and so we include a reference to `maven-assembly-plugin`. Again, the configuration for the plug-in is defined in the parent *pom.xml*.

The *single-event-stage pom.xml* looks almost the same as the *bulk-events-stage pom.xml*, but with fewer dependencies.

With the Maven POM files complete, we then create *src* directories within each module. The end result of our project directory tree looks as follows:

```
.
+--> bulk-events-stage
|    +--> src/main/java/book/pipeline/bulk
|    |                            +--> BulkEventsLambda.java
|    +--> pom.xml
+--> common-code
|    +--> src/main/java/book/pipeline/common
|    |                            +--> WeatherEvent.java
|    +--> pom.xml
+--> single-event-stage
|    +--> src/main/java/book/pipeline/single
|    |                            +--> SingleEventLambda.java
|    +--> pom.xml
+--> src/assembly
|         +--> lambda-zip.xml
+--> pom.xml
+--> template.yaml
```

Running `mvn package` for this multimodule project will create separate *lambda.zip* files in each of the two Lambda module directories.

Since we have parallel modules that don't depend on each other we can actually tune our use of Maven a little to increase build performance. Running `mvn package -T 1C` will make Maven use multiple OS threads, one per core of your machine, when it can.

Infrastructure

Despite the significant change in the structure of our Java project, our SAM template doesn't change all that much. Let's look at how it does change, plus the other AWS resources that we use in Example 5-13.

Example 5-13. SAM template for data pipeline

```
AWSTemplateFormatVersion: 2010-09-09
Transform: AWS::Serverless-2016-10-31
Description: chapter5-data-pipeline

Globals:
```

```yaml
  Function:
    Runtime: java8
    MemorySize: 512
    Timeout: 10

Resources:
  PipelineStartBucket:
    Type: AWS::S3::Bucket
    Properties:
      BucketName: !Sub ${AWS::StackName}-${AWS::AccountId}-${AWS::Region}-start

  FanOutTopic:
    Type: AWS::SNS::Topic

  BulkEventsLambda:
    Type: AWS::Serverless::Function
    Properties:
      CodeUri: bulk-events-stage/target/lambda.zip
      Handler: book.pipeline.bulk.BulkEventsLambda::handler
      Environment:
        Variables:
          FAN_OUT_TOPIC: !Ref FanOutTopic
      Policies:
        - S3ReadPolicy:
            BucketName: !Sub ${AWS::StackName}-${AWS::AccountId}-${AWS::Region}-start
        - SNSPublishMessagePolicy:
            TopicName: !GetAtt FanOutTopic.TopicName
      Events:
        S3Event:
          Type: S3
          Properties:
            Bucket: !Ref PipelineStartBucket
            Events: s3:ObjectCreated:

  SingleEventLambda:
    Type: AWS::Serverless::Function
    Properties:
      CodeUri: single-event-stage/target/lambda.zip
      Handler: book.pipeline.single.SingleEventLambda::handler
      Events:
        SnsEvent:
          Type: SNS
          Properties:
            Topic: !Ref FanOutTopic
```

First, while it's still fresh in our minds, let's look at the differences caused by the multimodule Maven project. They are solely the updates to the `CodeUri` properties on the Lambda functions—where we used to have the same `target/lambda.zip` value for both functions in the API example, it's now `bulk-events-stage/target/lambda.zip` for `BulkEventsLambda`, and `single-event-stage/target/lambda.zip` for the `Single EventLambda`.

OK, now let's go back to the top.

The `Globals` section is a little smaller this time. That's because there are no shared environment variables across the Lambda functions, and we don't need any API configuration.

Under `Resources`, first we declare our S3 bucket. There are a whole lot of properties you can add here—access control–related properties are particularly popular. One thing we typically like to add is server-side encryption as well as lifecycle policies. But here we keep it to the defaults. One thing that's here is an explicitly declared name. Normally we wouldn't want to do this, and instead have CloudFormation generate a unique name for us, but due to an annoying aspect of CloudFormation's S3 resource, if we don't declare a name, then we get a circular dependency with some of the other elements of the file.

S3 bucket names have to be globally unique across all AWS regions and accounts. If you create a bucket named *sheep* in the us-east-1 region, then you can't also create another one named *sheep* in us-west-2 (unless you first delete the one in us-east-1), and I can't create a bucket named "sheep" at all. This means that when you create a bucket name explicitly via an automated tool like CloudFormation, you need to include various context-unique aspects to avoid a naming collision.

For example, we use the following declared bucket name:

```
!Sub ${AWS::StackName}-${AWS::AccountId}-${AWS::Region}-start
```

There's some CloudFormation smarts happening here, so let's unpack that a little.

First of all `!Sub` is another *intrinsic function* (*https://oreil.ly/NaRtL*), just like `!Ref` in the first example. `!Sub` substitutes variables in a string. Often you will use variables you declare yourself in template parameters, but in this case we are using CloudFormation *pseudo parameters* (*https://oreil.ly/LUtMC*)—variables that CloudFormation defines on our behalf. Say I created a stack named *my-stack*, our account ID was 123456, and we had created the stack in us-west-2, then the bucket name in this stack would be *my-stack-123456-us-west-2-start*.

The next resource is our SNS Topic. Look—no properties! SNS is partly configurable, but it's also super simple to use with no configuration at all.

And then we have our two Lambda functions.

`BulkEventsLambda` has an environment variable referring to the Amazon Resource Name (ARN) of the SNS topic. The SNS Topic CloudFormation documentation (*https://oreil.ly/r6oVW*) tells us that calling `!Ref` on a Topic resource returns its ARN.

For the security side of this Lambda we both need to read from the S3 bucket—which we refer to with the same name as we used when declaring the bucket in the first place—and we need to write (or publish) to the SNS topic. For the SNS topic, the security policy doesn't need the ARN (which is what is returned when we call !Ref on the Topic resource); it needs the Topic's name. To get that, we use a third intrinsic function—!GetAtt. !GetAtt allows us to read secondary return values from a Cloud-Formation resource. Again, when looking at the SNS documentation, we can see that the name is returned when asking for TopicName, hence the value !GetAtt FanOut Topic.TopicName.

Finally, for BulkEventsLambda we need to declare the event source. This is the S3 bucket, and we declare the type of S3 events we care about in the Events fields. You can be much more prescriptive here if you like, for example including filter patterns to only trigger events for certain S3 keys.

As you'd expect, SingleEventLambda is simpler since it doesn't call any AWS resources. For this function, we just need to declare the event source, which is the SNS Topic, referred to by the Topic's ARN.

Deployment

Deployment is similar to what you've seen before. Again, we're using the principles of a serverless application in that we collectively deploy all of the components together.

There's one small change for deploying this app. Because we're using the stack name in the manually defined S3 bucket name, we have to use only lowercase letters in the stack name (because S3 buckets can't be named with uppercase letters):

```
$ sam deploy \
    --s3-bucket $CF_BUCKET \
    --stack-name chapter-five-data-pipeline \
    --capabilities CAPABILITY_IAM
```

Once the application is deployed, you can explore the deployed components via the Lambda Applications console, or the CloudFormation console. Figure 5-11 shows what it looks like in Lambda applications.

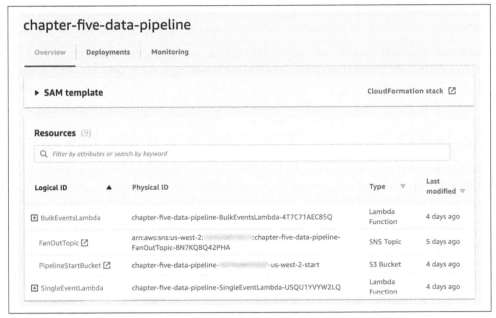

Figure 5-11. Serverless Application view for data pipeline

Clicking the resources will take you through to their own parts of the AWS Console. To test this application, we need to upload a file to S3. One option is to do that manually through the web console.

A more automated approach is as follows.

First, query CloudFormation to get the name of the S3 bucket, and assign that to a shell variable:

```
$ PIPELINE_BUCKET="$(aws cloudformation describe-stack-resource \
    --stack-name chapter-five-data-pipeline \
    --logical-resource-id PipelineStartBucket \
    --query 'StackResourceDetail.PhysicalResourceId' \
    --output text)"
```

Now use the AWS CLI to upload the sample file:

```
$ aws s3 cp sampledata.json s3://${PIPELINE_BUCKET}/sampledata.json
```

Now look at the logs for the `SingleEventLambda` function, and you'll see, after a few seconds, each of the weather events separately logged.

Congratulations—you've built your second serverless application!

As you can imagine, with the vast number of services available on AWS, the different types of serverless application that can be built are innumerable. And that's before we even consider the perfectly valid capability of calling services outside of AWS from Lambda!

We hope that this chapter has given you a taste of what's possible. The ability to deploy complete, multicomponent, applications with just a few text files, in minutes or seconds, and then tear them down again, makes for an extraordinarily valuable "application sandbox" environment that can also scale to real production use.

Summary

We started this chapter by looking at how to trigger Lambda functions from other AWS services. Understanding this is an important first step to embracing serverless architecture.

We then explored two example serverless applications—wholly contained groups of AWS resources that can be collectively deployed. The first example was a database-backed HTTP API, using two synchronously invoked Lambda functions, along with the AWS services API Gateway and DynamoDB.

The second example was a serverless data pipeline consisting of two asynchronous processing stages, including a fan-out design. This example used Lambda, S3, and SNS. In this example, we also explored using multimodule Maven projects to create a "serverless application MiniMono."

You now have a framework for building serverless AWS applications:

1. Identify the *behavior* you want your application to have.
2. Design the *architecture* of your application by choosing which services will implement the different aspects of your system, and how those services will interact.
3. Program *Lambda code* to:
   - Consume the correct event types.
   - Perform the necessary side effects on downstream services.
   - Where relevant, return the correct response.
4. Configure your *infrastructure* using a CloudFormation/SAM template.
5. Execute *deployment* using the correct AWS tooling.

So far all of our testing has been very manual. How can we do better, using automated testing techniques? That's what we explore in the next chapter.

Exercises

1. Another great event source for "getting started" with Lambda is CloudWatch Scheduled Events, which we can use to build "serverless cron jobs." We describe this use of Lambda in "Example: Lambda "cron jobs"" on page 227. Build a Lambda function that will run every minute, and for now that just writes out a log statement when it's called. See the SAM documentation (*https://oreil.ly/C_FhY*) on how to set up this trigger.

2. Update your scheduled event Lambda from the previous exercise to post a message to SNS, similar to how we did so in BulkEventsLambda earlier in this chapter. Update your SNS topic to send an SMS, or text, message to your mobile phone (see the AWS documentation (*https://oreil.ly/TrQct*) on how to do this).

3. Reimplement the data pipeline example from this chapter to use an SQS queue, rather than an SNS topic, between the two Lambdas. A couple of good starting places to help with this are here (*https://oreil.ly/LKekx*) and here (*https://oreil.ly/Cbvb3*) in the Lambda documentation.

CHAPTER 6
Testing

A good test suite, like the solid foundation of a house, provides a known baseline of system behavior on top of which we can build confidently. That baseline gives us confidence to add features, fix bugs, and refactor without worrying that we'll break other parts of the system. When integrated into a development workflow, that same test suite also encourages good practices by making it easier to maintain existing tests and add new ones.

Of course, foundations aren't free. The effort of maintaining tests must be balanced with the value that the tests provide. If we spend all of our effort on testing, we'll have none left to work on the rest of the system.

For serverless applications, drawing the line between valuable tests and brittle technical debt is harder than ever. Fortunately, we can use a familiar model to help consider the trade-offs.

The Test Pyramid

The classic "Test Pyramid" (from the 2009 book *Succeeding with Agile* by Mike Cohn, shown in Figure 6-1) is a useful guide in helping us decide which kinds of tests to write. The pyramid metaphor illustrates the trade-offs between the number of tests in a given slice, the value of those tests, and the costs to write, run, and maintain them.

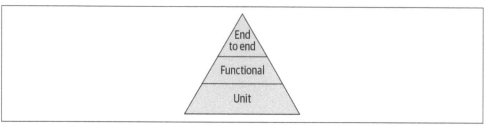

Figure 6-1. The Test Pyramid

Testing in a serverless world isn't substantively different than in a traditional application, especially nearer the base of the pyramid. However, as with any distributed system made up of different components and services, higher-level "end-to-end" testing is more challenging. In this chapter, we'll address testing from the bottom of the pyramid to the top, with plenty of examples along the way.

Unit Tests

At the base of the pyramid are unit tests—these tests should exercise specific pieces of our components of our application, without relying on any external dependencies (like databases). Unit tests should execute quickly, and we should be able to run them regularly (or even automatically) during the course of development, with a minimum of configuration and no network access. We should have as many unit tests as necessary to give us confidence that our code is working correctly. Unit tests not only cover the "happy paths," but thoroughly address edge cases and error handling. Even a small application might have dozens or hundreds of unit tests.

Functional Tests

In the middle of the pyramid are the functional tests. Like unit tests, these tests should execute quickly, and shouldn't rely on external dependencies. Unlike unit tests, we might have to mock or stub those external dependencies to meet the runtime requirements of the component under test.

Rather than attempting to exhaustively exercise every logical branch of our code, our functional tests address the major code paths for a component, paying particular attention to failure modes.

End-to-End Tests

At the top of the pyramid are the end-to-end tests. An end-to-end test submits input to the application (often via the normal user interface or API) and then makes assertions on the output or side effects. Unlike a functional test, an end-to-end test runs against the complete application and all of its external dependencies, in a production-like environment (although often isolated from production).

Because end-to-end tests are more expensive to run than functional and unit tests (in terms of runtime and infrastructure cost), you typically should only test a few important scenarios. A good rule of thumb is to have at least one end-to-end test that covers the most important path through an application (e.g., the purchase path in an online shopping application).

Refactoring for Testing

We're going to use the serverless data pipeline we built in Chapter 5 as the basis to build out a suite of unit, functional, and end-to-end tests. Before we jump in, let's do a little refactoring to make our data pipeline Lambdas easier to test.

Recall from the previous section that unit tests exercise specific pieces of components of our application. In our case, we're referring to methods within the Java classes that make up our Lambda functions. We want to write tests that provide input to certain methods, and assert that the output (or side effects) of those methods are what we expect.

Side Effects

In computer science, a *side effect* can be thought of as something that is observable outside of the scope of the invoking function or method. For example, if a Java method writes output to a file or makes an HTTP call, that method is said to have a side effect. Even "read-only" operations might have observable side effects like modifying a system file descriptor or opening a network socket.

When testing applications, it's important to validate both the application and the result of any side effects it may perform.

To start, let's review BulkEventsLambda, keeping in mind the unit and functional slices of the Test Pyramid. This relatively simple Lambda function is interacting with two external AWS services (S3 and SNS), as well as serializing and deserializing JSON data.

Revisiting BulkEventsLambda

BulkEventsLambda is triggered whenever a file is uploaded to a specific S3 bucket. The handler method is invoked with an S3Event object. For each S3EventNotificationRecord within that event, the Lambda retrieves a JSON file from an S3 bucket. That JSON file contains zero or more JSON objects. The Lambda deserializes the JSON file into a collection of WeatherEvent Java objects. Each of those Java objects is then serialized into a String and published to an SNS topic. Finally, the Lambda function writes a log entry to STDOUT (and hence to CloudWatch Logs) stating the number of weather events that were sent to SNS.

The code you saw in Chapter 5 was written and organized for clarity, but not necessarily for ease of testing. Let's take a look at the four methods in the BulkEvents Lambda class.

First, the handler method, which receives an S3Event object:

```
public void handler(S3Event event) {
    event.getRecords().forEach(this::processS3EventRecord);
}
```

This is the only method accessible from outside the class—without refactoring, it means that any tests for this class *must* invoke this method with an S3Event object. Furthermore, the method has a void return type, so asserting success or failure is difficult.

Moving on, we see that this method calls processS3EventRecord for each incoming event record:

```
private void processS3EventRecord(
    S3EventNotification.S3EventNotificationRecord record) {

  final List<WeatherEvent> weatherEvents = readWeatherEventsFromS3(
    record.getS3().getBucket().getName(),
    record.getS3().getObject().getKey());

  weatherEvents.stream()
    .map(this::weatherEventToSnsMessage)
    .forEach(message -> sns.publish(snsTopic, message));

  System.out.println("Published " + weatherEvents.size()
    + " weather events to SNS");
}
```

This method is private, so it can't be tested at all without changing the visibility to "package-private" (by removing the private keyword). Like the handler function, it has a void return type, so any assertions we make will be on the side effects rather than the return value of the method. This method has two explicit side effects:

- The System.out.println call.
- The sns.publish call, which sends an SNS message to the topic named by the snsTopic field. Because this is an AWS SDK call, a number of other environment and system attributes must be accounted for:
  - The appropriate AWS configuration must be in place and correct.
  - The AWS API endpoint for the configured region must be accessible over the network.

— The named SNS topic must exist.

— The AWS credentials we're using must have access to write to that SNS topic.

To invoke processS3EventRecord as written, we have to address all of those items ahead of time. For a unit test, this is unacceptable overhead.

Furthermore, if we also want to assert that processS3EventRecord has run correctly, we need a way of knowing that the SNS message was sent to the correct topic. One way to do that would be to subscribe to the SNS topic within our test process and wait for the expected message to show up. As before, this is unacceptable overhead for a unit test.

A common way to test these side effects in Java is to mock or stub the classes responsible for those side effects using tools like Mockito (*https://site.mockito.org*). This allows us to test our own application classes that produce side effects, by replacing things like the AWS SDK with a mock that looks and acts similarly but allows us to avoid actually setting up a real SNS topic. Using techniques like argument capture (*https://oreil.ly/GPdlH*), mocks can also save the parameters used to call them, which allows us to make assertions about how they are called—in this case we could assert that the sns.publish method was called with the correct topic name and message.

To use a mock AWS SDK object like this, we need a way to inject it into the class under test—typically this is done via a constructor that accepts the appropriate parameters. BulkEventsLambda doesn't have such a constructor, so we'll need to add one to be able to use mock objects.

The readWeatherEventsFromS3 method is another example of a method with a side effect, in this case a remote API call. In this case, it uses the AWS S3 SDK client's getObject call to download data from the S3.

That data is then deserialized into a collection of WeatherEvent objects and returned to the caller:

```
private List<WeatherEvent> readWeatherEventsFromS3(String bucket, String key) {
  try {
    final S3ObjectInputStream s3is =
      s3.getObject(bucket, key).getObjectContent();
    final WeatherEvent[] weatherEvents =
      objectMapper.readValue(s3is, WeatherEvent[].class);
    s3is.close();
    return Arrays.asList(weatherEvents);
  } catch (IOException e) {
    throw new RuntimeException(e);
  }
}
```

This method does two distinctly different things—it downloads data from S3 *and* deserializes that data. That combination of actions makes it harder for us to test each piece of functionality in isolation. If we want to test how errors are handled during JSON deserialization, we still have to make sure that the input to the method has the correct S3 bucket and key even though that information isn't relevant to the JSON processing.

Finally, `weatherEventToSnsMessage` is an example of a method that should be easy to test (if made visible outside of the `BulkEventsLambda` class). It takes a single `Weather Event` object and returns a `String`, and it doesn't cause any side effects.

Refactoring BulkEventsLambda

Having reviewed the four methods in `BulkEventsLambda`, here are some things we can do to better enable unit and functional testing:

- Enable injection of mock AWS SDK classes via constructor arguments.
- Isolate side effects, so most methods can be tested without using mocks.
- Split methods up so most methods just do one thing.

Add Constructors

With those things in mind, let's start by adding some constructors:

```
public BulkEventsLambda() {
  this(AmazonSNSClientBuilder.defaultClient(),
    AmazonS3ClientBuilder.defaultClient());
}

public BulkEventsLambda(AmazonSNS sns, AmazonS3 s3) {
  this.sns = sns;
  this.s3 = s3;
  this.snsTopic = System.getenv(FAN_OUT_TOPIC_ENV);

  if (this.snsTopic == null) {
    throw new RuntimeException(
      String.format("%s must be set", FAN_OUT_TOPIC_ENV));
  }
}
```

We now have two constructors. As we learned in Chapter 3, the no-arguments default constructor will be invoked by the Lambda runtime when our function is run for the first time. That default constructor creates an AWS SDK SNS client and an S3 client and passes those two objects to the second constructor (this technique is called *constructor chaining*).

The second constructor takes those client objects as parameters. In tests we can use this constructor to instantiate the `BulkEventsLambda` class with mock AWS SDK clients. That second constructor also reads the FAN_OUT_TOPIC environment variable, and throws an exception if it isn't set.

Isolate Side Effects

We noted three side effects from the BulkEventsLambda review:

- Download a JSON file from S3.
- Publish messages to an SNS topic.
- Write a log entry to STDOUT.

The first two impose a number of prerequisites on the test environment, slow down test execution, and make tests more complex to write. While we definitely want to test those side effects (using both mocks *and* the actual AWS services), isolating them to as few methods as possible will help make our unit tests simple and fast.

With that in mind, let's look at two new methods that isolate AWS side effects:

```
private void publishToSns(String message) {
  sns.publish(snsTopic, message);
}

private InputStream getObjectFromS3(
      S3EventNotification.S3EventNotificationRecord record) {

  String bucket = record.getS3().getBucket().getName();
  String key = record.getS3().getObject().getKey();
  return s3.getObject(bucket, key).getObjectContent();
}
```

The first method, publishToSns, takes a String parameter and publishes a message to an SNS topic. The second, getObjectFromS3, takes an S3EventNotification Record and downloads the corresponding file from S3.

These two methods are now called from a refactored handler method, which is where the actual isolation of side effects is realized:

```
public void handler(S3Event event) {

  List<WeatherEvent> events = event.getRecords().stream()
    .map(this::getObjectFromS3)
    .map(this::readWeatherEvents)
    .flatMap(List::stream)
    .collect(Collectors.toList());

  // Serialize and publish WeatherEvent messages to SNS
  events.stream()
    .map(this::weatherEventToSnsMessage)
    .forEach(this::publishToSns);
```

```
System.out.println("Published " + events.size()
  + " weather events to SNS");
}
```

There's more going on in this new handler method, but for now just note that get ObjectFromS3 and publishToSns are called from here (and nowhere else).

Split Methods

In addition to isolating our side effects, the new handler method now also contains much of our processing logic. This might seem contrary to our goal, but this "glue" logic orchestrates a number of simpler, single-purpose methods that are easier to unit test. In this case, the readWeatherEvents method no longer requires access to S3 (or to a mock S3 client). Its only purpose is to deserialize an InputStream into a collection of WeatherEvent objects and handle errors (by rethrowing a RuntimeException, which will halt the Lambda function).

```
List<WeatherEvent> readWeatherEvents(InputStream inputStream) {
  try (InputStream is = inputStream) {
    return Arrays.asList(
      objectMapper.readValue(is, WeatherEvent[].class));
  } catch (IOException e) {
    throw new RuntimeException(e);
  }
}
```

Note that we're now using Java's try-with-resources feature (*https://oreil.ly/LxRNY*) to automatically close the input stream. We also removed the private keyword from this and the weatherEventToSnsMessage method, so those can both be accessed from our test classes as necessary.

Testing BulkEventsLambda

Now that we've refactored, let's add some unit tests for BulkEventsLambda.

Unit Testing

These tests are completely isolated from side effects—we don't have to configure or connect to any AWS services or any other external dependencies. That isolation also means that these tests execute quickly, in just a few milliseconds. We have only a few, because BulkEventsLambda is fairly simple, but even hundreds of unit tests written in this style could be run in a few seconds.

Here's a unit test for the readWeatherEvents method of BulkEventsLambda:

```java
public class BulkEventsLambdaUnitTest {

  @Test
  public void testReadWeatherEvents() {

    // Fixture data
    InputStream inputStream =
      getClass().getResourceAsStream("/bulk_data.json");

    // Construct Lambda function class, and invoke
    BulkEventsLambda lambda =
      new BulkEventsLambda(null, null);
    List<WeatherEvent> weatherEvents =
      lambda.readWeatherEvents(inputStream);

    // Assert
    Assert.assertEquals(3, weatherEvents.size());

    Assert.assertEquals("Brooklyn, NY",
      weatherEvents.get(0).locationName);
    Assert.assertEquals(91.0,
      weatherEvents.get(0).temperature, 0.0);
    Assert.assertEquals(1564428897L,
      weatherEvents.get(0).timestamp, 0);
    Assert.assertEquals(40.7,
      weatherEvents.get(0).latitude, 0.0);
    Assert.assertEquals(-73.99,
      weatherEvents.get(0).longitude, 0.0);

    Assert.assertEquals("Oxford, UK",
      weatherEvents.get(1).locationName);
    Assert.assertEquals(64.0,
      weatherEvents.get(1).temperature, 0.0);
    Assert.assertEquals(1564428897L,
      weatherEvents.get(1).timestamp, 0);
    Assert.assertEquals(51.75,
      weatherEvents.get(1).latitude, 0.0);
```

```
    Assert.assertEquals(-1.25,
      weatherEvents.get(1).longitude, 0.0);

    Assert.assertEquals("Charlottesville, VA",
      weatherEvents.get(2).locationName);
    Assert.assertEquals(87.0,
      weatherEvents.get(2).temperature, 0.0);
    Assert.assertEquals(1564428897L,
      weatherEvents.get(2).timestamp, 0);
    Assert.assertEquals(38.02,
      weatherEvents.get(2).latitude, 0.0);
    Assert.assertEquals(-78.47,
      weatherEvents.get(2).longitude, 0.0);
  }

}
```

For convenience, we're reading the input data from a JSON file on disk. We then create an instance of BulkEventsLambda—notice that we're simply passing in null for the SNS and S3 clients, because they're not needed by this test at all. The readWeatherEvents method is called, and we assert that it produced the right objects.

We can test the failure case with even less code:

```
public class BulkEventsLambdaUnitTest {

  @Rule
  public ExpectedException thrown = ExpectedException.none();

  @Rule
  public EnvironmentVariables environment = new EnvironmentVariables();

  @Test
  public void testReadWeatherEventsBadData() {

    // Fixture data
    InputStream inputStream =
      getClass().getResourceAsStream("/bad_data.json");

    // Expect exception
    thrown.expect(RuntimeException.class);
    thrown.expectCause(
      CoreMatchers.instanceOf(InvalidFormatException.class));
    thrown.expectMessage(
      "Can not deserialize value of type java.lang.Long from String");

    // Invoke
    BulkEventsLambda lambda = new BulkEventsLambda(null, null);
    lambda.readWeatherEvents(inputStream);
  }

}
```

Here we use a JUnit Rule (*https://oreil.ly/YeLiW*) to assert that an exception of the expected type is thrown by our method.

As unit tests go, these are simple and effective. For a more complex Lambda function, we might have dozens of tests like these to test as many logical paths and edge cases as necessary.

Functional Testing

Like the unit tests, we want our functional tests to run without having to connect to AWS. However, unlike the unit tests, we want to test our Lambda function as a single component, and doing so means that we have to convince our code that it's talking to the cloud! To accomplish this feat of trickery and deceit, we'll use Mockito to build "mock" instances of the AWS SDK clients configured to return prearranged responses to method calls. For example, if our code calls the getObject method on the S3 client, our mock will return an S3Object complete with fixtured test data.

Here's a functional test for the "happy path":

```
public class BulkEventsLambdaFunctionalTest {

    @Test
    public void testHandler() throws IOException {

        // Set up mock AWS SDK clients
        AmazonSNS mockSNS = Mockito.mock(AmazonSNS.class);
        AmazonS3 mockS3 = Mockito.mock(AmazonS3.class);

        // Fixture S3 event
        S3Event s3Event = objectMapper
          .readValue(getClass()
          .getResourceAsStream("/s3_event.json"), S3Event.class);
        String bucket =
          s3Event.getRecords().get(0).getS3().getBucket().getName();
        String key =
          s3Event.getRecords().get(0).getS3().getObject().getKey();

        // Fixture S3 return value
        S3Object s3Object = new S3Object();
        s3Object.setObjectContent(
          getClass().getResourceAsStream(String.format("/%s", key)));
        Mockito.when(mockS3.getObject(bucket, key)).thenReturn(s3Object);

        // Fixture environment
        String topic = "test-topic";
        environment.set(BulkEventsLambda.FAN_OUT_TOPIC_ENV, topic);

        // Construct Lambda function class, and invoke handler
        BulkEventsLambda lambda = new BulkEventsLambda(mockSNS, mockS3);
        lambda.handler(s3Event);
```

```
        // Capture outbound SNS messages
        ArgumentCaptor<String> topics =
          ArgumentCaptor.forClass(String.class);
        ArgumentCaptor<String> messages =
          ArgumentCaptor.forClass(String.class);
        Mockito.verify(mockSNS,
          Mockito.times(3)).publish(topics.capture(),
            messages.capture());

        // Assert
        Assert.assertArrayEquals(
          new String[]{topic, topic, topic},
          topics.getAllValues().toArray());
        Assert.assertArrayEquals(new String[]{
          "{\"locationName\":\"Brooklyn, NY\",\"temperature\":91.0,"
            + "\"timestamp\":1564428897,\"longitude\":-73.99,"
            + "\"latitude\":40.7}",
          "{\"locationName\":\"Oxford, UK\",\"temperature\":64.0,"
            + "\"timestamp\":1564428898,\"longitude\":-1.25,"
            + "\"latitude\":51.75}",
          "{\"locationName\":\"Charlottesville, VA\",\"temperature\":87.0,"
            + "\"timestamp\":1564428899,\"longitude\":-78.47,"
            + "\"latitude\":38.02}"
        }, messages.getAllValues().toArray());
    }
}
```

The first thing you should note is that this test is *much* longer than our unit tests. Most of that additional code is setting up the mock objects and configuring the environment so that our Lambda function's handler method thinks it's running in the cloud.

The second thing to note is that we're reading the input data from a file on disk. *s3_event.json* is a file that was generated using this sam command:

```
$ sam local generate-event s3 put > src/test/resources/s3_event.json
```

We then changed the key field to reference another local file, *bulk_data.json*, which represents the weather data that would be stored on S3:

```
{
  "Records": [
    {
      ...
      "s3": {
        "bucket": {
          "name": "example-bucket",
          ...
        },
        "object": {
          "key": "bulk_data.json",
```

```
          }
        }
      }
    ]
  }
```

Our mock S3 client returns the contents of the *bulk_data.json* file when the `s3.getOb` `ject` method is called, and our Lambda function is none the wiser.

JSON Files to Java Objects

Some event types can be easily deserialized from JSON files using the out-of-the-box functionality provided by the Jackson library (*https://oreil.ly/P07R8*). This allows us to use the sample events generated by the `sam` CLI or copied from various AWS Web Console sources.

However, some events use legacy JSON formats that aren't parseable without extra configuration. For an example of this, take a look at the following `Single Event` `LambdaFunctionalTest`:

```java
public class SingleEventLambdaFunctionalTest {

    private final ObjectMapper objectMapper = new ObjectMapper()
        .registerModule(new JodaModule())
        .enable(MapperFeature.ACCEPT_CASE_INSENSITIVE_PROPERTIES);

    ...

    @Test
    public void testHandler() throws IOException {

        // Fixture SNS event
        SNSEvent snsEvent = objectMapper.readValue(getClass()
          .getResourceAsStream("/sns_event.json"), SNSEvent.class);

        // Construct Lambda function class, and invoke handler
        SingleEventLambda lambda = new SingleEventLambda();
        lambda.handler(snsEvent);

        ...

    }

}
```

Here we have to configure the Jackson `ObjectMapper` to use a different module for date handling and parse property names without regard to capitalization. If you're trying to test with an event type that is difficult to parse from JSON, remember that you can always fall back to simply building the Java object in your test code!

We could rewrite the previous test as follows and avoid having to deal with JSON deserialization:

```
@Test
public void testHandlerNoJackson() throws IOException {

  // Fixture SNS content, record, and event
  SNSEvent.SNS snsContent = new SNSEvent.SNS()
    .withMessage("{\"locationName\":\"Brooklyn, NY\","
      + "\"temperature\":91.0,\"timestamp\":1564428897,"
      + "\"longitude\":-73.99,\"latitude\":40.7}");
  SNSEvent.SNSRecord snsRecord =
    new SNSEvent.SNSRecord().withSns(snsContent);
  SNSEvent snsEvent =
    new SNSEvent()
      .withRecords(Collections.singletonList(snsRecord));

  // Construct Lambda function class, and invoke handler
  SingleEventLambda lambda = new SingleEventLambda();
  lambda.handler(snsEvent);

  Assert.assertEquals(
    "Received weather event:\nWeatherEvent{"
      + "locationName='Brooklyn, NY', temperature=91.0, "
      + "timestamp=1564428897, longitude=-73.99, "
      + "latitude=40.7}\n"
    , systemOutRule.getLog());
  }

}
```

This avoids the Jackson configuration, but the result is a fair amount of boilerplate to build up the required SNSEvent object. We recommend using a combination of these two approaches, depending on the circumstances and the complexity of the event objects.

Lastly, we want to assert that BulkEventsLambda publishes messages to SNS, but without actually sending messages to AWS. Here we use our mock SNS client and capture the parameters that are passed to the sns.publish method. If that method is called the expected number of times with the right parameters, our test passes.

Another functional test asserts that the Lambda function throws an exception if it receives bad input data. The last test asserts that an exception is thrown if the FAN_OUT_TOPIC environment variable isn't set.

These functional tests are more complex to write and take somewhat longer to run, but they give us confidence that BulkEventsLambda will behave as we expect it to when the Lambda runtime calls the handler function with an S3Event object.

End-to-End Testing

With the confidence gained from our suite of unit and functional tests, we can focus our most complex and costly testing methodology on the critical path for our application. We can also take advantage of our infrastructure-as-code approach to deploy a complete version of our serverless application and infrastructure to AWS, for the sole purpose of running an end-to-end test. When the test has completed successfully, we'll clean up and tear it all down.

To run the end-to-end test, we simply need to execute the mvn verify command. This uses the Maven Failsafe plug-in, which finds test classes that end in *IT and runs them using JUnit. In this case, IT stands for integration test, but that's just Maven nomenclature—we could configure the Failsafe plug-in to use a different suffix.

For our end-to-end test, we exercise our application exactly as it would be used in production. We upload a JSON file to an S3 bucket and then assert that the Single EventLambda produces the correct CloudWatch Logs output. From the perspective of the test, our serverless application is a black box.

Here's the main body of the test method:

```java
@Test
public void endToEndTest() throws InterruptedException {
  String bucketName = resolvePhysicalId("PipelineStartBucket");
  String key = UUID.randomUUID().toString();
  File file = new File(getClass().getResource("/bulk_data.json").getFile());

  // 1. Upload bulk_data file to S3
  s3.putObject(bucketName, key, file);

  // 2. Check for executions of SingleEventLambda
  Thread.sleep(30000);
  String singleEventLambda = resolvePhysicalId("SingleEventLambda");
  Set<String> logMessages = getLogMessages(singleEventLambda);
  Assert.assertThat(logMessages, CoreMatchers.hasItems(
    "WeatherEvent{locationName='Brooklyn, NY', temperature=91.0, "
      + "timestamp=1564428897, longitude=-73.99, latitude=40.7}",
    "WeatherEvent{locationName='Oxford, UK', temperature=64.0, "
      + "timestamp=1564428898, longitude=-1.25, latitude=51.75}",
    "WeatherEvent{locationName='Charlottesville, VA', temperature=87.0, "
      + "timestamp=1564428899, longitude=-78.47, latitude=38.02}"
  ));

  // 3. Delete object from S3 bucket (to allow a clean CloudFormation teardown)
  s3.deleteObject(bucketName, key);

  // 4. Delete Lambda log groups
  logs.deleteLogGroup(
    new DeleteLogGroupRequest(getLogGroup(singleEventLambda)));
  String bulkEventsLambda = resolvePhysicalId("BulkEventsLambda");
```

```
logs.deleteLogGroup(
    new DeleteLogGroupRequest(getLogGroup(bulkEventsLambda)));
}
```

Here are a few points worth noting from this example:

- The test resolves the actual name (in AWS parlance, the "Physical ID") of the S3 bucket from our CloudFormation stack. This technique for resource discovery is useful because it allows us to deploy named stacks that don't explicitly specify names for resources (or that use the stack name as part of the resource name). This means that we can deploy the same application multiple times in the same account and even the same region, using different names each time for the CloudFormation stack.

- For simplicity's sake, our test simply sleeps for 30 seconds before checking if the SingleEventLambda has executed. Another approach would be to poll Cloud-Watch Logs proactively, which would be more reliable, but obviously more complex.

- We clean up some resources at the end of the test method. We do this so if the test fails, those resources remain available for our investigation into the test failure. If we had used JUnit's @After functionality, that cleanup would happen even if the test failed, thus hampering an investigation.

Now that you've seen the test method itself, let's look at how we set up and tear down the test infrastructure. We need to make sure that the S3 bucket, SNS topic, and Lambda functions are in place for our test to run, but we don't want to create those resources individually. Instead, we want to use the same SAM *template.yaml* file as we use for production.

For this example, we're using the Maven "exec" plug-in to hook into the build lifecycle's "pre-integration" phase, which will execute before the end-to-end test. Don't be put off by the fact that we're using Maven here. You could just as easily do this with a simple shell script or Makefile. What's important is that we use the same *template.yaml* file as we would use for production, and if possible, the same AWS CLI commands to deploy our application.

```
<plugin>
  <groupId>org.codehaus.mojo</groupId>
  <artifactId>exec-maven-plugin</artifactId>
  <executions>
    <execution>
      <id>001-sam-deploy</id>
      <phase>pre-integration-test</phase>
      <goals>
        <goal>exec</goal>
      </goals>
      <configuration>
```

```
      <basedir>${project.parent.basedir}</basedir>
      <executable>sam</executable>
      <arguments>
        <argument>deploy</argument>
        <argument>--s3-bucket</argument>
        <argument>${integration.test.code.bucket}</argument>
        <argument>--stack-name</argument>
        <argument>${integration.test.stack.name}</argument>
        <argument>--capabilities</argument>
        <argument>CAPABILITY_IAM</argument>
      </arguments>
    </configuration>
  </execution>
</executions>
</plugin>
```

It takes several lines of XML to describe, but in this example we're calling the SAM CLI binary with the same arguments that we used in Chapter 5.

The `${integration.test.code.bucket}` and `${integration.test.stack.name}` properties come from the top-level *pom.xml* file and are defined like this:

```
<properties>
  <maven.build.timestamp.format>
    yyyyMMddHHmmss
  </maven.build.timestamp.format>
  <integration.test.code.bucket>
    ${env.CF_BUCKET}
  </integration.test.code.bucket>
  <integration.test.stack.name>
    chapter6-it-${maven.build.timestamp}
  </integration.test.stack.name>
</properties>
```

Our Maven process populates the value of `${integration.test.code.bucket}` with the value of the `$CF_BUCKET` environment variable, which we've used in previous chapters. The `${maven.build.timestamp.format}` *pom.xml* documentation (*https://oreil.ly/FIl7J*) tells Maven to construct a human-readable numeric timestamp, which we then use as part of the `${integration.test.stack.name}`. This gives us a (nearly) unique CloudFormation stack name, so multiple end-to-end tests could be run simultaneously using the same AWS account and region (as long as they're not started in the same second!).

What we don't see in this Maven configuration are any AWS credentials. Processes started by the Maven "exec" plug-in will pick up environment variables automatically, so this will use the AWS environment variables that we've been using for the last several chapters without any additional configuration on our part.

In most cases you should use separate AWS accounts for your test environments to isolate test infrastructure and data. To achieve that here, simply supply a different set of AWS credentials via environment variables.

After our end-to-end test runs, teardown of the CloudFormation stack works in the same way, as part of Maven's "post-integration-test" lifecycle phase:

```xml
<execution>
  <id>001-cfn-delete</id>
  <phase>post-integration-test</phase>
  <goals>
    <goal>exec</goal>
  </goals>
  <configuration>
    <basedir>${project.parent.basedir}</basedir>
    <executable>aws</executable>
    <arguments>
      <argument>cloudformation</argument>
      <argument>delete-stack</argument>
      <argument>--stack-name</argument>
      <argument>${integration.test.stack.name}</argument>
    </arguments>
  </configuration>
</execution>
```

We've now reached the very top of the Test Pyramid. The end-to-end test brings a lot of value: it deploys and runs the entire application. It tests the critical path just as it would be executed in production. However, with that value comes a fairly high cost—we need a lot of extra configuration and setup and teardown code to make sure the test can be run repeatedly and without any affinity to a particular AWS account or region. Despite those efforts, this test is still vulnerable to vendor outages, environment changes, and the indeterminate behavior inherent in operating over a global network.

In other words, our end-to-end test is brittle and costly to maintain compared to the unit and functional tests. For this reason, you should try to write as few end-to-end tests as possible and instead rely on more, lower-cost tests to fully exercise your application.

Local Cloud Testing

For years, an inherent and unassailable property of a good development workflow was the ability to run the entire application or system locally, without touching any external resources. For a traditional desktop or server application, this might mean just running the application itself, or perhaps the application and a database. For a web application, the list of requirements might include a reverse proxy, a web server, and a job queue.

But what happens when we start using vendor-managed cloud services? Our initial reaction might be to try to achieve the same fully local development workflow we were used to before, using tools like localstack (*https://oreil.ly/TbcEo*) and `sam local` ("sam local invoke" on page 154). This approach might seem tenable at first, but it quickly puts us at odds with a cloud-first architecture in which we want to take full advantage of scalable, reliable, fully managed services provided by a cloud vendor. Most importantly, we don't want to limit our service choices to only those that enable our development workflow. This is the tail wagging the dog!

What are the difficulties with fully local development in a world of vendor-managed cloud services? The fundamental issue is fidelity: it is simply impossible for a local version of a service (like S3 or DynamoDB or Lambda) to have the same properties as the cloud version. Even if the local analogue is provided by the vendor (in this case AWS), it will have at least some of the following issues:

- Missing features
- Different (or absent) control plane behavior (e.g., creating DynamoDB tables)
- Different scaling behavior
- Different latency (e.g., extremely low latency for the local analogue compared to the cloud service)
- Different failure modes
- Different (or no) security controls

Having run into these issues time after time, we advocate for the pragmatic testing approach taken in this chapter. We rely extensively on unit tests to verify the behavior of specific pieces of functionality, and we use those tests to rapidly iterate during development of individual Lambda functions. Functional tests exercise the capability of a Lambda function using mocks or stubs in place of AWS SDK clients and other external dependencies. Finally, a few full-fledged end-to-end tests let us execute the entire application in the cloud, using the same SAM infrastructure template and CLI commands that we would use in production.

---

sam local invoke

The SAM CLI provides a few different methods to execute Lambda functions locally, with or without an API Gateway layer. While these methods can be useful for a brief ad hoc test, they fall victim to the issues described in this section. The local execution environment of a Lambda function lacks fidelity compared to the actual cloud service. We can see this lack of fidelity manifested in a couple of different ways, using `sam local invoke`.

First, while `sam local invoke` parses the *template.yaml* file to find the relevant Lambda resources and paths to local code artifacts, it doesn't perform any kind of higher-level validation of SAM (or CloudFormation) resources or of the structure of the template in general.

Second, the runtime environment itself differs from the real Lambda platform. For example, we can configure our Lambda functions to use less (or more) memory than would be allowed by the Lambda platform, and `sam local invoke` won't pick that up.

These issues (and others like them) aren't significant in isolation. The real danger, however, is that tools like `sam local invoke` allow developers to build up a sense of confidence that a Lambda that correctly executes locally will run without errors in the cloud. In many cases, those developers are then confronted by new issues when they finally deploy their applications to the cloud.

Given the simplicity of the Lambda programming model, it's unclear that `sam local invoke` adds enough value (over the unit and functional tests described in this chapter) to make it part of a local testing process.

Cloud Test Environments

For the unit and functional testing we've described in this chapter, a local environment with Java, Maven, and your favorite IDE will suffice nicely. For the end-to-end tests, you need access to an AWS account. This is all straightforward for a single developer working in isolation, but when working as part of a larger team, it can get more complex.

When you're working as a part of a larger team, what's the best way to work with cloud resources? We have found that a good place to start is for each developer to have an isolated development account and for the team as a whole to have one account per shared integration environment (e.g., dev, test, staging). Things can get tricky when relying on truly shared resources (such as databases or S3 buckets), but in general maintaining isolation during rapid development prevents an entire class of issues ranging from accidental deletion to resource contention.

A rigorous infrastructure-as-code approach makes managing resources in multiple accounts much easier. Taking it a step further, an infrastructure-as-code approach to setting up build pipelines means that standing up and deploying a serverless application in a new account might be as simple as deploying a single CloudFormation stack representing the build pipeline, which will then pull the latest source code and deploy the application.

Canary Testing with CloudWatch Synthetics

CloudWatch Synthetics (*https://oreil.ly/XbXfP*) is a new service (in preview at the time of writing) that allows developers to create small scripts, called *canaries*, that exercise a deployed application in the same way a user might. Canaries can be run on a schedule or just once, and they can trigger CloudWatch alarms if they fail. The code for a canary is written in JavaScript and has access to the Synthetics library as well as Puppeteer (*https://oreil.ly/SUDHt*) and Chromium (*https://www.chromium.org/Home*). As you might have guessed, behind-the-scenes canaries are simply managed Lambda functions, and as such they have access to 1GB of RAM and up to a 10-minute timeout.

You might think that this new capability could take the place of end-to-end tests. While it can certainly be used across multiple environments (e.g., you can run a canary in your end-to-end test environment), keep in mind that Synthetics is meant to exercise an application from the user's perspective. This means that a canary shouldn't have access to components or services that a user doesn't have access too, which precludes testing asynchronous operations and side effects. Furthermore, Synthetics tightly couples canary failures to alarms, which isn't the mechanism by which test failures should be surfaced.

Once Synthetics is generally available, we strongly recommend considering it as part of your application monitoring strategy (see Chapter 7).

Summary

Testing serverless applications is not substantively different than testing traditional applications—it's all about finding the right balance of coverage, complexity, cost, and value, and scaling our testing approach to work for a team.

In this chapter, you learned that the Test Pyramid can guide your testing strategy for a serverless application. We refactored our Lambda code to ease unit testing and to enable functional testing without a network connection. The end-to-end test demonstrated the efficacy of an infrastructure-as-code approach as well as the high degree of complexity inherent in testing a distributed application.

You saw that trying to run cloud services for local testing is subject to a host of issues, especially the lack of fidelity that can be achieved locally. If you want to test a cloud-based application, at some point you have to actually run it in the cloud! Finally, for a team to work effectively in this way, developers should have isolated cloud accounts, and teams should have shared integration environments.

Through testing, we now have confidence that our application will behave as expected. In the next chapter, we'll explore how to gain insight into the behavior of our deployed applications through logging, metrics, and tracing.

Exercise

The code and tests in this chapter exercise S3 and SNS. Write an integration test for the Chapter 5 application that makes HTTP calls from Java to the deployed API Gateway and then asserts on the responses (and side effects). For extra credit, use Java 11's new native HTTP client (*https://oreil.ly/ctKPo*)!

CHAPTER 7

Logging, Metrics, and Tracing

In this chapter, we'll explore how to enhance the observability of Lambda functions through logging, metrics, and tracing. Through logging, you'll learn how to gain information from specific events occuring during the execution of your Lambda functions. Platform and business metrics will give insight into the operational health of our serverless application. Finally, distributed tracing will let you see how requests flow to the different managed services and components that make up our architecture.

We'll use the Weather API from Chapter 5 to explore the wide variety of logging, metrics, and tracing options available for serverless applications on AWS. Similar to the data pipeline changes we made in Chapter 6, you'll notice that the Weather API Lambda functions have been refactored to use the `aws-lambda-java-events` library.

Logging

Given the following log message, what can we infer about the state of the application that generated it?

```
Recorded a temperature of 78 F from Brooklyn, NY
```

We know the values of some of the data (the temperature measurement and location), but not much else. When was this data received or processed? In the larger context of our application, what request generated this data? Which Java class and method produced this log message? How can we correlate this with other, possibly related, log messages?

Fundamentally, this is an unhelpful log message. It lacks context and specificity. If a message like this was repeated hundreds or thousands of times (perhaps with different temperature or location values), it would lose meaning. When our log messages are prose (e.g., a sentence or phrase), they are more difficult to parse without resorting to regular expressions or pattern matching.

As we explore logging in our Lambda functions, keep in mind a few properties of high-value log messages:

Data rich
> We want to capture as much data as is feasible and cost-effective. The more data we have, the more questions we can ask without having to go back and add more logging after that fact.

High cardinality
> Data values that make a particular log message unique are especially important. For example, a field like Request ID will have a large number of unique values, whereas a field like Thread Priority may not (especially in a single-threaded Lambda function).

Machine readable
> Using JSON or another standardized format that is easily machine readable (without custom parsing logic) will ease analysis by downstream tools.

CloudWatch Logs

CloudWatch Logs is, as the name would suggest, AWS's log collection, aggregation, and processing service. Through a variety of mechanisms, it receives log data from applications and other AWS services and makes that data accessible through a web console as well as via an API.

The two main organizational components of CloudWatch Logs are log groups and log streams. A log group is a top-level grouping for a set of related log streams. A log stream is a list of log messages, usually originating from a single application or function instance.

Lambda and CloudWatch Logs

In a serverless application, by default there is one log group per Lambda function, which contains many log streams. Each log stream contains the log messages for all the function invocations for a particular function instance. Recall from Chapter 3 that the Lambda runtime captures anything written to standard output (`System.out` in Java) or standard error (`System.err`), and forwards that information to CloudWatch Logs.

The log output for a Lambda function looks something like this:

```
START RequestId: 6127fe67-a406-11e8-9030-69649c02a345
  Version: $LATEST
Recorded a temperature of 78 F from Brooklyn, NY
```

```
END RequestId: 6127fe67-a406-11e8-9030-69649c02a345
REPORT RequestId: 6127fe67-a406-11e8-9030-69649c02a345
    Duration: 2001.52 ms
    Billed Duration: 2000 ms
    Memory Size: 512 MB
    Max Memory Used: 51 MB
```

The START, END, and REPORT lines are automatically added by the Lambda platform. Of particular interest is the UUID value labeled RequestId. This is an identifier that's unique for each *requested* Lambda function invocation. The most common source of repeated RequestId values in logs is when our functions have an error and the platform retries the execution (see "Error Handling" on page 183). Aside from that, since the Lambda platform (like most distributed systems) has "at least once" semantics, the platform may occasionally invoke a function with the same RequestId more than once even when there are no errors (we examine "at least once" behavior in "At-Least-Once Delivery" on page 227).

LambdaLogger

The log line between the START and END lines above was generated using System.out.println. This is a perfectly reasonable way to get started with logging from simple Lambda functions, but there are several other options that provide a combination of sensible behavior and customization. The first of these options is the LambdaLogger (*https://oreil.ly/lXGJB*) class that AWS provides.

This logger is accessed via the Lambda Context object, so we'll have to alter our WeatherEvent Lambda handler function to include that parameter, as follows:

```
public class WeatherEventLambda {
    …
    public APIGatewayProxyResponseEvent handler(
        APIGatewayProxyRequestEvent request,
        Context context
        ) throws IOException {

        context.getLogger().log("Request received");
        …
    }
}
```

The output of this log statement looks just as if it had been generated using Sys tem.out.println:

```
START RequestId: 4f40a12b-1112-4b3a-94a9-89031d57defa Version: $LATEST
Request received
END RequestId: 4f40a12b-1112-4b3a-94a9-89031d57defa
```

You can see the difference between LambdaLogger and the System println methods when we have output that includes newlines, like a stack trace:

```
public class WeatherEventLambda {
    …
    public APIGatewayProxyResponseEvent handler(
        APIGatewayProxyRequestEvent request,
        Context context
        ) throws IOException {

        StringWriter stringWriter = new StringWriter();
        Exception e = new Exception();
        e.printStackTrace(new PrintWriter(stringWriter));

        context.getLogger().log(stringWriter);
        …
    }
}
```

Using `System.err.println` the stack trace is printed on multiple lines, as multiple CloudWatch Logs entries (Figure 7-1).

```
▶   16:47:58                        START RequestId: 0cac6088-aa76-45da-8709-9c1c44009f1e Version: $LATEST
▼   16:47:58                        System.err: java.lang.Exception

System.err: java.lang.Exception

▼   16:47:58                                at book.api.WeatherEventLambda.handler(WeatherEventLambda.java:28)

at book.api.WeatherEventLambda.handler(WeatherEventLambda.java:28)

▼   16:47:58                                at sun.reflect.NativeMethodAccessorImpl.invoke0(Native Method)

at sun.reflect.NativeMethodAccessorImpl.invoke0(Native Method)

▼   16:47:58                                at sun.reflect.NativeMethodAccessorImpl.invoke(NativeMethodAccessorImpl.java:62)

at sun.reflect.NativeMethodAccessorImpl.invoke(NativeMethodAccessorImpl.java:62)
```

Figure 7-1. Stack trace output in CloudWatch Logs using System.err.println

Using LambdaLogger, that stack trace is a single entry (which can be expanded in the web console, as shown in Figure 7-2).

This feature alone is a compelling reason to use `LambdaLogger` instead of `System.out.println` or `System.err.println`, especially when printing exception stack traces.

```
▼   16:47:58                    LambdaLogger: java.lang.Exception at book.api.WeatherEventLambda.handler(WeatherEve

LambdaLogger: java.lang.Exception
at book.api.WeatherEventLambda.handler(WeatherEventLambda.java:28)
at sun.reflect.NativeMethodAccessorImpl.invoke0(Native Method)
at sun.reflect.NativeMethodAccessorImpl.invoke(NativeMethodAccessorImpl.java:62)
at sun.reflect.DelegatingMethodAccessorImpl.invoke(DelegatingMethodAccessorImpl.java:43)
at java.lang.reflect.Method.invoke(Method.java:498)
at lambdainternal.EventHandlerLoader$PojoMethodRequestHandler.handleRequest(EventHandlerLoader.java:259)
at lambdainternal.EventHandlerLoader$PojoHandlerAsStreamHandler.handleRequest(EventHandlerLoader.java:178)
at lambdainternal.EventHandlerLoader$2.call(EventHandlerLoader.java:888)
at lambdainternal.AWSLambda.startRuntime(AWSLambda.java:293)
at lambdainternal.AWSLambda.<clinit>(AWSLambda.java:64)
at java.lang.Class.forName0(Native Method)
at java.lang.Class.forName(Class.java:348)
at lambdainternal.LambdaRTEntry.main(LambdaRTEntry.java:114)
```

Figure 7-2. Stack trace output in CloudWatch Logs using LambdaLogger

Java Logging Frameworks

LambdaLogger is often sufficient for simple Lambda functions. However, as you'll see later in this chapter, it's often useful to customize log output to meet specific requirements, like capturing business metrics or generating application alerts. While it's certainly possible to generate this kind of output using Java's standard library, like String.format (*https://oreil.ly/9qlLO*), it's easier to use an existing logging framework like Log4J or Java Commons Logging. These frameworks provide conveniences like log levels, property or file-based configuration, and a variety of output formats. They also make it easy to include relevant system and application context (like the AWS request ID) with each log message.

When Lambda was first made available, AWS provided a custom appender for a very old, unsupported version of Log4J. Using this old version of a popular logging framework made it challenging to integrate newer logging features in Lambda-based serverless applications. As a result, we spent a fair amount of time and effort to build a more modern logging solution for Lambda functions called lambda-monitoring, which uses SLF4J and Logback.

However, AWS now provides a library (*https://oreil.ly/rywdy*) with a custom log appender, which uses LambdaLogger under the covers (*https://oreil.ly/CrRoX*), for the most recent version of Log4J2 (*https://oreil.ly/8UEaw*). We now recommend using this setup as AWS has outlined in the Java logging section (*https://oreil.ly/2YP8h*) of the Lambda documentation. Setting up this method of logging simply involves adding a few additional dependencies, adding a *log4j2.xml* configuration file, and then using org.apache.logging.log4j.Logger in our code.

Here are the *pom.xml* additions for our Weather API project:

```xml
<dependencies>
  <dependency>
    <groupId>com.amazonaws</groupId>
    <artifactId>aws-lambda-java-log4j2</artifactId>
    <version>1.1.0</version>
  </dependency>
  <dependency>
    <groupId>org.apache.logging.log4j</groupId>
    <artifactId>log4j-core</artifactId>
    <version>2.12.1</version>
  </dependency>
  <dependency>
    <groupId>org.apache.logging.log4j</groupId>
    <artifactId>log4j-api</artifactId>
    <version>2.12.1</version>
  </dependency>
</dependencies>
```

The *log4j2.xml* configuration file should be familiar to anyone who has used Log4J. It uses the `Lambda` appender provided by AWS, and allows customization of the log pattern:

```xml
<?xml version="1.0" encoding="UTF-8"?>
<Configuration packages="com.amazonaws.services.lambda.runtime.log4j2">
  <Appenders>
    <Lambda name="Lambda">
      <PatternLayout>
        <pattern>
          %d{yyyy-MM-dd HH:mm:ss} %X{AWSRequestId} %-5p %c{1}:%L—%m%n
        </pattern>
      </PatternLayout>
    </Lambda>
  </Appenders>
  <Loggers>
    <Root level="info">
      <AppenderRef ref="Lambda"/>
    </Root>
  </Loggers>
</Configuration>
```

Notice that the log pattern includes the Lambda request ID (`%X{AWSRequestId}`). In our previous logging examples, that request ID wasn't included in most output lines —it just showed up at the beginning and end of an invocation. By including it in every line, we can tie each piece of output to a specific request, which is helpful if we inspect these logs using another tool or download them for offline analysis.

In our Lambda function, we set up the logger and use its `error` method to log out a message at ERROR level (*https://oreil.ly/pygbx*), as well as the exception:

```
import org.apache.logging.log4j.LogManager;
import org.apache.logging.log4j.Logger;

public class WeatherEventLambda {
  private static Logger logger = LogManager.getLogger();
  …
  public APIGatewayProxyResponseEvent handler(
    APIGatewayProxyRequestEvent request, Context context)
    throws IOException {

    Exception e = new Exception("Test exception");
    logger.error("Log4J logger", e);
    ...
  }
}
```

The output from the Lambda Log4J2 appender is shown in Figure 7-3.

```
▼   18:12:50              2019-09-01 18:12:50 5b6bc661-73bb-435b-b187-595273626441 ERROR WeatherEventLambda:39

2019-09-01 18:12:50 5b6bc661-73bb-435b-b187-595273626441 ERROR WeatherEventLambda:39 - Log4J logger
java.lang.Exception: Test exception
at book.api.WeatherEventLambda.handler(WeatherEventLambda.java:32) [task/:?]
at sun.reflect.NativeMethodAccessorImpl.invoke0(Native Method) ~[?:1.8.0_201]
at sun.reflect.NativeMethodAccessorImpl.invoke(NativeMethodAccessorImpl.java:62) ~[?:1.8.0_201]
at sun.reflect.DelegatingMethodAccessorImpl.invoke(DelegatingMethodAccessorImpl.java:43) ~[?:1.8.0_201]
at java.lang.reflect.Method.invoke(Method.java:498) ~[?:1.8.0_201]
at lambdainternal.EventHandlerLoader$PojoMethodRequestHandler.handleRequest(EventHandlerLoader.java:259) [LambdaSand
at lambdainternal.EventHandlerLoader$PojoHandlerAsStreamHandler.handleRequest(EventHandlerLoader.java:178) [LambdaSc
at lambdainternal.EventHandlerLoader$2.call(EventHandlerLoader.java:888) [LambdaSandboxJava-1.0.jar:?]
at lambdainternal.AWSLambda.startRuntime(AWSLambda.java:293) [LambdaSandboxJava-1.0.jar:?]
at lambdainternal.AWSLambda.<clinit>(AWSLambda.java:64) [LambdaSandboxJava-1.0.jar:?]
at java.lang.Class.forName0(Native Method) ~[?:1.8.0_201]
at java.lang.Class.forName(Class.java:348) [?:1.8.0_201]
at lambdainternal.LambdaRTEntry.main(LambdaRTEntry.java:114) [LambdaJavaRTEntry-1.0.jar:?]
```

Figure 7-3. Stack trace output in CloudWatch Logs using Log4J2

It includes the timestamp, the AWS request ID, the log level (ERROR in this case), the file and line that called the logging method, and a correctly formatted exception. We can use Log4J-provided bridge libraries to route log messages from other logging frameworks to our Log4J appender. The most useful application of this technique, at least for our `WeatherEventLambda`, is to gain insight into the behavior of the AWS Java SDK, which uses Apache Commons Logging (previously known as Jakarta Commons Logging, or JCL).

First, we add the Log4J JCL bridge library to the `dependencies` section of our *pom.xml* file:

```
<dependency>
  <groupId>org.apache.logging.log4j</groupId>
  <artifactId>log4j-jcl</artifactId>
  <version>2.12.1</version>
</dependency>
```

Next, we enable debug logging in the `Loggers` section of our *log4j2.xml* file:

```
<Loggers>
  <Root level="debug">
    <AppenderRef ref="Lambda"/>
  </Root>
</Loggers>
```

Now we can see detailed log information from the AWS Java SDK (Figure 7-4).

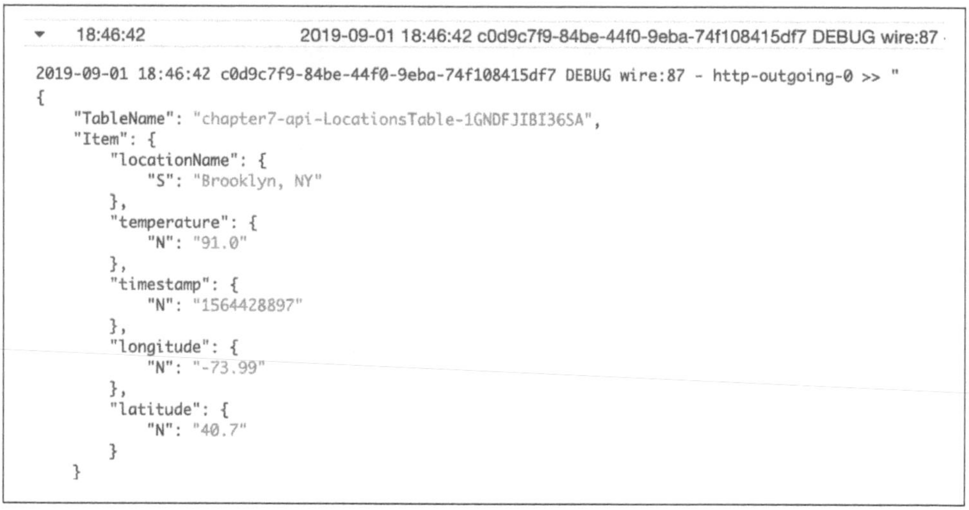

```
▼   18:46:42                  2019-09-01 18:46:42 c0d9c7f9-84be-44f0-9eba-74f108415df7 DEBUG wire:87

2019-09-01 18:46:42 c0d9c7f9-84be-44f0-9eba-74f108415df7 DEBUG wire:87 - http-outgoing-0 >> "
{
    "TableName": "chapter7-api-LocationsTable-1GNDFJIBI36SA",
    "Item": {
        "locationName": {
            "S": "Brooklyn, NY"
        },
        "temperature": {
            "N": "91.0"
        },
        "timestamp": {
            "N": "1564428897"
        },
        "longitude": {
            "N": "-73.99"
        },
        "latitude": {
            "N": "40.7"
        }
    }
}
```

Figure 7-4. Detailed debug logging from the AWS SDK

We probably don't want this information all the time, but it's useful for debugging if there's a problem—in this case we see exactly what the body of the DynamoDB `PutItem` API call contains.

By using more sophisticated logging frameworks, we gain additional insight into the context surrounding our log output. We can separate the logs for different Lambda requests using the request ID. Using the log level, we can understand if some log lines represent errors, or warnings about the state of our application, or if other lines might be ignored (or analyzed later) because they contain voluminous but less relevant debugging information.

CloudWatch Logs Costs

One word of caution—the cost of logging at high volume from Lambda functions is often surprising. At the time of writing, CloudWatch Logs costs $0.50 per GB of data ingested. If your Lambda functions generate 100KB of log output per invocation (perhaps by processing a batch of one thousand records from Kinesis and generating a single line of output for each record), and are invoked 1M times, that's 100GB of log output, which will cost $50. At 1M invocations per day, that's $1,500 of CloudWatch Logs in a month!

The admonition here is not to eliminate logging from your Lambda functions but to generate meaningful log output that's worth the cost. We'll discuss how to gain maximum value from log output in the next section.

Structured Logging

Our logging system as described in the previous section is capturing a great deal of useful information and context, ready to be used to inspect and improve our application.

However, when it comes time to extract some value from this great store of log data, it's often difficult to access, it's tricky to query, and because the actual messages are still essentially free-form text, you usually have to resort to a series of inscrutable regular expressions to find exactly the lines you're looking for. There are some standardized formats that have established conventions for the values of certain space or tab-delimited fields, but inevitably the regexes make an appearance in downstream processes and tooling.

Rather than continue with the free-text free-for-all, we can use a technique called *structured logging* to standardize our log output and make all of it easily searchable via a standard query language.

Take this JSON log entry as an example:

```
{
  "thread": "main",
  "level": "INFO",
  "loggerName": "book.api.WeatherEventLambda",
  "message": {
    "locationName": "Brooklyn, NY",
    "action": "record",
    "temperature": 78,
    "timestamp": 1564506117
  },
  "endOfBatch": false,
  "loggerFqcn": "org.apache.logging.log4j.spi.AbstractLogger",
  "instant": {
```

```
    "epochSecond": 1564506117,
    "nanoOfSecond": 400000000
  },
  "contextMap": {
    "AWSRequestId": "d814bbbe-559b-4798-aee0-31ddf9235a76"
  },
  "threadId": 1,
  "threadPriority": 5
}
```

Rather than relying on an ordering of fields to extract information, we can use JSON path specifications. For example, if we want to extract the `temperature` field, we can use the JSON path `.message.temperature`. The CloudWatch Logs service supports this both for searching in the web console (see Figure 7-5), and for creating Metric Filters, which we'll discuss later in this chapter.

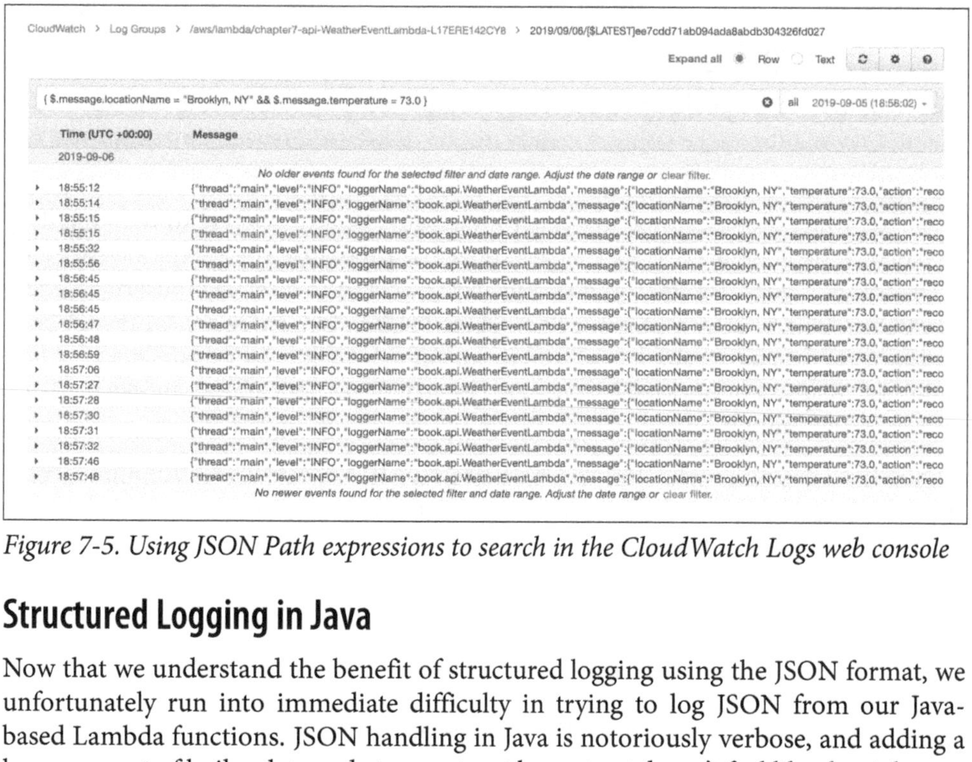

Figure 7-5. Using JSON Path expressions to search in the CloudWatch Logs web console

Structured Logging in Java

Now that we understand the benefit of structured logging using the JSON format, we unfortunately run into immediate difficulty in trying to log JSON from our Java-based Lambda functions. JSON handling in Java is notoriously verbose, and adding a large amount of boilerplate code to construct log output doesn't feel like the right way to go.

Fortunately, we can use Log4J2 to generate JSON log output (Log4J2 `JSONLayout` (*https://oreil.ly/G4EYb*)). The following *log4j2.xml* configuration will enable JSON-formatted output to `STDOUT`, which for our Lambda functions means that the output will be sent to CloudWatch Logs:

```xml
<?xml version="1.0" encoding="UTF-8"?>
<Configuration packages="com.amazonaws.services.lambda.runtime.log4j2">
  <Appenders>
    <Lambda name="Lambda">
      <JsonLayout
        compact="true"
        eventEol="true"
        objectMessageAsJsonObject="true"
        properties="true"/>
    </Lambda>
  </Appenders>
  <Loggers>
    <Root level="info">
      <AppenderRef ref="Lambda"/>
    </Root>
  </Loggers>
</Configuration>
```

In our Lambda code, we set up the Log4J2 logger as a static field:

```
...
private static Logger logger = LogManager.getLogger();
...
```

Rather than logging a string like `Recorded a temperature of 78 F from Brooklyn, NY`, we'll instead build up a `Map` with keys and values, as follows:

```
HashMap<Object, Object> message = new HashMap<>();
message.put("action", "record");
message.put("locationName", weatherEvent.locationName);
message.put("temperature", weatherEvent.temperature);
message.put("timestamp", weatherEvent.timestamp);

logger.info(new ObjectMessage(message));
```

Here's the output from that log line:

```
{
  "thread": "main",
  "level": "INFO",
  "loggerName": "book.api.WeatherEventLambda",
  "message": {
    "locationName": "Brooklyn, NY",
    "action": "record",
    "temperature": 78,
    "timestamp": 1564506117
  },
  "endOfBatch": false,
  "loggerFqcn": "org.apache.logging.log4j.spi.AbstractLogger",
  "instant": {
    "epochSecond": 1564506117,
    "nanoOfSecond": 400000000
  },
  "contextMap": {
```

```
    "AWSRequestId": "d814bbbe-559b-4798-aee0-31ddf9235a76"
  },
  "threadId": 1,
  "threadPriority": 5
}
```

A caveat worth noting—the information relevant to our application is there under the `message` key, but it's buried in a sea of other output. Unfortunately, most of that output is baked into the Log4J2 `JsonLayout`, so we can't remove it without some work. As we'll see in the next section, however, the benefits of JSON-formatted log events are well worth the increase in verbosity.

CloudWatch Logs Insights

Structured logging enables us to use far more sophisticated tools to analyze our logs, both in real time as well as after incidents. While the original CloudWatch Logs web console has some support for using JSONPath expressions to query log data (as shown earlier), truly sophisticated analysis has, until recently, required either downloading logs directly, or forwarding them to another service.

CloudWatch Logs Insights (*https://oreil.ly/mPqKe*) is a new addition to the CloudWatch Logs ecosystem, providing a powerful search engine and purpose-built query language ideally suited to analyzing structured logs. Taking our example JSON log line from the previous section, let's now imagine that we had a month's worth of hourly data that has been logged out to CloudWatch Logs. We might want to do some quick analysis of that log data to see what the minimum, average, and maximum temperatures for each day was, but only for Brooklyn.

The following CloudWatch Logs Insights query accomplishes just that:

```
filter message.action = "record"
    and message.locationName = "Brooklyn, NY"
| fields date_floor(concat(message.timestamp, "000"), 1d) as Day,
    message.temperature
| stats min(message.temperature) as Low,
    avg(message.temperature) as Average,
    max(message.temperature) as High by Day
| order by Day asc
```

Let's look at what this query is doing, line by line:

1. First we filter the data down to log events that have a value of `record` in the `message.action` field, and a value of "Brooklyn, NY" in the `message.locationName` field.

2. In the second line, we pick out the `message.timestamp` field and add three zeroes to the end before passing it to the `date_floor` method, which will replace a timestamp value (in milliseconds, hence needing to add zeroes) with the earliest

timestamp value for the given day. We also pick out the `message.temperature` field.

3. The third line calculates the minimum, average, and maximum value of the `message.temperature` field, for a day's worth of log events.

4. The last line orders the data by day, starting with the earliest day.

We can see the results of this query in the CloudWatch Logs Insights web console (Figure 7-6).

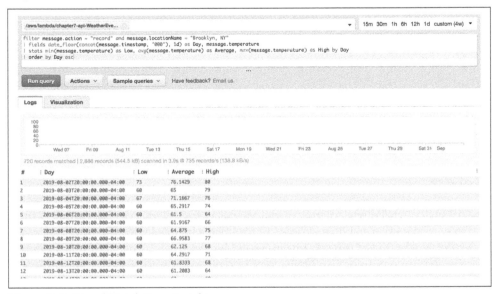

Figure 7-6. CloudWatch Logs Insights

These results can be exported as a CSV file, or graphed using the built-in visualization tool (Figure 7-7).

There are a few caveats to keep in mind with regard to CloudWatch Logs Insights. First, while the tool can be used quite effectively for ad hoc exploration of log data, it cannot (yet) be used to directly generate additional custom metrics or other data products (although we'll see how to generate custom metrics from JSON log data in the next section!). There is an API interface for running queries and accessing results, however, so it is possible to roll your own solution. Last but not least, pricing for queries is based on the amount of data scanned.

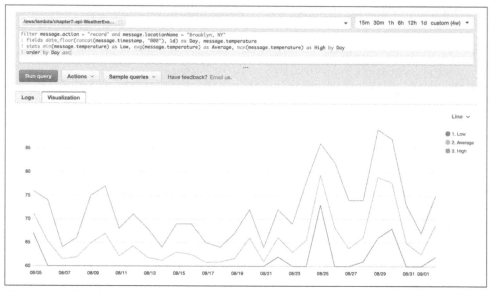

Figure 7-7. CloudWatch Logs Insights visualization

Metrics

Log messages are discrete snapshots into the state of a system at a given point in time. Metrics, on the other hand, are meant to produce a higher-level view of the state of a system over a period of time. While an individual metric is a snapshot in time, a series of metrics shows trends and behaviors of a system as it runs, over long periods of time.

CloudWatch Metrics

CloudWatch Metrics is AWS's metrics repository service. It receives metrics from most AWS services. At the most fundamental level, a metric is simply a set of time-ordered data points. For example, at a given moment, the CPU load of a traditional server might be 64%. A few seconds later, it might be 65%. Over a given time period, a minimum, a maximum, and other statistics (such as percentiles) can be calculated for the metric.

Metrics are grouped by namespace (e.g., /aws/lambda), and then by metric name (e.g., WeatherEventLambda). Metrics can also have associated dimensions, which are simply more granular identifiers—for example given a metric tracking application errors in a nonserverless application, one dimension might be server IP.

CloudWatch metrics are a primary tool for monitoring the behavior of AWS's services as well as our own applications.

Lambda Platform Metrics

Right out of the box, AWS provides a myriad of function and account-level metrics with which to monitor the overall health and availability of your serverless applications. We'll refer to these as platform metrics, because they're provided by the Lambda platform without requiring any extra configuration from us.

For individual functions, the Lambda platform provides the following metrics:

Invocations
> The number of times a function is invoked (whether successful or not).

Throttles
> The number of times an invocation attempt is throttled by the platform.

Errors
> The number of times a function invocation returns an error.

Duration
> The number of milliseconds of "elapsed wall clock time" from when a function begins executing to when it stops. This metric also supports percentiles (*https:// oreil.ly/-Njgn*).

ConcurrentExecutions
> How many concurrent executions of a function are happening at a given point in time.

For functions that are invoked by Kinesis or DynamoDB stream event sources, an IteratorAge metric tracks the number of milliseconds between when the function received a batch of records and the time the last record in that batch was written to the stream. Effectively, this metric shows you how far behind the stream a Lambda function is at a given point in time.

For functions configured with a dead letter queue (DLQ), a DeadLetterErrors metric is incremented when the function is unable to write a message to the DLQ (see "Error Handling" on page 183 for more about DLQs).

Additionally, the platform aggregates the Invocations, Throttles, Errors, Duration, and ConcurrentExecutions metrics across all functions in the account and region. An UnreservedConcurrentExecutions metric aggregates the concurrent executions for all functions in the account and region that do not have a custom concurrency limit specified.

Metrics that are generated by the Lambda platform include the following extra dimensions: FunctionName, Resource (e.g., function version or alias) and Executed Version (for alias invocations, which are discussed in the next chapter). Each of the per-function metrics mentioned can have these dimensions.

Business Metrics

Platform metrics and application logging are important tools for monitoring our serverless applications, but neither is useful in assessing whether our application is performing its business functions correctly and completely. For example, a metric capturing the duration of a Lambda execution is useful to catch unexpected performance issues, but it doesn't tell us if the Lambda function (or the application as a whole) is processing events correctly for our customers. On the other hand, a metric capturing the number of weather events successfully processed for our most popular location tells us that the application (or at least the part related to processing weather events) is working correctly, regardless of the underlying technical implementation.

These *business metrics* can serve not only as a finger on the pulse of our business logic but also as an aggregate metric that's not tied to specifics of an implementation or platform. Using our earlier example, what does it mean if Lambda execution time increases? Are we simply processing more data, or did a configuration or code change impact the performance of our function? Does it even matter? However, if the number of weather events our application processes decreases unexpectedly, we know something is wrong and it warrants an immediate investigation.

In a traditional application, we might use the CloudWatch Metrics API directly, by using the `PutMetricData` API call (*https://oreil.ly/zLHuA*) to proactively push these custom metrics as they're generated. More sophisticated applications might push small batches of metrics at regular intervals instead.

Lambda functions have two qualities that make the `PutMetricData` approach untenable. First, a Lambda function can scale to hundreds or thousands of concurrent executions very quickly. The CloudWatch Metrics API will throttle the `PutMetricData` call (CloudWatch limits (*https://oreil.ly/q2jmF*)), so there's a danger that the very action that's attempting to persist important data may in fact cause a dropout of metrics. Second, because Lambda functions are ephemeral, there is little opportunity or benefit to batching metrics during a single execution. There is no guarantee that a subsequent execution will take place in the same runtime instance, so batching across invocations isn't reliable.

Fortunately, there are two features of CloudWatch metrics that handle this situation in a scalable and reliable manner by moving the generation of CloudWatch metrics data outside of the Lambda execution entirely. The first and newest, called the Cloud-Watch Embedded Metric Format (*https://oreil.ly/pkNXB*), uses a special log format to automatically create metrics. This special log format isn't yet supported by Log4J (without a lot of extra work), so we won't use it here, but in other cases this is the preferred method for generating metrics in Lambda.

The other feature, CloudWatch metric filters (*https://oreil.ly/beOVU*), can also use CloudWatch Logs data to generate metrics. Unlike the embedded metric format, it can access data in columnar and arbitrarily nested JSON structures. This makes it a better choice for situations like ours where we can't easily add JSON keys to the top level of our log statements. It generates metric data by scraping CloudWatch Logs and pushing metrics in batches to the CloudWatch Metrics service.

Our use of structured logging makes setting up a metric filter trivial, using the following addition to our *template.yaml* file:

```
BrooklynWeatherMetricFilter:
  Type: AWS::Logs::MetricFilter
  Properties:
    LogGroupName: !Sub "/aws/lambda/${WeatherEventLambda}"
    FilterPattern: '{$.message.locationName = "Brooklyn, NY"}'
    MetricTransformations:
      - MetricValue: "1"
    MetricNamespace: WeatherApi
    MetricName: BrooklynWeatherEventCount
    DefaultValue: "0"
```

This metric filter will increment the `BrooklynWeatherEventCount` metric every time a JSON log line contains a `message.locationName` field with a "Brooklyn, NY" value. We can access and visualize this metric via the CloudWatch Metrics web console, and we can configure CloudWatch alarms and actions just as with regular platform metrics.

In this example we're effectively incrementing a counter every time an event occurs, but it's also possible (when it makes sense to do so with the data) to use an actual value from the captured log line. See the `MetricFilter MetricTransformation` documentation (*https://oreil.ly/ksKJu*) for more details.

Alarms

As with all CloudWatch metrics, we can use the data to build out alarms to warn us in case something is going wrong. At a minimum, we recommend setting alarms for the `Errors` and `Throttles` platform metrics, if not on a per-account basis, then certainly for production functions.

For functions invoked by Kinesis or DynamoDB stream event sources, the `Iterator Age` metric is a critical indication of whether a function is keeping up with the number of events in the stream (which is a function of the number of shards in the stream, the batch size configured in the Lambda event source, the `ParallelizationFactor` (*https://oreil.ly/ogUdK*), and the performance of the Lambda function itself).

Given the `BrooklynWeatherEventCount` metric we configured in the previous section, here's how the associated CloudWatch alarm is configured. This alarm will alert us (via an SNS message) if that metric value drops to zero (indicating we've stopped receiving weather events for "Brooklyn, NY") for longer than 60 seconds:

```
BrooklynWeatherAlarm:
  Type: AWS::CloudWatch::Alarm
  Properties:
    Namespace: WeatherApi
    MetricName: BrooklynWeatherEventCount
    Statistic: Sum
    ComparisonOperator: LessThanThreshold
    Threshold: 1
    Period: 60
    EvaluationPeriods: 1
    TreatMissingData: breaching
    ActionsEnabled: True
    AlarmActions:
      - !Ref BrooklynWeatherAlarmTopic

BrooklynWeatherAlarmTopic:
  Type: AWS::SNS::Topic
```

Figure 7-8 shows a view of that alarm in the CloudWatch web console.

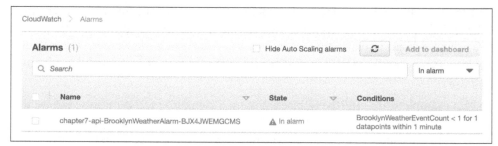

Figure 7-8. BrooklynWeatherAlarm CloudWatch alarm

The SNS message generated when the previous alarm is "breached" can be used to send a notification email, or to trigger a third-party alert system like PagerDuty (*https://www.pagerduty.com*).

As with application components like Lambda functions and DynamoDB tables, we strongly recommend keeping CloudWatch metric filters, alarms, and all other infrastructure in the same *template.yaml* file as everything else. This not only allows us to take advantage of intra-template references and dependencies, but it also keeps our metrics and alarm configurations tied closely to the application itself. If you don't want to generate these operational resources for development versions of your stacks, you can use CloudFormation's Conditions functionality (*https://oreil.ly/iXXkw*).

Distributed Tracing

The metrics and logging capabilities that we've covered thus far provide insight into individual application components like Lambda functions. However, in the case of nontrivial applications with many components, we would have a hard time piecing together the log output and metrics for a request flow that might involve an API Gateway, two Lambda functions, and a DynamoDB table.

Fortunately, this use case is covered by AWS's distributed tracing service, X-Ray. This service will essentially "tag" events either coming into or generated by our application and will keep track of those events as they flow through our application. When a tagged event triggers a Lambda function, X-Ray can then keep track of external service calls that the Lambda function makes and add information about those calls to the trace. If the called service is also X-Ray enabled, the tracing will continue through. In this way, X-Ray not only traces specific events but generates a service map of all of the components in our application and how they interact with each other.

CloudWatch ServiceLens

CloudWatch ServiceLens (*https://oreil.ly/kRn0I*) is a new service (at the time of writing) that integrates CloudWatch and X-Ray to provide a comprehensive, end-to-end overview of your application. In general, almost everything that can be done from the X-Ray console can now also be achieved through ServiceLens.

Over time, we anticipate that this will supersede the X-Ray console, so we encourage you to try it! This AWS blog post (*https://oreil.ly/Vr1AX*) offers an excellent overview of ServiceLens' capabilities and usage.

For AWS Lambda, there are two modes for X-Ray tracing (*https://oreil.ly/juSOL*). The first is `PassThrough`, which means that if an event triggering a Lambda function has already been "tagged" by X-Ray, the invocation of the Lambda function will be tracked by X-Ray. If a triggering event hasn't been tagged, then no trace information will be recorded from Lambda. Conversely, `Active` tracing proactively adds X-Ray trace IDs to all Lambda invocations.

In the following example, we've enabled tracing in our API Gateway, which will tag incoming events with an X-Ray trace ID. The Lambda function is configured in `Pass Through` mode, so when it's triggered by a tagged event from the API Gateway, it will propagate that trace ID to downstream services. Note that *PassThrough* mode is enabled by default if the Lambda's IAM execution role has permission to send data to the X-Ray service; otherwise, it can be configured explicitly as we've done here (in which case SAM adds the appropriate permissions to the Lambda execution role).

Here's the `Globals` section from our SAM *template.yaml* file from Chapter 5, updated to enabled API Gateway tracing:

```
Globals:
  Function:
    Runtime: java8
    MemorySize: 512
    Timeout: 25
    Environment:
      Variables:
        LOCATIONS_TABLE: !Ref LocationsTable
    Tracing: PassThrough
  Api:
    OpenApiVersion: '3.0.1'
    TracingEnabled: true
```

With tracing enabled, we can also add the X-Ray libraries to our *pom.xml* file. By adding these libraries, we'll get the benefit of X-Ray tracing for all of the interactions our Lambda function has with services like DynamoDB and SNS, without having to make any changes to our Java code.

Like the AWS SDK, X-Ray provides a bill of materials (BOM), which keeps version numbers in sync across whichever X-Ray libraries we end up using in our project. To use the X-Ray BOM, add it to the `<dependencyManagement>` section of the top-level *pom.xml* file:

```
<dependency>
  <groupId>com.amazonaws</groupId>
  <artifactId>aws-xray-recorder-sdk-bom</artifactId>
  <version>2.3.0</version>
  <type>pom</type>
  <scope>import</scope>
</dependency>
```

Now we need to add the three X-Ray libraries that will instrument our Java-based Lambda functions:

```
<dependency>
  <groupId>com.amazonaws</groupId>
  <artifactId>aws-xray-recorder-sdk-core</artifactId>
</dependency>
<dependency>
  <groupId>com.amazonaws</groupId>
  <artifactId>aws-xray-recorder-sdk-aws-sdk</artifactId>
</dependency>
<dependency>
  <groupId>com.amazonaws</groupId>
  <artifactId>aws-xray-recorder-sdk-aws-sdk-instrumentor</artifactId>
</dependency>
```

Figure 7-9 shows the X-Ray service map for our API from Chapter 5, showing the API Gateway, Lambda platform, Lambda function, and DynamoDB table:

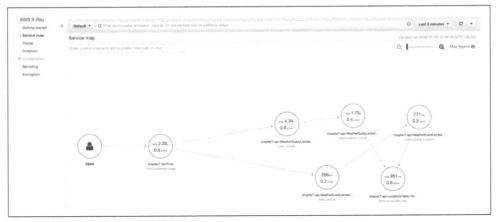

Figure 7-9. X-Ray service map

We can also view a trace for an individual event (in this case, our HTTP POST), which traversed the API Gateway, Lambda, and DynamoDB (Figure 7-10).

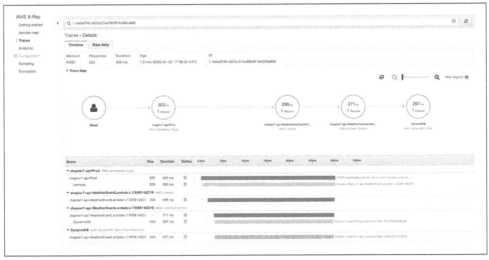

Figure 7-10. X-Ray trace

Finding Errors

What happens when our Lambda function throws an error? We can investigate errors via the X-Ray console, through both the service map and the traces interface.

First, let's introduce an error into the WeatherEvent Lambda, by removing that Lambda's permission to access DynamoDB:

```
WeatherEventLambda:
  Type: AWS::Serverless::Function
  Properties:
    CodeUri: target/lambda.zip
    Handler: book.api.WeatherEventLambda::handler
#      Policies:
#        - DynamoDBCrudPolicy:
#            TableName: !Ref LocationsTable
    Events:
      ApiEvents:
        Type: Api
        Properties:
          Path: /events
          Method: POST
```

After deploying our serverless application stack, we can send an HTTP POST event to the /events endpoint. When the WeatherEvent Lambda attempts to write that event to DynamoDB, it fails and throws an exception. Figure 7-11 shows what the X-Ray service map looks like after that happens.

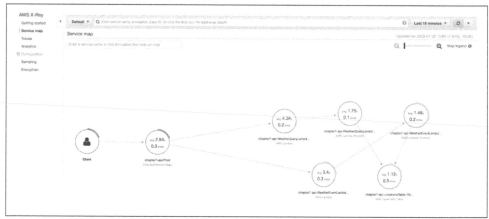

Figure 7-11. X-Ray service map showing an error

And when we drill into the specific request that caused the error, we can see that our POST request returned an HTTP 502 error (Figure 7-12).

Figure 7-12. X-Ray trace showing an error

We can then easily see the specific Java exception that caused the Lambda function to fail by hovering on the error icon next to the portion of the trace that shows the Lambda invocation (Figure 7-13).

Figure 7-13. X-Ray trace showing a Java exception

Clicking through will then show us the full stack trace, right from the X-Ray trace console (Figure 7-14).

Figure 7-14. X-Ray showing a Java exception stack trace

Summary

In this chapter, we covered the variety of ways we can gain insight into exactly how our serverless application is performing and functioning, both at the individual function or component level and as a complete application. We showed how using structured JSON logging enables observability and gives us the ability to surface meaningful business metrics from our highly scalable Lambda functions without overwhelming the CloudWatch API.

Finally, we added a few dependencies to our Maven *pom.xml* and unlocked fully featured distributed tracing capabilities, which not only trace individual requests but also automatically build out a map of all the components of our serverless application and allow us to easily drill into errors or unexpected behavior.

With the basics now covered, in the next chapter we'll dive into the advanced Lambda techniques that will make our production serverless systems robust and reliable.

Exercises

1. This chapter builds on the API Gateway code from Chapter 5. Add X-Ray instrumentation to the updated data pipeline code from Chapter 6, and observe how the interactions with SNS and S3 show up in the X-Ray console.

2. In addition to incrementing a metric as we've done in this chapter, CloudWatch Logs metric filters can parse a metric value from a log line. Use this technique to generate a CloudWatch Logs metric for the temperature in Brooklyn, NY. For extra credit, add an alarm for when the the temperature goes below 32 degrees Fahrenheit!

CHAPTER 8

Advanced AWS Lambda

As we start getting towards the end of the book, it's time to learn some of the aspects of Lambda that are important as you start to build production-ready applications—error handling, scaling, plus a few capabilities of Lambda that we don't use all the time, but are there—and important—when you need them.

Error Handling

All of our examples so far have lived in the wonderful world of rainbows and unicorns where no systems fail and no one makes a mistake in writing code. Of course, back in the real world, Things Go Wrong, and any useful production application and architecture needs to handle the times when errors occur, whether those be errors in our code or in the systems we rely on.

Since AWS Lambda is a "platform," it has certain constraints and behavior when it comes to errors, and in this section we'll dig into what kind of errors can happen, for which contexts, and how we can handle them. As a language note, we use the words *error* and *exception* interchangeably, without the nuance that comes between the two terms in the Java world.

Classes of Error

When using Lambda, there are several different classes of error that can occur. The primary ones are as follows, in order roughly of the time in which they can occur through the processing of an event:

1. Error initializing the Lambda function (a problem loading our code, locating the handler, or with the function signature)

2. Error parsing input into specified function parameters

3. Error communicating with an external downstream service (database, etc).

4. Error generated within the Lambda function (either within its code or within the immediate environment, like an out-of-memory problem)

5. Error caused by function timeout

Another way we can break up errors is into *handled* errors and *unhandled* errors.

For example, let's consider the case where we communicate with a downstream microservice over HTTP, and it throws an error. In this case, we may choose to catch the error within the Lambda function and process it there (a handled error), or we may let the error propagate out to the environment (an unhandled error).

Alternatively, say we specified an incorrect method name in our Lambda configuration. In this case, we are unable to catch the error in the Lambda function code, so this is always an unhandled error.

If we handle an error ourselves, within code, then Lambda really has nothing to do with our particular error handling strategy. We can log to standard error if like, but as we saw in Chapter 7, standard error is treated identically to standard output as far as Lambda as concerned, and no alarms are raised if content is sent to it.

Therefore, the nuances that come with handling errors in Lambda are all about unhandled errors—those that bubble out of our code to the Lambda runtime via an uncaught exception or that happen externally to our code. What happens to these errors? Interestingly, this depends significantly on the type of event source that triggers our Lambda function in the first place, as we will now examine.

The Various Behaviors of Lambda Error Processing

Lambda divides what it does with errors according to the event source that triggers invocation. Every event source is placed into one of the event source types we listed in Chapter 5 (Table 5-1):

- Synchronous event sources (e.g., API Gateway)
- Asynchronous event sources (e.g., S3 and SNS)
- Stream/queue event sources (e.g., Kinesis Data Streams and SQS)

Each of these categories has a different model for processing errors thrown by a Lambda function, as follows.

Synchronous event sources

This is the simplest model. For Lambda functions invoked in this way, the error is propagated back up to the caller, and no automatic retry is performed. How the error is exposed to the upstream client depends on the precise nature of how the Lambda function was called, so you should try forcing errors within your code to see how such problems are exposed.

For example, if API Gateway is the event source, then errors thrown by a Lambda function will result in an error being sent back to API Gateway. API Gateway in turn returns a 500 HTTP response to the original requestor.

Asynchronous event sources

Since this model of invocation is asynchronous, or event oriented, there is no upstream caller that can do anything useful with an error, so Lambda has a more sophisticated error handling model.

First, if an error is detected in this model of invocation, then Lambda will (by default) retry processing the event up to twice further (for a total of three attempts), with a delay between such retries (the precise delay is not documented, but we'll see an example a little later).

If the Lambda function fails for all retry attempts, then the event will be posted to the function's error destination and/or dead letter queue if either is configured (more on this later); otherwise, the event is discarded and lost.

Stream/queue event sources

In the absence of a configured error-handling strategy (see "Handling Kinesis and DynamoDB Stream Errors" on page 191), if an error bubbles up to the Lambda runtime when processing an event from a stream/queue event source, then Lambda will keep retrying the event until either (a) the failing event expires in the upstream source or (b) the problem is resolved. This means that the processing of the stream or queue is effectively blocked until the error is resolved. Note that there are particular nuances here when using streams that are scaled to multiple shards, which we recommend you research if this applies to you.

The following documentation pages are useful when you are considering error handling with Lambda:

- Error Handling and Automatic Retries in AWS Lambda (*https://oreil.ly/4wxMf*)
- AWS Lambda Function Errors in Java (*https://oreil.ly/ag0cu*)

Deep Dive into Asynchronous Event Source Errors

Asynchronous event sources are a popular use of Lambda and have a complicated error processing model, so let's look at this topic a little deeper by way of an example.

Retries

We start with the following code:

```
package book;

import com.amazonaws.services.lambda.runtime.events.S3Event;

public class S3ErroringLambda {
  public void handler(S3Event event) {
    System.out.println("Received new S3 event");
    throw new RuntimeException("This function unable to process S3 Events");
  }
}
```

We wire this up to an S3 bucket in the same way that we did for the `BatchEvents` `Lambda` function in Chapter 5, and we'll see the SAM template for that a little later.

If we upload a file to the S3 bucket attached to this function, we see Figure 8-1 in our logs.

Notice that Lambda tries to process the S3 event three times—once at 20:44:00, then about a minute later, and then about two minutes after that. These are the three total attempts to process an event that Lambda promises for an asynchronous event source.

We are able configure the number of retries that Lambda will perform—0, 1, or 2— using a separate CloudFormation resource. For example, let's configure Lambda not to attempt any retries for the `SingleEventLambda` function from "Example: Building a Serverless Data Pipeline" on page 111. We can add the following resource to the application template:

```
SingleEventInvokeConfig:
  Type: AWS::Lambda::EventInvokeConfig
  Properties:
    FunctionName: !Ref SingleEventLambda
    Qualifier: "$LATEST"
    MaximumRetryAttempts: 0
```

```
2019-08-05T20:44:00.756000 START RequestId: 0a5ea9bf-4dbf-4270-bb67-d69f02922a59 Version: $LATEST
2019-08-05T20:44:01.390000 Received new S3 event
2019-08-05T20:44:01.673000 This function unable to process S3 Events: java.lang.RuntimeException
java.lang.RuntimeException: This function unable to process S3 Events
        at book.S3ErroringLambda.handler(S3ErroringLambda.java:8)
        at sun.reflect.NativeMethodAccessorImpl.invoke0(Native Method)
        at sun.reflect.NativeMethodAccessorImpl.invoke(NativeMethodAccessorImpl.java:62)
        at sun.reflect.DelegatingMethodAccessorImpl.invoke(DelegatingMethodAccessorImpl.java:43)
        at java.lang.reflect.Method.invoke(Method.java:498)
2019-08-05T20:44:02.894000 END RequestId: 0a5ea9bf-4dbf-4270-bb67-d69f02922a59
2019-08-05T20:44:02.894000 REPORT RequestId: 0a5ea9bf-4dbf-4270-bb67-d69f02922a59 ...

2019-08-05T20:45:01.063000 START RequestId: 0a5ea9bf-4dbf-4270-bb67-d69f02922a59 Version: $LATEST
2019-08-05T20:45:01.068000 Received new S3 event
2019-08-05T20:45:01.069000 This function unable to process S3 Events: java.lang.RuntimeException
java.lang.RuntimeException: This function unable to process S3 Events
        at book.S3ErroringLambda.handler(S3ErroringLambda.java:8)
        at sun.reflect.NativeMethodAccessorImpl.invoke0(Native Method)
        at sun.reflect.NativeMethodAccessorImpl.invoke(NativeMethodAccessorImpl.java:62)
        at sun.reflect.DelegatingMethodAccessorImpl.invoke(DelegatingMethodAccessorImpl.java:43)
        at java.lang.reflect.Method.invoke(Method.java:498)
2019-08-05T20:45:01.074000 END RequestId: 0a5ea9bf-4dbf-4270-bb67-d69f02922a59
2019-08-05T20:45:01.074000 REPORT RequestId: 0a5ea9bf-4dbf-4270-bb67-d69f02922a59 ...

2019-08-05T20:47:06.235000 START RequestId: 0a5ea9bf-4dbf-4270-bb67-d69f02922a59 Version: $LATEST
2019-08-05T20:47:06.238000 Received new S3 event
2019-08-05T20:47:06.239000 This function unable to process S3 Events: java.lang.RuntimeException
java.lang.RuntimeException: This function unable to process S3 Events
        at book.S3ErroringLambda.handler(S3ErroringLambda.java:8)
        at sun.reflect.NativeMethodAccessorImpl.invoke0(Native Method)
        at sun.reflect.NativeMethodAccessorImpl.invoke(NativeMethodAccessorImpl.java:62)
        at sun.reflect.DelegatingMethodAccessorImpl.invoke(DelegatingMethodAccessorImpl.java:43)
        at java.lang.reflect.Method.invoke(Method.java:498)
2019-08-05T20:47:06.242000 END RequestId: 0a5ea9bf-4dbf-4270-bb67-d69f02922a59
2019-08-05T20:47:06.242000 REPORT RequestId: 0a5ea9bf-4dbf-4270-bb67-d69f02922a59 ...
```

Figure 8-1. Lambda logs during S3 error

If we don't make any further changes, Lambda won't do anything more after all the retries (if any) are complete—brief data about the original event will be logged, but eventually it will be discarded. For something like S3 this isn't too bad—we can always list all of the objects in S3 later. But for other event sources, this might be a problem if we can't go and regenerate the events once the cause of the error is fixed. There are two solutions to this problem—DLQs and destinations. DLQs have been around longer, so we'll describe them first, but destinations have more capabilities.

Dead letter queues

Lambda provides the capability of automatically forwarding events (for asynchronous sources) that fail all of their retries to a dead letter queue (DLQ). This DLQ can be either an SNS topic or an SQS queue. Once the event is in SNS or SQS, you can do whatever you want with it either immediately, or manually later, in the case of SQS. For example, you may register a separate Lambda function as an SNS topic listener that posts a copy of the failing event to an operations Slack channel for manual processing.

DLQs can be configured along with all the other properties of a Lambda function. For example, we can add a DLQ to our example app, and also add a DLQ processing function, with the SAM template.

Example 8-1. SAM template with DLQ and DLQ listener

```yaml
AWSTemplateFormatVersion: 2010-09-09
Transform: AWS::Serverless-2016-10-31
Description: chapter8-s3-errors

Resources:
  DLQ:
    Type: AWS::SNS::Topic

  ErrorTriggeringBucket:
    Type: AWS::S3::Bucket
    Properties:
      BucketName: !Sub ${AWS::AccountId}-${AWS::Region}-errortrigger

  S3ErroringLambda:
    Type: AWS::Serverless::Function
    Properties:
      Runtime: java8
      MemorySize: 512
      Handler: book.S3ErroringLambda::handler
      CodeUri: target/lambda.zip
      DeadLetterQueue:
        Type: SNS
        TargetArn: !Ref DLQ
      Events:
        S3Event:
          Type: S3
          Properties:
            Bucket: !Ref ErrorTriggeringBucket
            Events: s3:ObjectCreated:*

  DLQProcessingLambda:
    Type: AWS::Serverless::Function
    Properties:
      Runtime: java8
      MemorySize: 512
      Handler: book.DLQProcessingLambda::handler
      CodeUri: target/lambda.zip
      Events:
        SnsEvent:
```

```
Type: SNS
Properties:
  Topic: !Ref DLQ
```

The important elements to observe here are as follows:

- We define our own SNS topic to act as a DLQ.
- Within the application function (S3ErroringLambda), we tell Lambda that we want a DLQ for the function, that it's of type SNS, and that DLQ messages should be sent to the topic we created in this template.
- We also define a separate function (DLQProcessingLambda) that is triggered by events sent to the DLQ.

Our code for DLQProcessingLambda is as follows:

```
package book;

import com.amazonaws.services.lambda.runtime.events.SNSEvent;

public class DLQProcessingLambda {
  public void handler(SNSEvent event) {
    event.getRecords().forEach(snsRecord ->
        System.out.println("Received DLQ event: " + snsRecord.toString())
    );
  }
}
```

Now if we upload a file to S3, we see the following in the logs for DLQProcessing Lambda after the final delivery attempt to S3ErroringLambda:

```
Received DLQ event: {sns: {messageAttributes:
    {RequestID={type: String,value: ff294606-e377-4bad-8f2a-4c5f88042656},
    ErrorCode={type: String,value: 200}, ...
```

The event sent to the DLQ processing function includes the full original event that failed, allowing you to save this off and process later. It also includes the RequestID of the original event, which allows you to search within the application Lambda function's log for clues as to what went wrong.

While in this example we included all of the DLQ resources within the same template as the application itself, you may choose to use resources outside of the application and therefore share those DLQ elements across applications.

Destinations

At the end of 2019 AWS introduced an alternative to DLQs for capturing failed events: *destinations* (*https://oreil.ly/XT6Ds*). Destinations are actually a more powerful feature than DLQ since you can capture both errors *and* successfully processed asynchronous events.

Further, destinations support more types of target than DLQs. SNS and SQS are supported, just as they are with DLQs, but you can also route directly to another Lambda function (skipping the message bus part) or EventBridge.

To configure a Destination, we use the same type of AWS::Lambda::EventInvokeConfig resource we created earlier when configuring retry counts (see "Retries" on page 186). For example, let's replace the DLQ in the previous example with a Destination:

```
AWSTemplateFormatVersion: 2010-09-09
Transform: AWS::Serverless-2016-10-31
Description: chapter8-s3-errors

Resources:
  ErrorTriggeringBucket:
    Type: AWS::S3::Bucket
    Properties:
      BucketName: !Sub ${AWS::AccountId}-${AWS::Region}-errortrigger

  S3ErroringLambda:
    Type: AWS::Serverless::Function
    Properties:
      Runtime: java8
      MemorySize: 512
      Handler: book.S3ErroringLambda::handler
      CodeUri: target/lambda.zip
      Events:
        S3Event:
          Type: S3
          Properties:
            Bucket: !Ref ErrorTriggeringBucket
            Events: s3:ObjectCreated:*
      Policies:
        - LambdaInvokePolicy:
            FunctionName: !Ref ErrorProcessingLambda

  ErrorProcessingLambda:
    Type: AWS::Serverless::Function
    Properties:
      Runtime: java8
      MemorySize: 512
      Handler: book.ErrorProcessingLambda::handler
      CodeUri: target/lambda.zip

  S3ErroringLambdaInvokeConfig:
    Type: AWS::Lambda::EventInvokeConfig
    Properties:
      FunctionName: !Ref S3ErroringLambda
      Qualifier: "$LATEST"
      DestinationConfig:
```

```
OnFailure:
    Destination: !GetAtt ErrorProcessingLambda.Arn
```

There are a few aspects to notice from this example:

- There are no explicit queues or topics.
- The Destination at the end defines that when `S3ErroringLambda` fails, we want events to be sent to `ErrorProcessingLambda`.
- The application function needs to be given permission to invoke the error handling function, which we enable via the `Policies` property on the `S3Erroring Lambda` resource.

The event that is sent to `ErrorProcessingLambda` is *not* the same type as that sent to a DLQ. At time of writing, the `aws-lambda-java-events` library has not been updated to include the Destination types, and deserializing these types is tricky due to some unfortunate naming of fields within the sent objects. Ideally by the time you read this book, this will have been fixed!

Destinations will likely replace most usages of DLQ, and we're also interested to see how people use the `OnSuccess` version of destinations to build interesting solutions.

Handling Kinesis and DynamoDB Stream Errors

In late 2019, AWS added a number of failure-handling features (*https://oreil.ly/ gWKX-*) to the Kinesis and DynamoDB stream event sources. These new features make it possible to avoid "poison pill" scenarios, where a single bad record could block stream (or shard) processing for up to a week (depending on how long the stream retains records).

The failure-handling features can be configured via SAM (or CloudFormation), and are applied when a Lambda function fails to process a batch of records from either a Kinesis or DynamoDB stream. The new features are as follows:

Bisect on Function Error
Instead of simply retrying the entire batch of records for a failed Lambda invocation, this feature splits the batch into two. These smaller batches are retried separately. This approach can automatically narrow failures down to whichever individual records are causing a problem, and those records can be dealt with via the other error-handling features.

Maximum Record Age
This instructs the Lambda function to skip records older than a specified Maximum Record Age (which can be from 60 seconds to 7 days).

Maximum Retry Attempts

This feature retries failed batches for a configurable number of times and then sends information about the batch of records to the configured *on-failure destination* (the next feature in this list).

Destination on Failure

This is an SNS topic or SQS queue that will receive information about failed batches. Note that it doesn't receive the actual failed records—those have to be extracted from the stream before they expire.

A comprehensive error-handling approach can (and should) combine all of these features. For example, a failed batch of records can be split (perhaps several times) until there is a single-record batch causing a failure. That single-record batch might be retried 10 times or until the record is 15 minutes old, at which point the details of the batch (with its single failed record) will be sent to an SNS topic. A separate Lambda could be subscribed to that SNS topic, automatically retrieve the failed record from the stream, and store it in S3 for later investigation.

Tracing Errors with X-Ray

If you are using AWS X-Ray (discussed in "Distributed Tracing" on page 175), then it will be able to show where errors are occurring in your graph of components. For more details, see "Finding Errors" on page 177, and the X-Ray documentation.

Error Handling Strategies

So given everything we now know about errors, and Lambda's capabilities and behaviors regarding them, how should we choose to deal with errors?

For unhandled errors, we should set up monitoring (see "Alarms" on page 173), and when errors occur, we will likely need some kind of manual intervention. The urgency of this will depend on the context, and also the type of the event source—remember in the case of stream/queue event sources that processing is blocked until the error is cleared.

For handled errors, though, we have an interesting choice. Should we process the error and rethrow, or should we capture the error and exit the function cleanly? Again, this will depend on the context and invocation type, but here are some thoughts.

For synchronous event sources, you will likely want to return some kind of error to the original caller. Typically you'll want to do that explicitly within the Lambda code and return a well-formatted error. A problem here, though, is that Lambda won't know if this is an error, so you'll need to track this metric manually. The problem with letting unhandled errors bubble out from synchronously called Lambdas is that you have no control over the error returned to the upstream client.

For asynchronous event sources, what you do will largely depend on whether you want to use a DLQ or Destination. If you do, then there's often no harm in either letting an error bubble out or throwing a custom error and then handling the error in whatever is processing messages from the DLQ/Destination. If you don't use a DLQ/Destination then you may want to at least log the failing input event if the error occurs within your code.

For Kinesis and DynamoDB stream event sources, using one of the failure-handling features described earlier allows processing to continue even if some records cause errors. With a properly configured *Destination on Failure*, this is an effective error-handling strategy, although it assumes that it is safe for your application to potentially process records out of order. If that isn't the case, then consider omitting the failure-handling features and relying on the platform's automatic retry behavior (which in this case would block processing until the error is resolved or the records expire).

For SQS you'll typically want to handle errors within your code, since otherwise further processing is blocked. An effective way to do this is to put a top-level `try-catch` block in your handler function. Within this block, you can set up your own retry strategy or log the failing event and exit the function cleanly. In certain situations, you really will want to block further event processing until the problem causing the error is resolved, in which case you can throw a new error from the top-level try-catch block and use the platform's automatic retry behavior.

Scaling

In Chapter 5 we touched on one of the most valuable aspects of Lambda—its ability to auto-scale without any effort (see Figure 5-10). In the data pipeline example we used this auto-scaling ability to implement a "fan-out" pattern—processing many small events in parallel.

This is the key to Lambda's scaling model—if all current instances of a function are currently in use when a new event occurs, then Lambda will automatically create a new instance, *scaling out* the function, to handle the new event.

Eventually, after a period of inactivity, function instances will be *reaped*, *scaling in* the function.

From a cost perspective, Lambda guarantees that we are only charged while our function is processing an event, so it costs the same to process one hundred Lambda events serially in one function instance as it does to process them in parallel in one hundred instances (subject to any extra time costs involved in cold start, which we describe later in this chapter).

Lambda scaling has limits, of course, which we'll examine in a moment, but first let's take a look at Lambda's magical auto-scaling.

Observing Lambda Scaling

Let's start with the following code:

```
package book;

public class MyLambda {
  private static final String instanceID =
    java.util.UUID.randomUUID().toString();

  public String handler(String input) {
    return "This is function instance " + instanceID;
  }
}
```

Static and instance members of a function handler's class are instantiated once per instance of a function. We discuss this further later, in the section about cold starts. Therefore, if we invoke the previous code five times in succession, it will always return the same value for the `instanceID` member.

Now let's change the code a little, adding a `sleep` statement:

```
package book;

public class MyLambda {
  private static final String instanceID =
    java.util.UUID.randomUUID().toString();

  public String handler(String input) throws Exception {
    Thread.sleep(5000);
    return "This is function instance " + instanceID;
  }
}
```

Make sure if you're deploying this code to include a `Timeout` configuration of at least six seconds; otherwise, you'll see a good example of a timeout error!

Now invoke the function several times in parallel. One way to do this is by running the same `aws lambda invoke` command from multiple terminal tabs. Depending on how quick on the draw you are for navigating terminal sessions, you'll now see that different container IDs are returned for different invocations.

This behavior is visible because when Lambda receives the second request to invoke your function, the previous container that was used for the first request is still processing that request, so Lambda creates a new instance, automatically scaling out, to handle the second request. This creation of a new instance happens for the third and fourth requests too, if you're fast enough.

This is an example of invoking the Lambda function directly, but this is the same scaling behavior we see when Lambda is invoked by most event sources, including API

Gateway, S3, or SNS, whenever one instance of a Lambda function is not sufficient to keep up with the event load. Magical auto-scaling, without any effort!

Scaling Limits and Throttling

AWS is not an infinite computer, and there are limits to Lambda's scaling. Amazon limits the number of concurrent executions across all functions per AWS account, per region. By default, at the time of writing, this limit is one thousand, but you can make a support request to have this increased. Partly this limit exists because of the physical constraints of living in a material universe and partly so that your AWS bill doesn't explode to astronomical proportions!

If you reach this limit, you'll start to experience *throttling*, and you'll know this because the account-wide `Throttles` CloudWatch metric for your Lambda functions will suddenly have an amount greater than zero. This makes it a great metric to set a Cloudwatch alarm for (we talked about built-in metrics and alarms in "Metrics" on page 170).

When your function is throttled, the behavior exhibited by AWS is similar to the behavior that occurs when your function throws an error (which we talked about earlier in this chapter—"The Various Behaviors of Lambda Error Processing" on page 184)—in other words, it depends on the type of event source. In summary:

- For synchronous event sources (e.g., API Gateway), throttling is treated as an error and passed back up to the caller as an HTTP status code 500 error.
- For asynchronous event sources (e.g., S3), Lambda will retry calling your Lambda function for up to six hours, by default. This is configurable, for example, by using the `MaximumEventAgeInSeconds` property of the `AWS::Lambda::EventInvo keConfig` CloudFormation resource (*https://oreil.ly/by8cO*) that we introduced in "Retries" on page 186.
- For stream/queue event sources (e.g., Kinesis), Lambda will block and retry until successful or the data expires.

Stream-based sources may also have other scaling restrictions, for example, based on the number of shards of your stream and the configured `ParallelizationFactor` (*https://oreil.ly/4RSoj*).

Since the Lambda concurrency limit is account-wide, one particularly important aspect to be aware of is that one Lambda function that has scaled particularly wide can impact every other Lambda function in the same AWS account + region pair. Because of this, it is strongly recommended that, at the very least, you use separate AWS accounts for production and testing—deliberately DoS'ing (denial-of-servicing) your production application because of a load test against a staging environment is a particularly embarrassing situation to explain!

But beyond the production versus test account separation, we also recommend using different AWS "subaccounts" within one AWS "organization" for different "services" within your ecosystem to further isolate yourself from the problems of account-wide limits.

Burst limits

The limits and throttling mentioned refer to the total capacity available to your Lambda functions. However, there's another limit to be occasionally aware of—the *burst limit*. This refers to *how quickly* (as opposed to *how wide*) your Lambda function can scale. By default Lambda can scale out a function by up to 500 instances every minute, with perhaps a small boost at the beginning. If your workload can burst faster than this (and we've seen some that can), then you'll need to be aware of burst limits and may want to consider asking AWS to increase your burst limit.

Reserved concurrency

We just mentioned earlier that one Lambda function that has scaled particularly wide can impact the rest of the account by using all of the available concurrency. Lambda has a tool to help with this—the optional *reserved concurrency* configuration that can be applied to a function's configuration.

Setting a reserved concurrency value does two things:

- It guarantees that the particular function will always have up to that available amount of concurrency, no matter what any other functions are doing in the account.

- It limits that function to scale *no wider* than that amount of concurrency.

This second feature has some useful benefits that we discuss in "Solution: Manage scaling with reserved concurrency" on page 232.

If you are using SAM to define your application's infrastructure, you can use the `ReservedConcurrentExecutions` property of the `AWS::Serverless::Function` resource type to declare a reserved concurrency setting.

Thread Safety

Because of Lambda's scaling model, we are guaranteed that at most one event will be processed per function instance at any one time. In other words, you never need to be concerned about multiple events being processed at the same time within a function's runtime, let alone within a function object instance. Therefore, unless you create any of your own threads, Lambda programming is entirely thread safe.

Lambda and Threading

Applications spawn threads for a few reasons, typically to:

- Provide scaling by enabling an application to handle multiple requests at one time in the same process
- Perform parallel computation across a number of CPU cores
- Perform nonblocking I/O against an external resource so that work can continue while the I/O request completes

Of these uses the first—spawning threads to scale to handle multiple requests—is unnecessary in Lambda. As we've just described, the Lambda platform uses a process-based scaling model, invoking a different instance of the Lambda runtime per request.

The second use is rare in Lambda development. However, if you do need this capability, then Lambda will provide two execution cores if you specify more than 1792MB for your memory size. Typically, however, if you need to perform parallel computation, you would "fan out" processing, like we did in "Example: Building a Serverless Data Pipeline" on page 111.

The final case is a common usage pattern, though, even in Lambda development, and one you may well come across. As such, it's important that you understand how Lambda interacts with threads that are spawned from your own code.

The key is this section from the AWS Lambda Execution Context documentation (*https://oreil.ly/K5Ukb*):

> Background processes or callbacks initiated by your Lambda function that did not complete when the function ended resume if AWS Lambda chooses to reuse the execution context. You should make sure any background processes or callbacks in your code are complete before the code exits.

What this means is that you are free to create your own threads, but you should know two things:

- When you return from your handler function, those threads will be "frozen."
- If the Lambda runtime where you spawned threads is reused, then those threads will continue where they left off *for the previously processed event*.

You'll typically want to make sure that all spawned threads have completed processing before you return from your handler. In the context of nonblocking external requests, this means that you'll want to wait until either those requests have completed, or have timed out, before continuing processing.

As a final note on this topic, remember that many Java libraries will create threads on your behalf, so be aware when using any libraries that may do so.

Vertical Scaling

Almost all of Lambda's scaling capability is "horizontal"—that is, its ability to scale wider to handle multiple events in parallel. This is in contrast to "vertical" scaling—the ability to handle more load by increasing the computational capability of an individual node.

Lambda also has a rudimentary vertical scaling option, however, in its memory configuration. We discussed this in "Memory and CPU" on page 59.

Versions and Aliases, Traffic Shifting

In your experiments with Lambda so far, you may have occasionally seen the string "$LATEST" appear. This is a reference to a Lambda function's *version*. There's more to versions than just $LATEST though, so let's take a look.

Lambda Versions

Whenever we've deployed a new configuration, or new code, for our Lambda functions, we've always overridden what came before. The old function was dead, long live the new function.

However, Lambda supports keeping those old functions around if you want it to, by way of a capability named Lambda Function Versioning.

Without using versioning explicitly, Lambda has exactly one version of your function at any one time. Its name is $LATEST, which you can reference explicitly; alternatively, if you don't specify a version (or alias, which we'll see in a moment), you are also referring implicitly to $LATEST.

When you create or update a function, however, you are able at the time, or some time later, to snapshot that function to a version. The identifier of the version is a linear counter, starting at 1. You can't edit a version, which means that it only ever makes sense to create a versioned snapshot from the current $LATEST version.

You invoke a version of a function when calling it explicitly by adding a `:VERSION-IDENTIFIER` to its ARN, or if using the AWS CLI, you can add a `--qualifier` *VERSION-IDENTIFIER* parameter to the `aws lambda invoke` command.

You can create a version using various AWS CLI commands or the web console. You can't create a version explicitly using SAM, but you can do so implicitly when you use *aliases*, which we'll explain next.

Lambda Aliases

While you are able to explicitly reference a numbered version of a Lambda function, when using versions, it's more typical to use an *alias*. An alias is a named pointer to a Lambda version—either $LATEST, or a numeric, snapshotted version. An alias can be updated at any time to point to a different version. For example, you may start off pointing to $LATEST, but then point to a specific version when you want to add stability to the alias.

You invoke an alias of a function in precisely the same way as you do with a function version—by specifying it in an ARN or in the --qualifier argument of the CLI. An event source can be configured to point to a specific alias, and if the underlying alias is updated to point to a new version, then events from the source will flow to that new version.

Be Careful If Introspecting the Invoked Alias

One useful thing to know if you're using aliases and versions is that a Lambda function is able to know which alias or version was used to invoke the function, if any, by calling the getInvokedFunctionArn() method on the handler Context object. For example, you may use this in your code to switch between different databases for two aliases named DEV or PROD.

However, if both your DEV *alias* and your PROD *alias* are pointing to the same function *version*, then one function instance can handle events for both aliases—this is because the Lambda platform will reuse instances for a version no matter the alias that was involved. Because of this, it's imperative that any alias-specific logic you may have in your Lambda function is sensitive to this scenario. For example, you might choose to reset connections for each event invocation, or keep multiple cross-invocation state objects for different aliases.

When you deploy a Lambda function with SAM, you can define an alias that is automatically updated to point to the latest, published version. You do this by adding the AutoPublishAlias property, and giving an alias name as a value.

However, there's a much more powerful way of using aliases with SAM.

Traffic Shifting

If you use the AutoPublishAlias property of a Lambda function with SAM, all events from an event source immediately get routed to the new version of the function. If something goes wrong, you can manually update the alias to point to the previous version.

Lambda and SAM also have functionality to improve this process first by giving the opportunity to split traffic, sending some to the new version and some to the old version. This means that if a problem occurs, and a rollback is required, not all traffic has been impacted by the problem.

The second improvement is that a rollback can automatically be performed if an error is detected, where you have the opportunity to define how the error is calculated in a couple of different ways.

There are a number of moving pieces involved in getting this working—Lambda aliases, Lambda alias update policies, and use of the AWS CodeDeploy (*https:// oreil.ly/t2gIB*) service. Fortunately, SAM does a good job of wrapping all of this up for you so that you don't need to worry about all of the gory details. The main thing you need to do is add a `DeploymentPreference` property to your Lambda function in your SAM template, which is thoroughly documented (*https://oreil.ly/EhJaS*).

A choice you need to make when using traffic shifting is how you want your traffic to be shifted to the new alias. This breaks down into four options:

All at once
> While this may sound the same at first glance as `AutoPublishAlias` it's actually a lot more powerful, since you have the opportunity to automatically roll back deployment through "hooks," as we'll describe in a moment. This is a fully automated implementation of *Blue Green Deployment* (*https://oreil.ly/qowK1*) for Lambda.

Canary
> Send a small percentage of traffic to the new version, and if it works, then send the remaining traffic; otherwise, roll back.

Linear
> Similar to Canary, but send increasing percentages of traffic to the new version, still allowing for rollback.

Custom
> Decide for yourself how you want traffic to split across the old and new aliases.

As we mentioned already, a powerful element to this feature is that automatic rollback can be implemented via two different mechanisms—*hooks* and *alarms*.

Hook-triggered rollback is available to any of the previous schemes. You can define *pretraffic hooks* and/or *posttraffic hooks*. These hooks are simply other Lambda functions that will run whatever logic they need to decide whether deployment has been successful—either before any traffic is routed to the new alias or after all traffic has been shifted.

Alarms are available with schemes that offer gradual traffic shifting. You can define any number of *CloudWatch Alarms* (which we discussed in "Alarms" on page 173), and if any of those alarms transition to their *alarm* state, then a rollback to the original alias will be performed.

For more details on Lambda traffic shifting, see the SAM documentation (*https://oreil.ly/SXGLS*).

When (Not) to Use Versions and Aliases

Lambda's traffic shifting capability is very powerful, and if you don't already have a canary release scheme upstream of your Lambda code, then it may well be useful for you.

However, apart from traffic shifting, we try to steer away from versions and aliases. We find that they typically add unnecessary complexity, and instead we prefer to use alternative techniques. For example, for separating development and production versions of code, we prefer to use different deployed stacks. For "rolling back" code, our preference is to use a fast-running deployment pipeline, and roll back at the source repository, triggering a new commit through the pipeline.

Very occasionally you'll see that some event sources use, and recommend, using Lambda aliases. One example of this is when integrating Lambda with AWS Application Load Balancer (ALB) (*https://oreil.ly/4U1ZD*).

If you do use versions and aliases, be aware of a couple of "gotchas," beyond the function instance warning earlier:

- Versions do not automatically clean up after themselves, so periodically you'll want to delete old versions. Otherwise, you may find you hit your account-level "function and layer storage" limit of 75GB.
- The default CloudWatch metrics views in the AWS Web Console for Lambda are a little odd when you're using aliases and versions. Make sure you're being explicit about which version(s) or alias(es) you want to view data for when you're using CloudWatch metrics in this way.

Cold Starts

Now we move on to the thorny subject of *cold starts*. Depending on who you talk to, cold starts may be a minor footnote in the life of a Lambda developer, or it may be a complete blocker to Lambda even being considered a valid computation platform. We find how best to approach cold starts is somewhere between these two points—worth understanding and treating with rigor, but not a deal-breaker in most situations.

But what are cold starts, when do they happen, what impact do they have, and how can we mitigate them? There's a lot of fear, uncertainty, and doubt (FUD) surrounding cold starts, and we hope to remove some of that FUD for you here. Let's dive in.

What Is a Cold Start?

Back in Chapter 3, we explored the chain of activity (Figure 3-1) that occurs when a Lambda function is invoked for the first time—from starting a host Linux environment through to calling our handler function. In between those two activities the JVM will be started, the Lambda Java Runtime will be started, our code will be loaded, and depending on the precise nature of our Lambda function, more may happen besides. We collectively group this chain into something we call a *cold start*, and it results in a new *instance* (an execution environment, a runtime, and our code) of our Lambda function being available to process events.

An important point here is that all of this activity occurs *when our Lambda function is invoked*, not before. In other words, Lambda doesn't create function instances solely when Lambda code is deployed—it creates them *on demand*.

However, cold starts are special occurrences, rather than something that happens on every invocation, because typically Lambda won't perform a cold start for every event that triggers our function. This is because once our function has finished executing, Lambda can *freeze* (*https://oreil.ly/YrC-W*) the instance and keep it around for a little while in case another event happens soon. If an event does happen soon, then Lambda will *thaw* the instance and call it with the event. For many Lambda functions, cold starts in fact occur less than 1% of the time, but it's still useful to know when they do occur.

When Does a Cold Start Occur?

A cold start is necessary whenever there is no existing function instance available to process an event. This situation happens at the following times:

1. When a Lambda function's code or configuration changes (including when the first version of a function is deployed)
2. When all previous instances have been expired due to inactivity
3. When all previous instances have been "reaped" due to age
4. When Lambda needs to scale out because all current instances for the required function are already processing events

Let's look at these four types of occurrence in a little more detail.

---

1. When we deploy our function for the first time, Lambda will create an instance of our function, as we've already seen. However, Lambda will also create a new instance whenever a function is invoked after we deploy a new version of the function code, or when we change the Lambda configuration of our functions. Such configuration doesn't just cover environment variables—it also covers runtime aspects like timeouts, memory settings, DLQ, etc.

   A corollary of this is that one instance of a Lambda function is guaranteed to have the same code and configuration no matter how many times it is called.

2. Lambda will keep function instances around for a little while in case another event happens "soon." The precise definition of *soon* is not documented, but it can be anywhere between a few minutes and a few hours (and is not necessarily constant). In other words, if your function processes an event, and then a minute later another event occurs, there's a very good chance the second event will be processed using the same instance of your function that was used to process the first event. However, if there's a day or more between events, your function will likely experience a cold start for every event. In the past, some people have used a "ping hack" to work around this and keep their function "alive," but in late 2019 AWS introduced Provisioned Concurrency (see "Provisioned Concurrency" on page 208) to solve this kind of concern.

3. Even if your Lambda event is fairly active, Amazon doesn't keep instances around forever, even if they're being used every few seconds. How long AWS will keep instances around is, again, undocumented, but at time of writing we see instances lasting five to six hours, and after that they're killed off.

4. Finally, a cold start will occur if all current instances of a function are already busy processing events and Lambda "scales out," as we described this earlier in this chapter.

Identifying Cold Starts

How can you tell when a cold start has occurred? There are many ways of doing so, but here are a few.

First, you'll notice a latency spike. Cold starts typically add anywhere from 100 milliseconds to 10 seconds to the latency of your function, depending on the makeup of your function. Therefore, if your function typically takes less than that, a cold start will be easy to see in the function's latency metrics.

Next you'll be able to tell when a cold start has occurred due to a way that Lambda's logging works. As we discussed in "Lambda and CloudWatch Logs" on page 158, when Lambda functions log, the output is captured in CloudWatch Logs. All of the log output for one function is available in one CloudWatch Log *group*, but each instance of a function will write to a separate log *stream*, within the log group. Therefore if you see the number of log streams within a log group increase then you know a cold start has occurred.

Also, you can track cold starts yourself within code. Since the Java object encapsulating your handler is instantiated only once per instance of the actual function runtime, any instance member or static member initialization will happen at cold start, and never again for the lifetime of the function instance. Therefore, if you add a constructor, or static initializer, to your code, it will be called only when the function is experiencing a cold start. You can add explicit logging to your handler class constructor to see a cold start occurring in your function logs. Alternatively, we saw examples of identifying cold starts earlier in this chapter.

You can also identify cold starts using X-Ray and some third-party Lambda monitoring tools.

Impact of Cold Starts

So far we've described what cold starts are, when they happen, and how you can identify them. But why should you care about cold starts?

As we just mentioned in the previous section, one way to identify a cold start is that you'll typically see a latency spike in your event processing when one occurs, and this is most often why people are concerned about them. While end-to-end latency of a small Lambda function might be 50 ms in a usual case, a cold start could add *at least* 200 ms to this amount, and, depending on various factors, may add seconds, or even tens of seconds. The reasons that cold starts add latency are because of all the steps that need to occur during creation of a function instance.

Does this mean that we *always* need to care about cold starts? That depends a lot on what your Lambda function is doing.

For instance, say your function is asynchronously processing objects created in S3, and you are ambivalent as to whether it takes minutes to process such objects. Do you care about cold starts in this situation? Probably not. Especially when you consider that S3 has no guaranteed subsecond delivery of events anyway.

Here's another example of where you likely won't care too much about cold starts: say that you have a function that is processing messages from Kinesis, that each event takes about 100 ms to process, and that there's typically always enough data to keep your Lambda functions busy. In this case, one instance of your Lambda function may process 200,000 events before it gets "reaped." In other words *cold starts might only affect 0.0005% of Lambda invocations*. Even if a cold start added 10 seconds to your startup latency, it's highly likely that you'll be OK with such an impact in this scenario, when you consider amortizing that time over the lifetime of an instance.

On the other hand, say you're building a web application, and there's a particular element that calls a Lambda function, but that function gets called in AWS only once per hour. This might mean you're getting a cold start every time the function is invoked. Further, let's say for this particular function that the cold start overhead is five seconds. Is this a problem? It might be. If so, can this overhead be reduced? Perhaps, and we'll talk about that in the next section.

Although the concern with cold starts is almost always about latency overhead, it's also important to note that if your function loads data from a downstream resource at startup, it will be doing that every time a cold start occurs. You may want to consider this when you're thinking about the impact your Lambda functions have on downstream resources, especially when all of your instances cold start after a deployment.

Mitigating Cold Starts

Cold starts will always occur with Lambda, and unless we use Provisioned Concurrency (described in the next section), such cold starts will always, occasionally, affect our function's performance. If cold starts are causing you a problem, there are various techniques you can use to mitigate their impact. Just make sure that they really are causing you a problem, though—like other forms of performance optimization, you want to make sure you do this work only if it's truly necessary.

Reduce artifact size

Often the most effective tool in reducing cold start impact is to reduce the size of our code artifact. We can do that in two main ways:

- Reduce the amount of our own code in the artifact to just that needed by the Lambda function (where "amount" means both size and number of classes).
- Prune dependencies so that only libraries that our Lambda function needs are stored in the artifact.

There are a couple of follow-on techniques here. First, create a different artifact for each of your Lambda functions, and execute the tasks for each artifact. This was the point of the effort we went to in Chapter 5 when we created the multimodule Maven project.

Second, if you want to optimize library dependencies further, then consider *breaking depended-upon libraries apart to just the code you need*. And perhaps even re-implement library functionality in your own code. Obviously there's some work necessary here to do this correctly and safely, but it might be a useful technique for you.

These techniques reduce cold starts in two ways. First, there's simply a smaller artifact to copy and unpack before the runtime starts. But furthermore, there's less code for your runtime to load and initialize.

All of these techniques are somewhat unusual in modern server-side software development. We've become used to being able to add dependencies willy-nilly to our projects, creating multi-hundred-megabyte deployment artifacts while Maven or NPM "download the internet." This is typically sufficient in traditional server-side development since disk space is cheap, networks are fast, and most importantly, we don't care too much about startup time for our servers, at least not on the order of a few seconds here and there.

But with functions as a service (FaaS), and Lambda in particular, we care about startup time to a much more significant extent, so we need to be more judicious with how we build and package our software.

To prune dependencies in JVM projects, you may want to consider using the Apache Maven Dependency plug-in (*https://oreil.ly/RZYMF*), which will report on how dependencies in your project are used, or a similar tool.

Use a more load-speed-efficient packaging format

As we called out in Chapter 4, AWS recommends (*https://oreil.ly/_S6Bb*) the ZIP file approach to packaging a Lambda function, over the uberjar approach, because it decreases the time Lambda needs to unpack your deployment artifact.

Reduce startup logic

Later in this chapter, we'll look at state in Lambda functions. Despite what you may have heard, Lambda functions aren't stateless; they just have an unusual model when it comes to thinking about state.

A fairly common thing to do with Lambda functions is to create or load various resources when the function is first invoked. We saw this to a small extent in the examples in Chapter 5 when we initialized our serialization libraries and SDKs. However for some functions, it makes sense to grab this idea by the horns and create a large local cache, loaded from some other resources, in the name of more quickly handling events during the lifetime of the instance.

Such startup logic doesn't happen for free though, and will increase cold start time. If you are loading initial resources at cold start, you may find that you have a trade-off to make between how much you improve the performance of subsequent invocations versus how long the initial invocation takes. If possible, you may want to consider if you can gradually "warm" your function's local cache over a series of initial invocations.

One big cause of slow startup is the use of application frameworks like Spring. As we discuss later (see "Lambda and Java Application Frameworks" on page 215), we strongly discourage the use of such frameworks with Lambda. If cold starts are causing you a problem, and you're using an application framework, then we recommend your first course of action should be to investigate whether you can remove the framework from your Lambda function.

Language choice

Another area that can impact cold start time is the choice of language runtime. JavaScript, Python, and Go simply take less time to start up than the JVM or .NET runtime. Therefore, if you're writing a small function that isn't called often, and you care about reducing cold start impact as much as possible, you may want to use either JavaScript, Python, or Go over Java, all other development aspects being equal.

Because of this difference in startup time, we often hear people dismiss the JVM and .NET runtimes as Lambda runtimes in general, but this is a short-sighted opinion. For instance, in the situation we described earlier with the Kinesis processing function, what if, on average, the JVM function took 80 ms to process an event, but a JavaScript equivalent took 120 ms? In this case, you would literally be paying twice as much for the JavaScript version of your code to run (since billable Lambda time is rounded up to the next 100 ms). In this situation, JavaScript may be the wrong choice of runtime.

It's perfectly possible to use alternative (non-Java) JVM languages within Lambda (which we talk about more at the end of this chapter). One important aspect to remember, though, is that typically these languages come with their own "language runtimes" and libraries, and both of these will increase cold start time.

Finally, on the topic of language choice, it's worth keeping some perspective when it comes to impact of language on cold start, or event-processing, performance. The most important factor in language choice is how effectively you can build and maintain your code—the human element of software development. The cost of runtime performance differences between Lambda language runtimes may pale in comparison with this.

Memory and CPU

Certain aspects of your function's configuration can also affect cold start time. One of the primary examples of this is the MemorySize setting you choose. A larger memory setting also gives more CPU resources, and therefore a larger memory setting may speed up the time it takes your JVM code to JIT compile.

Until late 2019, another configuration setting of a Lambda function that could significantly increase cold start time was whether you were using a *virtual private cloud (VPC)*. We discuss VPCs in general later in this chapter, but for now all you need to know is that if you see any documentation anywhere warning of awful Lamdba startup times because of VPCs, then you can sit happy in the knowledge that this has now been resolved. For more details on what AWS did to improve this, see this article (*https://oreil.ly/UnES6*).

Provisioned Concurrency

In late 2019 AWS announced a new Lambda feature—*Provisioned Concurrency*. Provisioned Concurrency (PC) allows an engineer to effectively "pre-warm" Lambda functions, thereby removing (almost) all of the impact of cold starts. Before we describe how to use this feature, here are some important caveats:

- PC breaks the request-based cost model of Lambda. With PC you pay whether your functions are invoked or not. Using Lambda with PC therefore negates one of the main benefits of serverless: costs that scale to zero (see "FaaS as Implemented by Lambda" on page 11).

- To avoid paying for costs related to peak usage, you need to manually configure AWS Auto Scaling with PC (see this AWS blog article on how to implement this (*https://oreil.ly/9x0D6*)). This is extra operational overhead on your part.

- PC adds significant deployment time overhead. In our experiments, at the time of writing, deploying a Lambda function with a PC setting of 1 (see below as to what this means) has an overhead of about four minutes. Using a setting of 10 or 100 is about seven minutes.

- PC requires using either versions or aliases, which we described earlier in this chapter (see "Versions and Aliases, Traffic Shifting" on page 198). As we mentioned in that section, we do not recommend using versions or aliases in most cases, due to the extra complexity they bring.

Given these significant caveats, our recommendation is that you only reach for Provisioned Concurrency if you *absolutely need to*. As we mention in the summary of this section, we find that most teams that are concerned initially about cold starts find that they are of no effective consequence once they start using Lambda at scale in production, especially if the teams follow the other advice we give in this chapter about cold start mitigation.

Now, we've told you why you almost certainly shouldn't use Provisioned Concurrency, let's talk about what it is!

PC, at its simplest, is a numerical value (n) that tells the Lambda platform to always have *at least n* execution environments of your function in a "warm" state. "Warm" here means that the execution environment has been created, and your Lambda function handler code has been instantiated. In fact, the entire execution chain (see Figure 3-1) is performed during warming, apart from actually calling your handler method.

Since under a PC context Lambda won't call a nonwarmed function (apart from one caveat about scaling, which we'll describe in a moment), this guarantees that you won't have any performance-impacting cold starts at all! In other words, *all* of your function invocations will respond in their regular "warm" time.

Another nice aspect to PC is that it is defined solely in deployment configuration—no change to your code is required to use it (although you may want to change your code, as we will describe about code instantiation in a moment).

Let's look at an example. Say that we have the following function configured in our SAM template:

```
HelloWorldLambda:
  Type: AWS::Serverless::Function
  Properties:
    Runtime: java8
    MemorySize: 512
    Handler: book.HelloWorld::handler
    CodeUri: target/lambda.zip
    AutoPublishAlias: live
    ProvisionedConcurrencyConfig:
      ProvisionedConcurrentExecutions: 1
```

The new lines here are those last three. First you'll see that we're using an alias—PC requires configuring a `ProvisionedConcurrentExecutions` value for each version or alias that we want PC for. We can't configure a `ProvisionedConcurrentExecutions` value for $LATEST—the default version.

In this example, we then specify that we want to always have one instance of our Lambda function pre-warmed.

When we deploy this function for the first time, Lambda will instantiate the Java class `HelloWorld`, which contains our handler, even before any invocations occur. Then, when an event is received for the function, Lambda calls this pre-warmed function. When we *redeploy* the function, Lambda will keep routing requests to the old (warm) version and start using the new version only once all the provisioned instances for that version have been created. Again, this makes sure that function invocation isn't impacted by cold starts.

In other third-party Lambda documentation, you may see recommendations to use a secondary, scheduled, "ping" function that calls the application function, to avoid cold starts. PC, with a setting of 1, in almost any case is a more effective replacement of such a mechanism.

Now, let's cover a few details you should be aware of.

First, pricing. As mentioned, PC has (at the time of writing) a different cost model to regular "on-demand" Lambda. As described in "How Expensive Is Lambda?" on page 60, on-demand Lambda costs are based on how many requests your Lambda function receives and how long your Lambda function is executing (duration). For PC you still pay the request cost, and a (smaller) amount for duration, but you *also* pay a charge for the entire time your function is deployed, not just when it is processing requests.

Let's build on "How Expensive Is Lambda?" on page 60, specifically the example for the web API. Our cost estimate for just on-demand Lambda was $21.60/month. How much does it cost using Provisioned Concurrency?

Again, we'll assume 512-MB RAM, less than 100 ms to process a request and 864,000 requests/day. Let's start with using a PC value of 10, since that's what we expect to peak up to. In this scenario, our Lambda costs are as follows:

- The request cost is unchanged at $5.18/month.
- The duration cost is $0.1 \times 864000 \times 0.5 \times \$0.000009722 = \$0.42$/day, or $12.60/month.
- The Provisioned Concurrency cost is $10 \times 0.000004167 \times 0.5 \times 86400 = \$1.80$/day, or $54/month.

The total cost therefore has increased by a little over three times from approximately $22/month to $72/month. Yikes!

Now, this is likely a "worst case" since we are setting PC at peak. One option we have is to manually configure auto-scaling for PC. This is described on the AWS blog introducing PC (*https://oreil.ly/8p8K6*). Let's say that doing this means our PC configuration averages around 2. In this case, our total costs are $29/month. This is still 30% more expensive than on-demand, plus now we have the added complexity of managing PC auto-scaling.

There are some scenarios where if you have a very consistent usage model, then PC works out cheaper than on-demand, but in most cases you should expect to pay a significant overhead to use PC.

Another issue related to costs is that you probably want to have different configuration for development versus production to avoid paying "always-on" costs for development environments. You can do this using CloudFormation techniques, but again this is extra mental overhead.

That's enough about costs. Let's move on to a different subject!

What happens if at a certain point in time you have more invocations than your PC configuration? As we looked at earlier in this chapter, we know that Lambda always increases the number of active execution environments to satisfy load. For example, say that Lambda needs to use an 11th execution environment for your function, but you have a PC setting of 10—what happens now? In this case, Lambda will spin up a new execution environment in the "traditional" on-demand model to cover the extra load. You will be charged for this extra capacity in the usual on-demand fashion, but be warned—the first event using that new extra environment will also incur cold-start latency in the normal way!

Finally, a quick note on making the most of PC. AWS has been doing a great job over the last few years in reducing the *platform* overhead of cold starts, so the main point of PC is mostly to mitigate *application* overhead—the time taken to instantiate your language runtime, code, and handler class. This last element—class instantiation—is important since your handler class constructor is called during pre-warming. Therefore, you'll want to move as much application setup as possible to class and object instantiation time and not do this in the handler method itself. We've used this pattern throughout the book, but it's especially important if you're using PC.

Given all of our dire warnings about using PC, when do we recommend using it? Here are a few scenarios where we can imagine PC being useful:

- When you have a Lambda function called very infrequently (say once per hour, or longer) that you always want to return quickly (subsecond), and you are willing to pay the cost overhead.
- If your application has extreme "burst" scale scenarios (see "Burst limits" on page 196) that Lambda can't handle by default, then you can pre-warm sufficient capacity.
- If your function itself has significant code-level cold-start time (e.g., several seconds) that is not sufficient for application performance, and you have no other way to mitigate this. This is typical if you're using a heavyweight application framework within your Lambda code.

Cold Start Summary

Cold starts might be nothing you need to ever spend too much effort on, depending on what you use Lambda for, but it's certainly a topic that you should be aware of, since how cold starts are mitigated often runs counter to how we typically build and package systems.

We mentioned *FUD* around cold starts earlier, and cold starts are also often "thrown under the bus" for latency problems that turn out to actually have nothing to do with cold starts at all. Remember to perform proper latency analysis if you're having latency concerns—make sure your actual problem isn't, for example, how your code is interacting with a downstream system.

Also make sure to continue to test latency over time, especially if you rule out a certain use of Lambda because of cold starts. AWS has made, and continues to make, significant improvements in this part of the Lambda platform.

In our experience, cold starts concern teams when they first use Lambda, especially under spiky development loads, but once they see how Lambda performs under production loads, they often never worry about cold starts again.

State

Almost any application needs to consider state. Such state may be *persistent*—in other words, it captures data that is required to fulfill subsequent requests. Alternatively, it may be *cached* state—a copy of data that is used to improve performance, where the persisted version is stored elsewhere.

Despite how it's occasionally perceived, Lambda is *not* stateless—data can be stored in memory and on disk both during and across requests.

In-memory state is available via a handler method's object and class members—any data loaded into such members is available the next time that function instance is invoked again, and a Lambda function can have up to a total of 3GB RAM (some of that will be used by the Lambda runtime).

Lambda function instances also have access to 512MB of local disk storage in */tmp*. While this state is not automatically shared across function instances, it will, again, be available for subsequent invocations of the same function instance.

However, the nature of Lambda's runtime model significantly impacts how such state can be used.

Persistent Application State

The way that Lambda creates function instances, especially in the way that it scales, has significant implications on architecture. For example, we have absolutely no guarantee that sequential requests, for the same upstream client, will be handled by the same function instance. There is no "client affinity" for Lambda functions.

This means that we *cannot assume* that any state that was available locally (in-memory, or on local disk) in a Lambda function for one request will be available for a subsequent request. This is true whether our function scales or not—scaling just underlines the point.

Therefore, all persistent application state that we want to keep across Lambda function invocations must be *externalized*. In other words, this means that any state we want to keep beyond an individual invocation has to be either stored downstream of our Lambda function—in a database, external file storage, or other downstream service—or it must be returned to the caller in the case of a synchronously called function.

This might sound like a massive restriction, but in fact this way of building server-side software is not new. Many people have been espousing the virtues of the *12-factor architecture (https://12factor.net/)* for years, and this aspect of externalizing state is expressed within the sixth factor of that paradigm.

That being said, this definitely is a constraint of Lambda, and may require you to significantly re-architect existing applications that you want to move to Lambda. It may also mean that some applications that require particularly low latency to state (for example, gaming servers) are not good candidate applications for Lambda, nor are those that require a large data set in memory in order to perform adequately.

There are various common services that people use to externalize their application state with Lambda:

DynamoDB

DynamoDB is the NoSQL database of AWS. We used DynamoDB in the API example in "Example: Building a Serverless API" on page 92. The benefits of DynamoDB are that it is fast, fairly easy to operate and configure, and has very similar scaling properties to Lambda. The chief drawback to DynamoDB is that modeling data can get tricky.

RDS

AWS has various relational databases that it groups in the Relational/SQL Database Service (RDS) family, and all of these are available for use from Lambda. One fairly new option within this family is *Aurora Serverless (https://oreil.ly/2Kc4E)*—an auto-scaling version of Amazon's own *Aurora* MySQL and Postgres engines, made for serverless applications. The benefits of using a SQL database over a NoSQL one are decades of experience building such applications. The drawbacks, versus DynamoDB at least, typically are higher latencies and more operational overhead (with nonserverless RDS).

S3

Simple Storage Service (S3)—which we've used several times throughout this book—can be used as a data store for Lambda. It's simple to use, but isn't particularly low latency, and also has limited querying capabilities in comparison with one of the database services, unless you also use Amazon Athena (*https:// aws.amazon.com/athena*).

ElastiCache

AWS offers a managed version of the Redis persistent cache application as part of its ElastiCache (*https://aws.amazon.com/elasticache*) family. Of these four options, ElastiCache typically offers the fastest performance, but since it isn't a true serverless service, it does require some operational overhead.

Custom downstream service

Alternatively, you may choose to implement your own in-memory persistence in a downstream service, built using traditional designs.

AWS continues to make interesting developments in this area, and we recommend that you investigate all recently announced advances whenever you pick a persistence solution.

Caching

While we can't rely on Lambda's state capabilities for persistent application state, we absolutely can use them for caching data that is also stored elsewhere. Put another way, while it's true that we have no guarantee that one Lambda function instance will be called multiple times, we do know that it *probably will be*, depending on invocation frequency. Because of this, cache state is a candidate for Lambda's local storage.

We can use either or both of Lambda's in-memory or on-disk locations for cached data. For example, say that we always need a set of fairly up-to-date reference data from a downstream service to process an event, but "fairly up-to-date" is on order of "valid within the last day." In this case, we can load the reference data once, for the first invocation of the function instance, and then store that data locally in a static or instance member variable. Remember—our handler function instance object will be instantiated only once per runtime environment.

As another example, say that we want to call an external program or library as part of our execution—Lambda gives us a full Linux environment with which to do this. That program/library may be too big to fit in either a Lambda code artifact (which is restricted to at most 250MB when uncompressed) or even a Lambda layer (see later in this chapter about layers). Instead, we can copy the external code from S3 to */tmp* the first time we need it for a function instance, and then for subsequent requests for that instance the code will be available locally already.

Both of these examples relate to state that consists of chunks of data—application data, or libraries and executables. Another form of state in our Lambda applications are the runtime structures of our code itself, including those that represent connections to external services. These runtime structures either may take some amount of time to create when the function is invoked, or in the case of connections to services may take time to initialize, e.g., for authentication procedures. In either case, in Lambda, we will very often store these structures in program elements that live longer than the call to the method itself—in Java this means storing them in instance or static members.

We showed examples of this earlier in the book. For example in Chapter 5 at Example 5-3 we store the following in instance members:

- The `ObjectMapper` instance, because that is a program structure that takes some time to instantiate
- The DynamoDB client, which is a connection to the external DynamoDB service

While we typically use this form of object caching for performance reasons in certain situations, it can also significantly improve the cost effectiveness of our overall system—see "Lambda Runtime Model and Cost Impact on Downstream Systems" on page 234 for more detail on this.

Sometimes Lambda's own state capabilities are insufficient—for example, our total cache state might be too large to fit in memory, too slow to load up during a cold start, or update frequently (updating a locally cached version in a Lambda function is a tricky thing to manage, although it can be done). In such a case, you may choose to use one of the persistence services mentioned in the previous section as a caching solution.

Lambda and Java Application Frameworks

So far in this book most of our guidance has been how to use AWS Lambda, with a few warnings along the way. We're now going to take a brief tangent and talk about something we *don't* recommend doing.

Over the last two decades it's been very common to build server-side Java applications using some kind of container and/or framework. Back in the early 2000s, "Java Enterprise Edition" (J2EE) was all the rage, with application servers like WebLogic, WebSphere, and JBoss allowing you to build your apps with the Enterprise JavaBeans (EJB) or Servlet framework. For those of you not around then we can promise you, from personal experience, that this was not a whole bunch of fun.

People realized that these big servers were often unwieldy and/or expensive, and so they have been largely replaced by more "lightweight" equivalents, of which Spring is the most common. Spring itself has evolved along the way, of course, into Spring Boot, and people also use various Java web frameworks to build applications.

Because there is so much institutional knowledge in our industry on how to build "Java applications" with these tools, there's a very large temptation to carry on using them, and just port the runtime from a running process to a Lambda function. AWS has even put significant effort into supporting precisely this way of thinking, via the serverless Java Container (*https://oreil.ly/T_ruW*) project.

While we admire AWS's desire to "meet people where they are" in this way, we *strongly discourage* the use of most Java frameworks when building applications with Lambda, for the following reasons.

First, building a complete app in a single Lambda function misses the fundamental point of Lambda. Lambda functions are meant to be small, individual, short-lived functions that are event-driven, and programmed to accept a specific input event. "Java applications," on the other hand, are literally servers that have a lifecycle and state, and are typically designed to handle multiple types of request. If you're building miniservers, you're not thinking serverlessly.

Next, most application servers assume that there is some amount of shared state from request to request. While it's possible not to work this way, it's not a natural-feeling way of working in these environments.

Another reason we think this is a bad idea is that it detracts from the value provided by other AWS serverless services. For example, with the AWS project mentioned earlier, API Gateway is used, but in a "full proxy" mode. Here's a snippet from the SAM template from the Spring Boot example (*https://oreil.ly/KZYj3*):

```
Resources:
  PetStoreFunction:
    Type: AWS::Serverless::Function
    Properties:
      Events:
        GetResource:
          Type: Api
          Properties:
            Path: /{proxy+}
            Method: any
```

Using API Gateway in this way means that all requests, no matter the path, are sent to one Lambda function, and routing behavior needs to be implemented in the Lambda function. While Spring Boot can do that, (a) API Gateway will give you that functionality for free, and (b) it clutters up your Java code to keep it in the Lambda function.

Earlier in the book we mentioned that on the whole we're wary of using too many API Gateway features; for example, see the discussion of request and response mapping in "API Gateway Proxy Events" on page 96. However, we feel that removing routing is typically a step too far down the line of abstracting out the use of API Gateway.

As we discussed earlier on in the section on cold starts, application frameworks typically slow down function initialization. While some people may argue that this is a good case to use Provisioned Concurrency, we would counter that this is a Band-Aid and not a solution.

Finally, container and framework-based apps tend to have large distributable artifacts —partly because of the number of libraries depended upon, and partly, again, because such apps usually implement a number of functions. Throughout this book we've been attempting to reduce the size of artifacts by minimizing dependencies, and dividing up applications into multiple distributable elements, all in the name of keeping our Lambda functions clean and lean. Using an application framework runs counter to this way of thinking.

In summary, building Java Lambda applications in this way is really a "square peg and round hole problem." Yes, you can make it work, but it's inefficient, and you won't get all the benefits of Lambda if you work in this way. There's a real danger of hitting a "local maximum" of value from Lambda, and assuming that there are no further upsides.

So if we don't recommend using these frameworks, how do we suggest you use your hard-earned knowledge and skills?

Typically we find that programmers switching to "pure" Lambda development don't take too long to shake off the frameworks they've been used to. There's a certain "lightness" that comes with just writing a handler function. Also, there's nothing wrong with bringing along old Java code to the party, as long as it's not too ingrained in an application framework. If you can extract your domain logic into something that just expresses your business needs, then you're on the right path.

Also, it's still fine to use an ethos of "dependency injection" (DI), which the frameworks often provide. You may choose to "hand roll" such DI (our preference), as you've seen in some of the examples (see "Add Constructors" on page 140). Alternatively, you can try to use a framework to provide just dependency injection, without the other features they often come with.

Virtual Private Clouds

In all of our examples so far any external resources called by a Lambda function have been secured via HTTPS/"layer 7" authentication. For example, when we called DynamoDB in the serverless API example in Example 5-3, that connection was secured solely by credentials that were passed to DynamoDB from our Lambda function.

In other words, DynamoDB is not a "firewalled" service—it sits open to the internet, and any machine anywhere else on the internet can connect to it.

While this brave new world of "firewall-less" computing is gathering pace, there are still many situations where a Lambda function is going to need to connect to a resource that is shielded behind some kind of IP-address limited protection. A common way of doing that with AWS is to use a VPC.

VPCs are a lower-level piece of infrastructure than anything else we've discussed so far in the book. They require understanding things like IP addresses, elastic network interfaces (ENIs), CIDR blocks, and security groups, and also expose the fact to us that AWS regions are made up of multiple AZs. In other words, "Here be dragons!"

Lambda functions can be configured to be able to access a VPC. Three typical reasons a Lambda function would need this are:

- To be able to access an RDS SQL database (see Figure 8-2)
- To be able to access ElastiCache
- To be able to call an internal microservice running on a container cluster using IP/VPC-based security

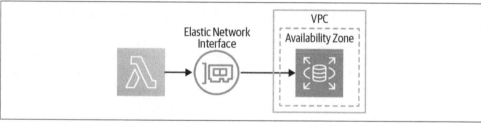

Figure 8-2. Lambda attached to VPC to access RDS database

You should configure Lambda to use a VPC only if it actually needs it. Adding a VPC is not "free"—it impacts other systems, it changes the behavior of how Lambda interacts with other services, and it adds complexity to your configuration and architecture.

Further, we recommend you configure Lambda to use a VPC only if either (a) you understand VPCs and the implications of doing so or (b) you've discussed this requirement with another team in your organization that understands this.

In the rest of this section, we assume that you understand, broadly, VPCs in general, but not necessarily any specifics with Lambda and VPCs. As such, there are certain VPC terms, like ENIs and security groups, which we'll mention but not explain.

Architectural Concerns of Using Lambda with a VPCs

Before you even enable Lambda to use a VPC, there are a few things to be aware of that might change your mind!

First, each *subnet* you specify in your VPC configuration is specific to an AZ. One of the nice things about Lambda is that we've completely ignored AZs until this point. If you're using Lambda + VPC, you need to make sure you configure enough subnets, across enough AZs, to allow you to continue to have the level of high availability (HA) you need.

Second, when a Lambda function is configured to use a VPC, then *all* network traffic from that Lambda will be routed through the VPC. That means if your Lambda function is using non-VPC AWS resources (like S3) or is using resources *external* to AWS, then you'll need to consider network routing for those resources, just like you would any other service within the VPC. For instance, for S3 you'll likely want to set up a VPC endpoint, and for external services you'll need to make sure your NAT Gateway is correctly configured.

Configuring Lambda to Use a VPC

You've read all the warnings, and you've figured out which subnets and security groups to use. How do you now actually configure your Lambda to use a VPC?

Fortunately, SAM comes to the rescue, and makes it fairly simple. By examining the example provided by AWS (*https://oreil.ly/388NC*) (slightly trimmed), we can see the additions that you need to make to each Lambda function:

```
AWSTemplateFormatVersion : '2010-09-09'
Transform: AWS::Serverless-2016-10-31

Parameters:
  SecurityGroupIds:
    Type: List<AWS::EC2::SecurityGroup::Id>
    Description: Security Group IDs that Lambda will use
  VpcSubnetIds:
    Type: List<AWS::EC2::Subnet::Id>
    Description: VPC Subnet IDs that Lambda will use (min 2 for HA)

Resources:
  HelloWorldFunction:
    Type: AWS::Serverless::Function
    Properties:
      Policies:
        - VPCAccessPolicy: {}
      VpcConfig:
        SecurityGroupIds: !Ref SecurityGroupIds
        SubnetIds: !Ref VpcSubnetIds
```

In summary, you need to:

- Add privileges for the Lambda function to attach to the VPC (e.g., by using `VPC AccessPolicy`)
- Add VPC configuration, with a list of security group IDs, and subnet IDs

And that's it! This particular example assumes that you'll use CloudFormation parameters (*https://oreil.ly/0xs3v*) to pass in the actual security group and subnet IDs at deployment time, but you should feel free to hardcode them in your template too.

Alternatives

Say that all of our dire warnings were enough to put you off of using VPCs with Lambda. What should you do instead? Here are a few approaches.

The first is to use roughly equivalent services that don't require a VPC. For example, if you were going to use a VPC to access an RDS database, consider using DynamoDB instead (although we do acknowledge that DynamoDB is not a relational database!). Or think about using Aurora serverless, and its Data API (*https://oreil.ly/uf2KE*).

Next is to re-architect your solution. For example, instead of calling a downstream resource directly, would it be possible to use a message bus as an intermediary?

Third—if what you needed to connect to was an internal service, then consider giving that internal service a "layer 7" authentication boundary. One way to do this is to add an API Gateway to your internal service (or update an existing API Gateway if it already has one), and then use API Gateway's IAM/Sigv4 authentication scheme (*https://oreil.ly/RJVSO*).

Finally, if you can't modify your service, you could do something similar to the previous idea, but in this case use API Gateway as a proxy (*https://oreil.ly/OKiid*) to your downstream service.

Of course, there is one more option—wait and see what AWS introduces next! For example, the Data API for serverless Aurora that we mentioned is fairly new, and signals that there may be more functionality coming that will help Lambda developers avoid the perils of VPCs!

Layers and Runtimes

If you take a look at one of your Lambda functions in the AWS Web Console, you'll now know what almost everything on there is for. Roles, environment variables, memory, VPCs, DLQs, reserved concurrency, and more. However, for the observant among you, you'll see that there's something towards the top of the page that is an omission so far: *layers*. To close out this chapter, we'll explain what layers are, why you (as a Java developer) probably won't care about them too much, and how they relate to another capability known as *custom runtimes*.

What Are Layers?

As you know by now, typically when you deploy a new version of a Lambda function, you package up the code and all of its dependencies into a ZIP file, and upload that file to the Lambda service. As your dependencies get bigger, however, this artifact gets bigger, and deployment slows down. Wouldn't it be nice to be able to speed this up?

This is where Lambda layers come in. A layer is part of the deployed resources of your Lambda function, which is deployed separately from the function itself. If your layer stays constant, then when you deploy your Lambda function, you only need to deploy the changes to your code that aren't within the layer.

Here's an example. Say that you are implementing the photo processing example from way back in Chapter 1 ("File processing" on page 15), and say that the actual part of your Lambda function that performs the image manipulation uses a third-party tool like ImageMagick (*https://imagemagick.org/index.php*).

Now, ImageMagick is probably a dependency that changes rarely. With Lambda layers you can define a layer (which is just a ZIP artifact containing any content that you want) that contains the ImageMagick tool, and then refer to that layer with your code in the photo processing Lambda. Now when you update your Lambda function, you'll only need to upload your own code, not your code *and* ImageMagick.

ImageMagick is often used by calling an external process from your application, rather than via a library API call. It's perfectly OK to call an external process like this from within a Lambda function—the Lambda runtime is a full Linux environment.

Another useful aspect to layers is that you can share layers across Lambda functions, and other AWS accounts—layers can in fact be shared publicly.

When to Use, and Not Use, Layers

When layers were announced, certain parts of the Lambda-using world were very excited, since they saw layers as a universal dependency system for Lambda functions. This was especially true for people using the Python language, since Python's dependency management tools can be a little tricky for some people (e.g., your authors!) to wrap their heads around. The Java ecosystem however, for all its faults, has a very strong story to tell around dependency management.

We feel that there are some specific times when layers are useful. However, there are also a number of concerns that we have about embracing them wholeheartedly, for example:

- Since layers are combined with your Lambda function after you've uploaded the function, it's not necessarily true that the version of a dependency you've used at test time (before deployment) is the same as that which is used with the deployed version. This, to us, is a (typically) unnecessary headache of coordination that needs to be managed.

- Lambda functions are limited to the number of layers that can be used (five), and so if you have more than five dependencies, you're going to need to use a local deployment tool anyway, so why add the extra complexity of layers?

- Layers don't particularly provide any functional benefit—they are a deployment optimization tool (we'll talk about cross-cutting behavior as a caveat for this).

- Particularly for developing Lambda in Java—Java does a pretty good job of defining its "own world." For example, it's usual to only depend on third-party code in Java that itself runs in the JVM, as opposed to calling out to system libraries or executables. Given this, and the ubiquity of Maven dependencies, it's easy to have one consolidated dependency management system with a Java application that doesn't include the use of Lambda layers.

- Some people like the fact that a layer can be manually updated for a function without having to deploy a new version of the function itself. We personally believe strongly that apart from extenuating circumstances, the best way to deploy any changes to production is through an automated continuous delivery process, and therefore the difference between changing an application library dependency versus a configured template layer dependency should almost always be moot.

We'd be remiss if we didn't also point out the places that layers can be useful.

First, if part of what a Lambda function executes is unrelated to the application, but more related to an organization's cross-cutting technical platform, then using layers as an alternative deployment path can be useful. For example, say that there is a security process that needs to be run, but as far as application developers are concerned, it's just a "fire-and-forget" call. In this case, publishing that code in a layer, and being able to query all the Lambda function configurations across an organization and making sure they're using the correct version of the layer, aids in organizational governance.

Another place where layers are useful is where a dependency is a large, system binary that rarely changes. In this case, the extra complexity of using layers may be worth the value of improved deployment speed, especially if the number of deployments of functions using that layer is on the order of hundreds per day or more.

A helpful example of this second case is where a Lambda function is using a custom runtime, which we'll explore now.

Custom Runtimes

Throughout this book we have been using the Java Lambda runtime, apart from our very first example, which used the Node 10 runtime. AWS offers a number of runtimes (*https://oreil.ly/uLMNz*) associated with different programming languages, and this list is frequently updated.

However, what happens if you want to use a language or runtime that AWS don't support? For example, what if you have some Cobol code you want to run in a Lambda function? Or, perhaps more likely, what if you want to run a highly customized JVM, rather than the one AWS provides?

The answer here is to use a *custom runtime*. A custom runtime is a Linux process that runs in a Lambda execution environment, and that can process Lambda events. There is a specific execution model (*https://oreil.ly/onv6J*) that a custom runtime needs to fulfill, but the basic idea is that when the runtime instance is started by the Lambda platform, it is configured with an instance-specific URL that it can query for the next event to process. In other words, custom runtimes use a polling architecture.

As a Java developer, it will typically be rare that you want or need to use a custom runtime for production usages. Two reasons for this are as follows:

- The custom runtime code itself needs to be part of your function's deployed assets. While you can package the runtime in a Lambda layer to avoid uploading it on every deployment, it will still be using up some of your 250MB total unpacked deployment package size limit (*https://oreil.ly/02nUm*). Most JVMs are going to use a considerable part of that, if you want to ship a custom JVM, and so this will cut into the space available for your application code.

- You will need to reimplement in your custom runtime a lot of what AWS has already implemented in its standard runtimes, such as deserialization/serialization of events and responses, error handling, and more.

That being said, for organizations of a certain size, building a custom runtime that handles various organizational-platform-related tasks might make actual Lambda development even more effective, but we would suggest a through analysis before jumping in!

This book has been focussed on the Java language, running on the Java runtime. However, there are many other languages that can run on the JVM—Scala, Clojure, Kotlin, and more. Since Lambda only specifies the Java *runtime*, it's perfectly reasonable to use alternative languages. In fact, we know of people using Scala and Lambda for significant load systems (thousands of concurrent executions).

From the Java Lambda runtime's point of view, all it cares is that you configure it with a valid handler method, so the way that most people use alternative JVM languages with Lambda is to use the Java runtime, and then an "interop" hook into their handler. Here's an example using Kotlin and Groovy on the AWS blog (*https://oreil.ly/4qUvM*). Depending on your specific language, the POJO serialization provided by the Java runtime may or may not play nicely, but alternatively you can use the Input Stream/OutputStream handler signature to get the raw bytes of a JSON event.

One drawback to using an alternative JVM language, especially one like Scala, is that it adds to your cold start time because the JVM has to JIT compile the language classes, as well as your application classes. But the general rules about cold starts that we discussed earlier in this chapter still hold, especially if your functions are high throughput.

An alternative to using the AWS Java runtime is to use a custom runtime to support your JVM language, but typically that isn't necessary, assuming the standard Java runtime can support your alternative JVM language.

Summary

In this chapter, we took a deep dive into some advanced aspects of Lambda. Some of these behaviors and configurations will be crucial as you deploy your serverless applications to production.

You learned about the following:

- The various different error handling strategies of Lambda and how you may choose to configure and program your functions to process errors
- The liberating way that Lambda scales without any effort on your part, how you can control that scaling, and what this behavior means in the context of multi-threaded programming
- What Lambda versions and aliases are, and how to use them with a "traffic shifting" approach for releasing new features

- What cold starts are, when they occur, whether you should be concerned about them, and how to mitigate them if you need to reduce their impact in your applications

- How to consider persistent and cache state in Lambda development

- How to use Lambda with AWS VPCs

- What Lambda layers and custom runtimes are, and when to think about using them

In the next chapter, we carry on rounding out our discussion of the more advanced aspects of Lambda, but this time in the context of how Lambda interacts with other services.

Exercises

1. Update `WeatherQueryLambda` in "Example: Building a Serverless API" on page 92 to throw an exception. What behavior do you see when you try to call the API?

2. If you implemented the exercise from Chapter 5 to use an SQS queue, then update the Lambda function that reads from SQS to throw an exception. Does Lambda's retry behavior do what you'd expect?

3. Investigate what happens with background threads and Lambda—start with the "Hello World" example from Chapter 2 (see "Lambda Hello World (the Proper Way)" on page 34) and within the handler use a `ScheduledExecutorService` (*https://oreil.ly/6cz67*) and its `scheduleAtFixedRate` method to repeatedly log the event that you received. What happens? Try using some `Thread.sleep` statements too.

4. Update "Example: Building a Serverless API" on page 92 to use traffic shifting, starting with the `Linear10PercentEvery10Minutes` deployment preference.

5. *Extended task*: If you program on the JVM with a different language—perhaps Clojure, Kotlin, or Scala—try building a Lambda function in one of those languages.

CHAPTER 9

Advanced Serverless Architecture

In Chapter 8 we looked at some more advanced aspects of Lambda that are important once you start thinking about productionizing your applications. In this chapter, we continue that theme, looking more broadly at the impact of Lambda on architecture.

Serverless Architecture "Gotchas"

First we look at areas of serverless architecture that might cause you problems if you don't consider them, and we offer different solutions for addressing these problems depending on your situation.

At-Least-Once Delivery

The Lambda platform guarantees that when an upstream event source triggers a Lambda function, or if another application explicitly calls the Lambda *invoke* API call (*https://oreil.ly/p1OWt*), then the corresponding Lambda function will be called. But one thing the platform doesn't guarantee is *how many times the function will be called*: "Occasionally, your function may receive the same event multiple times, even if no error occurs." This is known as "at-least-once delivery," and it exists due to the fact that the Lambda platform is a distributed system.

The vast majority of the time a Lambda function will be called only once per event. But sometimes, very occasionally (far less than 1% of the time), a Lambda function will be called multiple times. Why is this a problem? And how do you deal with this behavior? Let's take a look.

Example: Lambda "cron jobs"

If you've been developing software in industry long enough, you've probably come across a server host that runs multiple "cron jobs"—scheduled tasks that run perhaps every hour or every day. Because these tasks typically don't run all the time it would be inefficient to run only one on each host, so it's very typical to run multiple types of job on just one host. This is more efficient, but can cause operational headaches—dependency clashes, ownership uncertainties, security concerns, etc.

You can implement many kinds of activity that would otherwise be performed in a cron job as a Lambda function. To get the schedule behavior of cron, you can use a *CloudWatch Scheduled Event* as a trigger. SAM gives you a concise syntax (*https://oreil.ly/vFPnk*) to specify this as a trigger for a function, and you can even use cron syntax to specify a schedule expression (*https://oreil.ly/488um*). There are various benefits to using Lambda as a cron platform—including improving all the operational headaches from the previous paragraph.

The chief drawbacks to using Lambda to implement a cron task are if the function takes longer than 15 minutes to run (Lambda's maximum timeout) or if it needs more than 3GB memory. In either of these situations, if you can't break up your task into smaller chunks, then you may want to look at Step Functions (*https://oreil.ly/YDDyY*) and/or Fargate (*https://oreil.ly/NP0Sq*) instead.

But there is one other drawback to using Lambda: *very, very,* occasionally your cron job may run more than once at or near its scheduled time. Often this won't be a problem worth considering—maybe your task is a cleanup job where performing the same cleanup twice is slightly inefficient but functionally correct. Other times, though, this might be a big problem—what if your task is calculating mortgage interest for the month—you wouldn't want to charge that twice to a customer.

This *at-least-once delivery* characteristic of Lambda applies to all event sources and invocations, not just scheduled events. Fortunately, there are a number of ways to tackle this problem.

Solution: Build an idempotent system

The first, and typically the best, solution to this concern is to build an *idempotent* (*https://oreil.ly/rmaFI*) system. We say that this is "typically the best" solution because it embraces the idea that we are building distributed systems when we use Lambda. Instead of working around, or ignoring, the attributes of distributed systems, we actively design to work with them.

A system is idempotent when a specific operation can be applied one or more times, and have the same effect no matter how many times it was applied. Idempotence is a very common requirement when considering any distributed architecture, let alone a serverless one.

An example of an idempotent operation is uploading a file to S3 (ignoring any possible triggers!). Whether you upload the same file to the same location once or ten times, the net result is that the correct bytes will be stored in S3 at the expected key.

We can build an idempotent system with Lambda when any significant *side effects* of a function are, themselves, idempotent. For example, if our Lambda function uploads a file to S3, then the complete system of Lambda + S3 is idempotent. Similarly if you are writing to a database you can use an *upsert* operation ("update or insert"), like DynamoDB's `UpdateItem` (*https://oreil.ly/OTfZP*) method, to create idempotence. Finally, if you are calling any external APIs, you will likely want to look to see if they offer idempotent operations.

Solution: Accept duplicates, and perhaps deal with problems if/when they come up

Sometimes a perfectly reasonable way to deal with possible multiple invocations is to be aware that it can happen, and accept it, especially since it happens so rarely. For example, say you have a scheduled task that generates a report and then emails it to a company-internal mailing list. Do you care if that email occasionally goes out twice? Perhaps not.

Similarly, maybe the work to build an idempotent system would be significant, but dealing with the impact of very occasional task repetition is actually simple and cheap. In this case, rather than building in idempotence, it might be better to monitor for a job being run multiple times for one event and then have a manual or automated task that performs cleanup if it ever occurs.

Solution: Check for previous processing

If repeated side effects aren't ever acceptable, but your Lambda function is also using downstream systems that don't have idempotent operations, then you have another way to solve this problem. The idea is to make your Lambda function itself idempotent, rather than relying on downstream components to provide idempotence.

But how do you do this, knowing that Lambda may call a function multiple times for the same event? The key here is to also know that even if Lambda calls a function more than once for the same event, then the *AWS request ID* that Lambda attaches to an event will be the same for each call. We can read the AWS request ID by calling `.getAwsRequestId()` on the `Context` (*https://oreil.ly/gh-Bw*) object that we can choose to accept in our handler method.

Assuming we can keep track of these request IDs, we'll know if we've seen one before, and if we have we can choose to discard the second call, guaranteeing "exactly-once" overall semantics.

All we need now is a way of checking, for each invocation of our function, to see if the function has already seen the request ID before. Because multiple function invocations for an event could in theory overlap, we need a source of *atomicity* to provide this capability, and this suggests that using a database would help.

DynamoDB can provide this for us by way of its *conditional writes* (*https://oreil.ly/ DBne-*) feature. In a simple scenario, we could have a table with just a primary key of request_id; we could attempt to write to that table at the beginning of our handler with the event's request ID; immediately stop execution if the DynamoDB operation failed; and otherwise continue our Lambda's functionality as normal, knowing that this is the first time an event has been processed (see Figure 9-1).

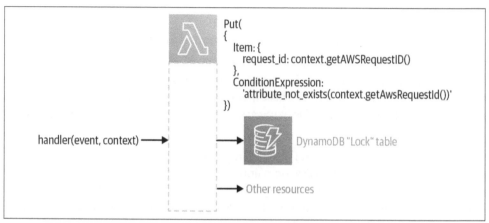

Figure 9-1. Checking for a previous event with DynamoDB

If you choose to go down this path, your actual solution will likely have some nuance. For example, you may choose to delete the row in DynamoDB if an error occurred (so as to continue to be able to use Lambda's retry semantics—the retried event will also have the same AWS request ID!). And/or you may choose to have a more complicated "lock with timeout" style of behavior to allow for overlapping calls where the first could fail.

There are also a few DynamoDB concerns to think about with this solution. For example, you probably want to set up a Time to Live (TTL) property (*https://oreil.ly/ JFDQg*) on the table to automatically delete rows after a certain period of time to keep things clean, typically set to a day or to a week. Also, you may want to consider the expected throughput of your Lambda function and use that to analyze costs of the DynamoDB table—if the costs are too high, you may want to choose an alternative solution. Such alternatives include using a SQL database; building your own (non-Lambda) service to manage this repetition; or, in extreme cases, replacing Lambda entirely for this particular function with a more traditional compute platform.

Impacts of Lambda Scaling on Downstream Systems

In Chapter 8 we looked at Lambda's "magical" auto-scaling ("Scaling" on page 193). To quickly summarize, Lambda will automatically create just as many instances as necessary of your function, and its environment, to handle all events to be processed.

It will do this, by default, up to one thousand Lambda instances per account, and more than that if you ask AWS to increase your limit.

This is, in general, a very useful feature, and one of the key reasons people find Lambda valuable. However, if your Lambda function interacts with downstream systems (and most do!), then you need to consider how such scaling could impact those systems. As an exercise, let's consider the examples in Chapter 5.

In "Example: Building a Serverless API" on page 92, we had two functions—Weather EventLambda and WeatherQueryLambda—that both called DynamoDB. We would need to know that DynamoDB could handle the load of however many upstream Lambda instances existed. Since we used DynamoDB's "on-demand" capacity mode (*https://oreil.ly/SHRmW*), we know that this is, in fact, the case.

In "Example: Building a Serverless Data Pipeline" on page 111, we also had two functions—BulkEventsLambda and SingleEventLambda. BulkEventsLambda calls SNS, specifically to publish messages, so we can look at the AWS service limits documentation (*https://oreil.ly/rv4GW*) to see how many publish calls we can make to the SNS API. That page says that the limit is between 300 and 30,000 "transactions per second," depending on the region we're in.

We can use that data to make a judgment call as to whether we think SNS can handle the load we may put on it from our Lambda function. Also, the documentation says that this is a *soft limit*—in other words, we can ask AWS to increase it for us. It's worth knowing that should we exceed the limit, then our use of SNS will be throttled—we could pass this error back up through our Lambda function as an *unhandled error* and therefore use Lambda's retry mechanism. It's also useful to know that this is an account-wide limit, so any other components using SNS in the same account would also be throttled if our Lambda function caused us to hit the SNS API limit.

SingleEventLambda only calls CloudWatch Logs indirectly via the Lambda runtime. CloudWatch Logs has limits, but they're very high, so for now we'll assume it has sufficient capacity.

In summary, the services that we've used in these examples scale up to high throughputs. That shouldn't be surprising—these examples were designed to be good examples of serverless architecture.

However, what happens if you're using downstream systems that either (a) don't scale as *much* as your Lambda function may scale or (b) don't scale as *quickly* as your Lambda function may scale? An example of (a) might be a downstream relational database—it may only be designed for one hundred concurrent connections, and five hundred connections might cause it serious problems. An example of (b) might be a downstream microservice using EC2-based auto-scaling—here the service may eventually scale wide enough to handle unexpected load, but Lambda can scale in *seconds*, as opposed to EC2, which will scale in *minutes*.

In either of these cases, unplanned scaling of your Lambda functions can cause performance impacts on downstream systems. Often times if such problems occur then the effects will also be felt by other clients of those systems, not just the Lambda function inflicting the load. Because of this concern, you should always consider Lambda's impact on downstream systems with regards to scaling. There are multiple possible solutions to dealing with this.

Solution: Use like-scaling infrastructure

One solution is, where possible, to use downstream systems that have similar scaling behaviors and capacities to Lambda itself. We chose DynamoDB and SNS in the Chapter 5 examples partly due to this design motivation. Similarly, sometimes we may choose to actively migrate away from certain solutions precisely because of scaling concerns. For example, if we can easily switch to using DynamoDB from an RDS database, it may make sense to do so.

Solution: Manage scaling upstream

Another way to solve the problem of Lambda scaling too wide for downstream systems is to make sure it never needs to scale in the first place, or in other words to restrict the number of events that trigger execution. If you're implementing a company-internal serverless API, then this might mean making sure the API's clients do not make too many requests.

Some Lambda event sources also offer functionality to help manage scale. API Gateway has rate limiting (with *usage plans* (*https://oreil.ly/FR4eX*) and *throttling limits*), and Lambda's SQS integration allows you to configure a batch size (*https://oreil.ly/LxNTp*).

Solution: Manage scaling with reserved concurrency

If you can't manage scale upstream, but still want to restrict how wide your function will scale, you can use Lambda's reserved concurrency feature that we looked at in "Reserved concurrency" on page 196.

When using reserved concurrency, the Lambda platform will only scale out your function at most as wide as the configured amount you have given. For example, if you set reserved concurrency to 10, then you'll have at most 10 instances of your Lambda function running at any one time. In this case, if 10 instances of your Lambda are already processing events when another event arrives, then your function is throttled, just as we looked at in Chapter 8.

This kind of scale limitation is great when you have event sources like SNS or S3 where you may easily have a "burst" of events—using reserved concurrency means that these events are processed over a period of time, rather than all immediately. And because of Lambda's retrying capability for throttling errors and asynchronous sources, you're guaranteed that all of the events will eventually get processed, as long as processing can occur within six hours.

One behavior you should know about reserved concurrency is that it doesn't just limit concurrency—it *guarantees* concurrency by removing the configured amount from the account-global Lambda concurrency pool. If you have 20 functions all with a reserved concurrency of 50, then you won't have any more capacity for other Lambda functions, assuming an account-wide concurrency limit of 1,000. This account-wide limit can be increased, but that's a manual task that you'll need to remember to perform.

Solution: Architect deliberately hybrid solutions

A final idea is to build *deliberately* "hybrid" solutions (as opposed to *accidentally* hybrid solutions) consisting of serverless and traditional components.

For example, if you used Lambda and Amazon's (nonserverless) RDS SQL database service, without considering the scaling concerns, we'd call this an "accidentally" hybrid solution. However, if you put thought into how your RDS database could be used more effectively with Lambda, then we'd call this "deliberately" hybrid. And to be clear—we think that some architectural solutions are going to be better with a mixture of serverless and nonserverless components, due to the nature of services like DynamoDB, and Lambda itself.

Let's consider an example where you are ingesting data into a relational database via a Lambda function, perhaps behind an API Gateway (Figure 9-2).

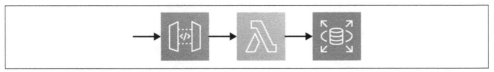

Figure 9-2. Direct writes to a relational database from a Lambda function

A concern with this design is that if you have too many inbound requests, then you may end up overloading your downstream database.

The first solution you may consider is to add reserved concurrency to the Lambda function backing the API, but the problem here is now your upstream clients will have to deal with throttling caused by your concurrency restrictions.

A better solution, therefore, might be to introduce a messaging topic, a new Lambda function, and use reserved concurrency on the second Lambda function (Figure 9-3).

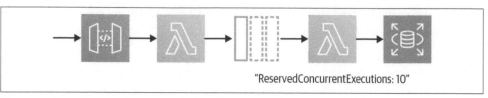

"ReservedConcurrentExecutions: 10"

Figure 9-3. Indirect writes to a relational database from a Lambda function via a topic

With this design, your API Lambda function can still, for example, perform input validation, returning an error message to the client if necessary. However, instead of writing directly to the database, it would instead publish a message to a topic, for example, with SNS, under the assumption that your messaging system can handle sudden load more effectively than your database. The listener of that message would then be another Lambda function, whose job is purely to perform the database write (or "upsert" to handle duplicate invocations!). But this time the Lambda function can have reserved concurrency applied to protect the database, while at the same time making use of the retry semantics within AWS itself, rather than requiring the original external client to perform a retry.

While this resulting design has more moving parts, it successfully solves the scaling concerns while still mixing serverless and nonserverless components.

> In late 2019 Amazon announced the RDS Proxy (*https://oreil.ly/ alAqq*) service. At the time of writing, it is still in "Preview" and so many of the details and capabilities it will have when it is released to general availability (GA) aren't yet known. However, it certainly should help with some of the concerns discussed in this chapter in connecting Lambda to RDS.

Lambda Runtime Model and Cost Impact on Downstream Systems

This section has been about the functional impacts of Lambda's scaling. It's also useful to consider how scale, external systems, and Lambda's runtime model impact overall system financial costs.

Say, for example, that you have the following piece of Lambda code. This particular handler uses the AWS service KMS (*https://aws.amazon.com/kms*) to decrypt an encrypted environment variable:

```java
public class LambdaWithApiKey {
  public void handler(Object event) {
    final String encryptedAPIKey = System.getenv("ENCRYPTED_API_KEY");
    final String apiKey = decryptWithKms(encryptedAPIKey);
    // ... use apiKey to process event
  }
}
```

```
    private String decryptWithKms(String encryptedCypherText) {
      // Use AWS to decrypt encryptedCypherText, and return the value
    }
  }
```

We're leaving out the actual KMS service implementation here for brevity's sake.

This Lambda function would work correctly. But say we changed the code to the following:

```
public class LambdaWithApiKey {
  private final String apiKey;

  public LambdaWithApiKey() {
    final String encryptedAPIKey = System.getenv("ENCRYPTED_API_KEY");
    apiKey = decryptWithKms(encryptedAPIKey);
  }

  public void handler(Object event) {
    // ... use apiKey to process event
  }

  private String decryptWithKms(String encryptedCypherText) {
    // USE AWS KMS TO DECRYPT, AND RETURN
  }
}
```

This code, functionally, does precisely what the first version did—we just moved some code to the constructor. So what is the difference? One difference is that at an average of 200 events per second the first version increases your AWS costs nearly $20,000/year in comparison to the second version! This is because the first version calls KMS to decrypt the API key on every event, but the second version calls KMS only once per function instance. AWS charges for KMS by the number of times we call its API, so KMS costs increase linearly with how many times the Lambda function calls it.

This is not a hypothetical situation—we've seen an example of the first version of the code. We recommended switching to the second version, saving one of our clients approximately $20,000/year.

While Lambda has a simple runtime model, how you use it can still have substantive impacts on other components and services, and also your AWS bill.

The "Fine Print" of Lambda Event Sources

The first couple of sections in this chapter have been about architectural concerns that come about because of nuances of Lambda itself. There are other areas that can impact a serverless design because of the services that exist upstream of Lambda. Just like the fact that "at-least-once" delivery isn't front and center of the first document you read about Lambda, you'll only find some of these nuances with upstream services through deep exploration of documentation, or hard-earned experience.

When you start to get beyond the "tinkering" stage with any Lambda event source, read as much AWS documentation as you can on the services you're using. Seek out non-AWS articles too—while they're not authoritative, and sometimes wrong, occasionally they can nudge you in a direction, architecturally, that you may not have considered otherwise.

New Patterns of Architecture Enabled by Serverless Thinking

Sometimes when we're building serverless systems, our architecture, viewed from a certain distance, might not look that different than how we could have designed it using containers or virtual machines (VMs). "Cloud-native" architecture is not the sole domain of Kubernetes, no matter what you may have otherwise heard!

For example, our serverless API that we built back in "Example: Building a Serverless API" on page 92, from a "black-box" point of view, looked just like any other microservice-style API. In fact, we could replace the Lambda functions with an application running in a container and, architecturally, the system would have been very similar.

As serverless starts to mature, however, we're seeing new architectural patterns that either wouldn't make sense with traditional services, or wouldn't even be possible. We alluded to one of these earlier in Chapter 5 when we talked about "Serverless Without Lambda" on page 102. To close out this chapter, we'll look at a couple of other patterns, using Lambda, that break into new territory.

Published Components with the Serverless Application Repository

We've talked a few times through the book about "serverless applications"—groups of components that we collectively deploy as one unit. We had our serverless API, using API Gateway, two Lambda functions, and a DynamoDB table, all grouped as a unit. We defined this collection of resources using a Serverless Application Model (SAM) template.

AWS provides a way to reuse and share these SAM applications, via the Serverless Application Repository (SAR) (*https://oreil.ly/Oa8HO*). With SAR you *publish* your application, and you can then *deploy* it later, multiple times, to different regions, accounts, or even different organizations if you choose to make the SAR application publicly available.

Traditionally you likely have either distributed code or a shipped environment–agnostic deployment configuration. With SAR the code (by way of packaged Lambda functions), the infrastructure definitions, and the (parameterizable) deployment configuration are all wrapped up in one shareable, *versioned*, component.

There are a couple of different ways that SAR apps can be deployed that make them useful in different situations.

First, they can be deployed as *standalone applications*, just as if you had called sam deploy directly on them, rather than using SAR. This is useful when you want to deploy the same application in multiple locations or across multiple accounts or organizations. In this case, SAR acts somewhat like a repository of application deployment templates, but by bundling the code, it also includes the actual application code.

Examples of SAR application suited to this type of usage abound in the public SAR repository (*https://oreil.ly/QyOkD*)—it's especially useful for third-party software providers who want to make it easier for customers to deploy integration components to their AWS account. A good example is this log forwarder from DataDog (*https://oreil.ly/z-s8e*).

SAR applications can also be used as *embedded* components within other, *parent*, serverless applications via CloudFormation nested stacks (*https://oreil.ly/1sJjI*). SAM enables nesting SAR components via the AWS::Serverless::Application resource type (*https://oreil.ly/aY0-G*). When using SAR in this way, you are abstracting higher-level components as SAR apps, and instantiating those components within multiple applications. Using SAR in this way is a little like using a "sidecar" (*https://oreil.ly/9k3Xl*) in container-oriented applications, but without the low-level network-oriented communication patterns that sidecars require.

These nested components may include Lambda functions that may be invoked directly, or indirectly (e.g., via SNS topic, perhaps also included in the SAR), by the parent application. Alternatively, these nested components may not contain any functions at all, and instead solely define infrastructural resources. A good example here are SAR applications that standardize monitoring resources.

We prefer the embedded deployment scheme in general, even if there are no other components in the parent application. This is because deploying SAR apps, along with their parameter values that can be defined as part of the AWS::Server less::Application resource in your template file, is no different than deploying any other SAM-defined serverless application. Further, if you choose to update the *version* of a deployed SAR app, then that too can be tracked in version control just like any other template update.

SAR apps can be secured so that they are accessible only to accounts within a particular AWS organization, and therefore they are a great way of defining standard components that can be used across a whole company. Examples of using this with the embedded component deployment scheme are custom authorizers for API Gateway, standard operational components (e.g., alarms, log filters, and dashboards), and common patterns of message-based inter-service communication.

SAR does have some limitations. For example, you can't use all CloudFormation resource types within it (for example, EC2 instances). However, this is an interesting way of building, deploying, and composing Lambda-based applications.

For details on how to publish SAM applications to SAR, see the documentation (*https://oreil.ly/nhOUb*), and for details of deploying SAR apps see the previous link for the AWS::Serverless::Application resource type.

Globally Distributed Applications

In days of yore (i.e., about 15 years ago), most of us building server-based applications often had a fairly good idea where our software was physically running, at least to within one hundred meters or so, and often closer than that. We could pinpoint the data centers, server rooms, and perhaps even the racks or individual machines where our code was humming along.

Along came the "cloud," and our understanding of the geographic deployment of our apps got a little, well, cloudy. With EC2, for example, we know, roughly, that our code is running in the region of "Northern Virginia" or "Ireland" and we also know when two servers are running in the same data center, via their Availability Zone (AZ) location. But it's extremely unlikely that we'd be able to point on a map to the building where our software is running.

Serverless computing immediately expands our radius of consideration a little further. Now we're *only* thinking of the region—the AZ concept is hidden in abstraction.

One of the reasons to know where your applications are running is when you consider availability. When we run applications in a data center, we would need to know that if the data center lost internet connectivity, then our applications would be unavailable.

For many companies, certainly those who are used to deploying to one data center, this regional level of availability we get with the cloud is sufficient, especially since serverless services guarantee high availability across a region.

But what if you want to think bigger? For example, what if you want to guarantee resilience of your application even if an entire region of AWS becomes unstable? This happens—just talk to anyone that's used us-east-1 for at least a couple of years. The good news is that it's very rare that AWS has any kind of *cross-region* outage. The vast majority of AWS downtime is constrained to one region.

Alternatively, looking beyond just availability, what if your users are spread around the world, from Sao Paulo to Seoul, and you want all of them to have low-latency access to your applications?

Solving these problems has been *possible* in the cloud ever since multiple regions became available. However, running applications in multiple regions is complicated, and can get expensive, especially as you add more regions.

Serverless, however, makes this problem significantly easier and cheaper. It's now possible to deploy your application to multiple regions around the world, without much added complexity, and without breaking your budget.

Global deployment

When you define your application in a SAM template, you don't typically hardcode any region-specific resources. If you need to refer to the region in which a stack is deployed in a CloudFormation string (as we did in the data pipeline example in Chapter 5), we recommend using the AWS::Region *pseudo parameter* (*https://oreil.ly/7Xe9-*). For any region-specific resources that you need to access, we recommend passing those by reference as a CloudFormation parameter.

With these techniques you can define your application template in a *region-neutral* way, and you can deploy it to as many AWS regions as you like.

Actually deploying your application to multiple regions isn't quite as easy as we'd like it to be. For example, when you deploy an application with CloudFormation (e.g., using sam deploy) any packages that you refer to in the CodeUri properties in the template file must be available in a S3 bucket that is located *within the same region you are deploying to*. Therefore, if you want to deploy an application to multiple regions, then its packaged artifacts need to be available in multiple S3 buckets, one per region. This is nothing a little scripting can't solve, but it's something that you have to think about.

AWS has improved the experience of multiregion deployment by enabling "cross-region actions" in CodePipeline (*https://oreil.ly/E_DJr*). CodePipeline is Amazon's "continuous delivery" orchestration tool and allows us to define the source control repository for a project; build and package an application by calling out to CodeBuild (*https://oreil.ly/fSD1_*); and finally deploy it using SAM/CloudFormation. CodePipeline is effectively an automation system on top of the commands we've been running manually in this book. It will do a lot more than this too—the flow here is just an example.

"Cross-region actions" (*https://oreil.ly/6X5vB*) within CodePipeline allow you to deploy to multiple regions, in parallel, to as many regions as currently support CodePipeline at the current time. This means that one CD pipeline can deploy an application to the US, Europe, Japan, and South America.

There's still some trickiness to setting all of this up. For more, please see our example project on Github (*https://oreil.ly/xzWiI*).

Another tool that helps multiregion deployment is the Serverless Application Repository, which we described in the previous section. When you publish an application to SAR via one region, it is made available globally to all regions. At the time of writing, this is only the case for publicly shared applications, but we hope that this feature will be enabled for private apps before too long.

Localized connectivity, with failover

Once you've deployed your application around the world, how do your users connect to a version that's near to them? One of the points of global deployment, after all, is to accept that the speed of light is limited, and therefore to route user requests to the closest geographic version of your application to their client, giving users the lowest latency experience you can.

One way is to hardcode the region-specific location, typically a DNS hostname, within the client itself. It's crude, but sometimes effective, especially for organization-internal apps.

An alternative that's usually better, because it adapts *dynamically* to the user's location, is to embrace Amazon's Route53 DNS Service, and specifically its *Geolocation* (*https://oreil.ly/4RCb2*) feature. For example, if users connect to your application via an API Gateway deployed in parallel to three different regions, then you can set up your DNS in Route53 such that the user is connected to the API Gateway in the region closest to them.

Since you're already using some advanced features of Route53 by this point, you may as well go one step further and use *Health Checks and DNS Failover* (*https://oreil.ly/XlUX9*). With this feature of Route53, if the version of your application nearest to a user becomes unavailable, then Route53 will instead reroute that user to the *next* nearest, available, version of the application.

Now we have active-active versions of our applications *and* localized routing. We have built an application that is resilient *and* has better performance. And so far there have been no updates to our application architecture, only operational updates. However, we should really address the elephant in the room.

Global state

We said earlier that serverless makes it possible to deploy your application to multiple regions around the world, without much added complexity. We just described the deployment process itself, and we talked about how users can access your application over the internet.

A big concern, however, with global applications is how to treat state. The simplest solution is to have your state in only one region and have your service using that state deployed to multiple regions (Figure 9-4).

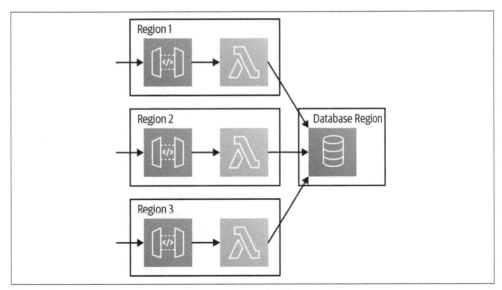

Figure 9-4. Multiple compute regions and one database region

This is the same model that content delivery networks (CDNs) (*https://oreil.ly/UaAj5*) use—there is one "origin" somewhere in the world, and then CDNs cache state in tens, or hundreds, of "points of presence" around the globe.

This is fine for cacheable state, but what about noncacheable situations?

In this case, the single-region-for-state model breaks down since all of your regions will be calling the centralized database region for *every request*. You've lost the benefit of localized latency, and you run the risk of a regional outage.

Fortunately, AWS and the other major cloud providers now provide globally replicated databases. A good example of this on AWS is DynamoDB global tables (*https://oreil.ly/fEZAG*). Say you're using the serverless API pattern from Chapter 5—you can replace the DynamoDB table in your design from that example with a *global* table. You can then happily deploy your API to multiple regions around the world, and AWS will do the hard work of moving your data safely around the planet. This gives you resilience, and improved user latency, since the table replication is performed by DynamoDB asynchronously (Figure 9-5).

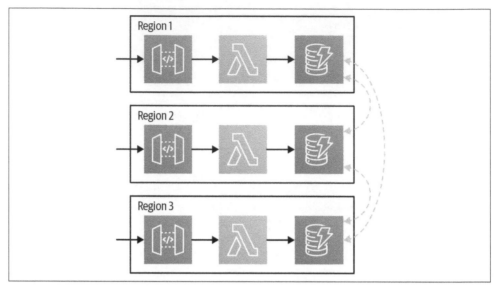

Figure 9-5. Multiple regions with a replicated database

AWS does charge a premium for global tables, but they're not too much more expensive than having a table per region, especially when compared with building a state replication system yourself.

Pay-per-use

On the subject of costs, this is where serverless computing really clinches the deal when it comes to multiregion deployment. Back in Chapter 1 we said that a specific differentiator of a serverless service is that it "has costs that are based on precise usage, up from and down to zero usage." This applies not just to one region but across regions.

Say, for example, you have deployed a Lambda application to three regions because you want to have two backup regions for disaster recovery. If you are using only one of those regions, then you are *paying* only for the Lambda usage in that one region—the backup versions you have in the other two regions are free! This is a huge difference from any other computing paradigm.

On the other hand, say you start off with an application deployed to one region, but then you deploy your API Gateway + Lambda application to ten regions, using the Geolocation DNS routing we discussed earlier. If you do this, your Lambda bill won't change—whether you run in one region or ten—because Lambda still only charges you by the amount of activity that occurs in your functions. Your previous usage hasn't increased; it's now just distributed across ten regions.

We think that this vastly different cost model, in comparison to traditional platforms, will make globally distributed applications much more common than they've been in the past.

 There's a slight caveat here to the "no change in costs" point for Lambda. AWS may charge slightly differently for Lambda for different regions. That's an element of region-specific pricing, however, not because of running your application across multiple regions.

Edge computing/"regionless"

The examples we've talked about in this section so far are all about deploying to multiple regions around the world, but they do still require us to understand that Amazon's entire cloud is broken up into those different regions.

What if you didn't need to think about regions at all? What if you were able to deploy your code to a global service, and then AWS just did whatever it needed to run your code, giving users the best latency possible, and guaranteeing availability even if one location went offline?

It turns out that this wild idea of the future is already here. Sort of. First, AWS already has some services that are "global services"—IAM and Route53 are two of them. But so is CloudFront: AWS's CDN (*https://oreil.ly/_0EUS*). While CloudFront does the thing you'd expect of any other CDN—caching HTTP traffic to enable faster websites—it also has the capability of being able to invoke a special class of Lambda functions via a service named Lambda@Edge (*https://oreil.ly/6D4yw*).

Lambda@Edge functions are mostly similar to Lambda functions—they have the same runtime model and mostly the same deployment tooling. When you deploy a Lambda@Edge function, AWS replicates your code around the world, so your application truly becomes "regionless."

There are, however, a number of significant limitations to Lambda@Edge, including:

- The only event source available is CloudFront itself—so you can only run Lambda@Edge as part of processing an HTTP request within a CloudFront distribution.
- Lambda@Edge functions, at the time of writing, can be written only in Node or Python.
- The Lambda@Edge environment has more restrictions with regard to memory, CPU, and timeout than regular Lambda functions.

Lambda@Edge functions are fascinating, and even at the time of writing are great for solving certain problems. But more than that, they point to a future of *truly* global cloud computing, where locality is completely abstracted. If AWS can bring Lambda@Edge closer in capability to regular Lambda, then as architects and developers we are well on the road to leaving region-thinking behind us. We might still need to think about locality when people are running applications on Mars, but we're a few years away from that yet. Lambda promises to be serverless, not planetless!

Summary

When we're building serverless systems, the amount of effort that we spend on code and operations decreases, but some of that effort needs to be exchanged for more architectural thinking than we have done in the past, especially about the capabilities and limitations of the managed services we're using. In this chapter, you learned more detail of some of these concerns, and examined a number of mitigation approaches.

Serverless computing also presents entirely new ways of architecting software. You learned about two such ideas—the Serverless Application Repository, and globally distributed applications. As Lambda, and serverless more generally, evolves over the coming years, we expect to see many more new models of architecting applications.

Exercises

1. Update the data pipeline example from "Example: Building a Serverless Data Pipeline" on page 111—set SingleEventLambda to have a reserved concurrency of 1. Now upload the sample data—you should see throttling occur (if necessary, add a few more elements to the *sampledata.json* file). Use the "Throttle" behavior from the Lambda web console to set reserved concurrency to zero.

2. Update "Example: Building a Serverless API" on page 92 to use a DynamoDB global table—make sure to separate the table itself into its own CloudFormation stack! Then deploy just the API component (with its Lambda functions) to multiple regions. Are you able to write data to one region and then read it from another?

CHAPTER 10

Conclusion

The goal of this book was for you to learn what it means to build and run applications using serverless technology on AWS, with AWS Lambda at the core of those systems. We hope that you feel empowered to do this, safe in the knowledge that Java is truly a first-class language choice in the serverless world.

We encourage you to reflect on some of the points we've tried to emphasize in this book:

- Above all, know that trying out ideas with serverless systems is quick, and cheap. If in doubt, experiment!

- Remember that Lambda code is "just code." Lambda is not a framework, or an "application server" in the traditional sense—your Lambda functions are just small pieces of Java that process a JSON event. This makes unit testing, and incremental development within your IDE, fast and nimble. Similarly, try not to bloat your functions with unnecessary libraries and frameworks that were designed for alternative runtime models.

- Automate the scripting of building and deploying your functions to the AWS Cloud. You want to be able to rapidly iterate in the same environment that will be processing production events. Use the techniques we've shown throughout the book with Maven, SAM, and CloudFormation to enable this.

- As we showed in Chapter 6, spend most of your testing time on quick unit and functional tests that run locally within one JVM along with functions under test, but also invest in the automation of end-to-end tests that exercise your functions running on the Lambda platform.

- Try to keep each of your Lambda functions focused on solving one task. Just include the code and libraries necessary to handle each function's own events.

Where necessary, use code sharing as we described in "Build and Package Using Multiple Modules and Isolated Artifacts" on page 122.

- Don't give in to the fear of cold starts! Typically either they won't be a concern for you once your application is in production, or you can use one or more remediation techniques if necessary.

- Secure your serverless applications appropriately, considering the principle of least privilege, using AWS IAM. Your organization may end up with thousands of deployed Lambda functions, so you want to reduce the blast radius of each to reduce the impact of bugs or perhaps malicious intent.

- Remember that logging and metrics work a little differently in this new world of Lambda. Use structured logging as much as you can; remember that you want to be able to observe behavior of your complete system, not just an individual function. Consider what metrics best indicate the health of the system as far as your users are concerned.

- As you build your serverless applications, embrace an "event-driven" mode of thinking. Even for functions invoked synchronously, consider how each invocation represents the passing of a self-contained message from one component to the next. And then think about how you can make your system as asynchronous as possible.

- Don't necessarily throw away your nonserverless services. Things like relational databases might still be the best way for you to solve certain problems, especially if they already exist in your larger ecosystem. But do think carefully about how to use them in a world where scale is handled very differently.

- Finally, serverless is a lot bigger than just Lambda—consider how you can lean on BaaS products from AWS and others to reduce the amount of code you need to write and operate. Even when you've settled on a particular service, investigate all of its features—it may have some hidden gems that can save you days or weeks of work.

We hope you've enjoyed this book, have found it valuable, and that it continues to be a useful resource to you over the coming months and years. We will continue to write and speak about what we learn and build with Lambda and other AWS technologies.

You can find our work at the following locations:

- On Twitter at *https://twitter.com/symphoniacloud*, *https://twitter.com/johnchapin*, and *https://twitter.com/mikebroberts*
- Our blog at *https://blog.symphonia.io*
- Our website at *https://www.symphonia.io*
- Our GitHub repositories at *https://github.com/symphoniacloud*

And of course, we'd love to hear how you get along. Please feel free to drop us a line at *johnandmike@symphonia.io*.

Thanks for reading, and go serverless!

Index

Symbols

$LATEST, 198

A

Access Key ID, 28
accounts, set up and use, 9
alarms, building for metrics, 173, 200
aliases
    introspecting, 199
    invoking, 199
    rolling back, 200
    traffic shifting, 199
    when not to use, 201
Amazon Resource Names (ARNs), 79
Amazon Web Services (AWS)
    account set up and use, 9
    capacity, 7
    command line interface (CLI), 10, 27-31
    free tier, 9
    global infrastructure, 7
    interacting through API, 10, 27
    types of service, 6
    uses for, 9
API Gateway
    as upstream event source, 86
    Integration versus Proxy events, 96
    purpose of, 14
    SAM resources, 76
    versions of, 94
APIs (see serverless APIs, building)
applications
artifacts
    isolating for packaging, 122-127
    reducing size of, 205

assumable identity, 78
asynchronous event sources
    error handling strategies, 193
    error processing, 185-191
    polling and, 91
    scaling limits and throttling, 195
at-least-once-delivery
    accepting duplicates, 229
    building idempotent systems, 228
    checking for previous processing, 229-230
    defined, 227
    using Lambda as a cron platform, 227
Auth0, 4
auto-provisioning, 5, 12
auto-scaling
    defined, 5
    DynamoDB and, 93
    fan-out pattern, 193
    impacts on downstream systems, 230
    transparency of, 12
Availability Zones (AZs), 12, 20
AWS (see Amazon Web Services (AWS))
AWS CLI
    acquiring credentials for, 28-30
    aws lambda invoke command, 43
    configuring, 31
    configuring for testing, 152
    installing, 27
    modifications for Windows users, 28
AWS Lambda (see also Lambda applications;
    Lambda functions)
    application overview, 13-16
    as cost-efficient choice, 60
    benefits of, xiii, 12, 60

constructor chaining, 140
contact information, xvii, 247
containers, 3
containers-as-a-service (CaaS), 3
content delivery networks (CDNs), 241
control plane, 42, 78
Corretto, 32
costs
    based on precise usage, 5, 12
    benefits of auto-scaling feature, 193
    benefits of Lambda, 60
    calling Lambda functions recursively, 115
    CloudWatch Logs, 165
    impact of runtime model on downstream
        systems, 234
    Lambda versus EC2, 60
    pay-per-use of globally distributed applica-
        tions, 242
    Provisioned Concurrency, 208-211
    request versus duration pricing, 60
credentials
    acquiring for AWS account set up, 9
    acquiring for AWS CLI, 28-30
    types of, 19
cron jobs, 227
cross-region actions, 239

D

data pipelines (see serverless data pipelines,
    building)
data plane, 42, 78
dead letter queues (DLQs), 187-189
deliberately hybrid solutions, 233
deployment
    infrastructure as code, 73
    methods of, 72
    serverless API example, 107-111
    Serverless Application Model (SAM), 74-76
    serverless data pipeline example, 130
destinations, 189
development environment
    AWS CLI configuration, 31
    AWS CLI credentials, 28
    AWS CLI installation, 27
    AWS SAM CLI installation, 33
    Java setup, 31
    pitfalls of fully-local development workflow,
        153
distributed tracing service, 175-180

Docker, 3
duplicate tasks, 229
duration pricing, 60
DynamoDB
    benefits of, 93
    conditional writes, 230
    Document model, 100
    error handling, 191, 193
    globally replicated database, 241
    scaling capabilities, 14
    support for, 76
    Time-to-Live (TTL) property, 230

E

EC2 (see Elastic Compute Cloud (EC2))
edge computing, 243
Elastic Compute Cloud (EC2), 1, 8
email-processing applications, 16
end-to-end tests, 136, 149-153
environment variables, 61
error handling
    asynchronous event source errors, 186-191
    classes of errors, 183
    documentation pages, 185
    errors versus exceptions, 183
    finding and investigating, 177
    Lambda error processing, 184
    strategies for, 192
    unhandled errors, 231
event sources
    asynchronous event sources, 91, 185-191
    at-least-once delivery and, 227-230
    configuring Lambda event sources, 90
    event notification failures, 235
    event source semantics, 91
    purpose of, 86
    stream/queue event sources, 91, 185
    synchronous event sources, 91, 185
    writing code to work with I/O, 86-90
Events key, 90
exceptions (see error handling)
execution environment
    autogenerated execution roles, 82
    invocation types, 43-45
    logging, 46, 79
    overview of, 42
exercises
    AWS account set up, 9, 18
    building serverless applications, 133

About the Authors

John Chapin has more than 15 years of experience as a technical executive and senior engineer. He was previously VP of Engineering, Core Services & Data Science, at Intent Media, where he helped teams transform how they delivered business value through serverless technology and Agile practices. Outside of Symphonia, he can be found running along the west side of Manhattan, surfing at Rockaway Beach, or planning his next trip abroad.

Mike Roberts is an engineering leader who has called New York City home since 2006. During his career he's been an engineer, a CTO, and other fun positions in between. Mike is a long time proponent of Agile and DevOps values and is passionate about the role that cloud technologies have played in enabling such values for many high-functioning software teams. He sees serverless as the next evolution of cloud systems and as such is excited about its ability to help teams, and their customers, be awesome.

Colophon

The bird on the cover of *Programming AWS Lambda* is a migratory shorebird called a red knot (*Calidris canutus*). Its vast range includes the Arctic Cordillera mountains from Canada to Russia in the summer and coastal areas of South America, Africa, Europe, Australia, and New Zealand in the winter. Red knots fly more than nine thousand miles each year.

In the winter, red knots are not red but gray. Their plumage takes on color in the spring when they breed. These birds are not dimorphic; both males and females have this gray to red coloring, as well as round bodies, small heads, and short dark beaks. Adults are about 9–10 inches long with a 19–21-inch wingspan. Red knots weigh 4.8 ounces on average and can double their weight before migration. They peck for insects, mussels, and crabs along the shores and tundra of their seasonal homes.

Male red knots build nests in the ground near the water where they forage for food. These birds are seasonally monogamous. Females typically lay three to four eggs, which are pale olive green with dark speckles, and both adults take shifts incubating.

Red knots have a conservation status of Near Threatened, with variation across different populations (in the United States, they are classified as Threatened). Many of the animals on O'Reilly's covers are endangered; all of them are important to the world.

The cover illustration is by Karen Montgomery, based on a black and white engraving from *Wood's Illustrated Natural History*. The cover fonts are Gilroy Semibold and Guardian Sans. The text font is Adobe Minion Pro; the heading font is Adobe Myriad Condensed; and the code font is Dalton Maag's Ubuntu Mono.